Robert M. Cutler

SOVIET AND POST-SOVIET FOREIGN POLICIES I

East-South Relations and the Political Economy of the Communist Bloc, 1971–1991

With a foreword by Roger E. Kanet

Bibliografische Information der Deutschen Nationalbibliothek
Die Deutsche Nationalbibliothek verzeichnet diese Publikation in der Deutschen Nationalbibliografie; detaillierte bibliografische Daten sind im Internet über http://dnb.d-nb.de abrufbar.

Bibliographic information published by the Deutsche Nationalbibliothek
Die Deutsche Nationalbibliothek lists this publication in the Deutsche Nationalbibliografie; detailed bibliographic data are available in the Internet at http://dnb.d-nb.de.

ISBN-13: 978-3-8382-1654-6
© *ibidem*-Verlag, Stuttgart 2023
Alle Rechte vorbehalten

Das Werk einschließlich aller seiner Teile ist urheberrechtlich geschützt. Jede Verwertung außerhalb der engen Grenzen des Urheberrechtsgesetzes ist ohne Zustimmung des Verlages unzulässig und strafbar. Dies gilt insbesondere für Vervielfältigungen, Übersetzungen, Mikroverfilmungen und elektronische Speicherformen sowie die Einspeicherung und Verarbeitung in elektronischen Systemen.

All rights reserved. No part of this publication may be reproduced, stored in or introduced into a retrieval system, or transmitted, in any form, or by any means (electronic, mechanical, photocopying, recording or otherwise) without the prior written permission of the publisher. Any person who does any unauthorized act in relation to this publication may be liable to criminal prosecution and civil claims for damages.

Printed in the EU

Soviet and Post-Soviet Politics and Society (SPPS)   Vol. 240
ISSN 1614-3515

General Editor: Andreas Umland,
Stockholm Centre for Eastern European Studies, andreas.umland@ui.se

Commissioning Editor: Max Jakob Horstmann,
London, mjh@ibidem.eu

EDITORIAL COMMITTEE*

DOMESTIC & COMPARATIVE POLITICS
Prof. **Ellen Bos**, *Andrássy University of Budapest*
Dr. **Gergana Dimova**, *Florida State University*
Prof. **Heiko Pleines**, *University of Bremen*
Dr. **Sarah Whitmore**, *Oxford Brookes University*
Dr. **Harald Wydra**, *University of Cambridge*

SOCIETY, CLASS & ETHNICITY
Col. **David Glantz**, *"Journal of Slavic Military Studies"*
Dr. **Marlène Laruelle**, *George Washington University*
Dr. **Stephen Shulman**, *Southern Illinois University*
Prof. **Stefan Troebst**, *University of Leipzig*

POLITICAL ECONOMY & PUBLIC POLICY
Prof. **Andreas Goldthau**, *University of Erfurt*
Dr. **Robert Kravchuk**, *University of North Carolina*
Dr. **David Lane**, *University of Cambridge*
Dr. **Carol Leonard**, *University of Oxford*
Dr. **Maria Popova**, *McGill University, Montreal*

FOREIGN POLICY & INTERNATIONAL AFFAIRS
Dr. **Peter Duncan**, *University College London*
Prof. **Andreas Heinemann-Grüder**, *University of Bonn*
Prof. **Gerhard Mangott**, *University of Innsbruck*
Dr. **Diana Schmidt-Pfister**, *University of Konstanz*
Dr. **Lisbeth Tarlow**, *Harvard University, Cambridge*
Dr. **Christian Wipperfürth**, *N-Ost Network, Berlin*
Dr. **William Zimmerman**, *University of Michigan*

HISTORY, CULTURE & THOUGHT
Dr. **Catherine Andreyev**, *University of Oxford*
Prof. **Mark Bassin**, *Södertörn University*
Prof. **Karsten Brüggemann**, *Tallinn University*
Prof. **Alexander Etkind**, *Central European University*
Prof. **Gasan Gusejnov**, *Free University of Berlin*
Prof. **Leonid Luks**, *Catholic University of Eichstaett*
Dr. **Olga Malinova**, *Russian Academy of Sciences*
Dr. **Richard Mole**, *University College London*
Prof. **Andrei Rogatchevski**, *University of Tromsø*
Dr. **Mark Tauger**, *West Virginia University*

ADVISORY BOARD*

Prof. **Dominique Arel**, *University of Ottawa*
Prof. **Jörg Baberowski**, *Humboldt University of Berlin*
Prof. **Margarita Balmaceda**, *Seton Hall University*
Dr. **John Barber**, *University of Cambridge*
Prof. **Timm Beichelt**, *European University Viadrina*
Dr. **Katrin Boeckh**, *University of Munich*
Prof. em. **Archie Brown**, *University of Oxford*
Dr. **Vyacheslav Bryukhovetsky**, *Kyiv-Mohyla Academy*
Prof. **Timothy Colton**, *Harvard University, Cambridge*
Prof. **Paul D'Anieri**, *University of California*
Dr. **Heike Dörrenbächer**, *Friedrich Naumann Foundation*
Dr. **John Dunlop**, *Hoover Institution, Stanford, California*
Dr. **Sabine Fischer**, *SWP, Berlin*
Dr. **Geir Flikke**, *NUPI, Oslo*
Prof. **David Galbreath**, *University of Aberdeen*
Prof. **Frank Golczewski**, *University of Hamburg*
Dr. **Nikolas Gvosdev**, *Naval War College, Newport, RI*
Prof. **Mark von Hagen**, *Arizona State University*
Prof. **Guido Hausmann**, *University of Regensburg*
Prof. **Dale Herspring**, *Kansas State University*
Dr. **Stefani Hoffman**, *Hebrew University of Jerusalem*
Prof. em. **Andrzej Korbonski**, *University of California*
Dr. **Iris Kempe**, *"Caucasus Analytical Digest"*
Prof. **Herbert Küpper**, *Institut für Ostrecht Regensburg*
Prof. **Rainer Lindner**, *University of Konstanz*

Dr. **Luke March**, *University of Edinburgh*
Prof. **Michael McFaul**, *Stanford University, Palo Alto*
Prof. **Birgit Menzel**, *University of Mainz-Germersheim*
Dr. **Alex Pravda**, *University of Oxford*
Dr. **Erik van Ree**, *University of Amsterdam*
Dr. **Joachim Rogall**, *Robert Bosch Foundation Stuttgart*
Prof. **Peter Rutland**, *Wesleyan University, Middletown*
Prof. **Gwendolyn Sasse**, *University of Oxford*
Prof. **Jutta Scherrer**, *EHESS, Paris*
Prof. **Robert Service**, *University of Oxford*
Mr. **James Sherr**, *RIIA Chatham House London*
Dr. **Oxana Shevel**, *Tufts University, Medford*
Prof. **Eberhard Schneider**, *University of Siegen*
Prof. **Olexander Shnyrkov**, *Shevchenko University, Kyiv*
Prof. **Hans-Henning Schröder**, *SWP, Berlin*
Prof. **Yuri Shapoval**, *Ukrainian Academy of Sciences*
Dr. **Lisa Sundstrom**, *University of British Columbia*
Dr. **Philip Walters**, *"Religion, State and Society", Oxford*
Prof. **Zenon Wasyliw**, *Ithaca College, New York State*
Dr. **Lucan Way**, *University of Toronto*
Dr. **Markus Wehner**, *"Frankfurter Allgemeine Zeitung"*
Dr. **Andrew Wilson**, *University College London*
Prof. **Jan Zielonka**, *University of Oxford*
Prof. **Andrei Zorin**, *University of Oxford*

While the Editorial Committee and Advisory Board support the General Editor in the choice and improvement of manuscripts for publication, responsibility for remaining errors and misinterpretations in the series' volumes lies with the books' authors.

Soviet and Post-Soviet Politics and Society (SPPS)
ISSN 1614-3515

Founded in 2004 and refereed since 2007, SPPS makes available affordable English-, German-, and Russian-language studies on the history of the countries of the former Soviet bloc from the late Tsarist period to today. It publishes between 5 and 20 volumes per year and focuses on issues in transitions to and from democracy such as economic crisis, identity formation, civil society development, and constitutional reform in CEE and the NIS. SPPS also aims to highlight so far understudied themes in East European studies such as right-wing radicalism, religious life, higher education, or human rights protection. The authors and titles of all previously published volumes are listed at the end of this book. For a full description of the series and reviews of its books, see www.ibidem-verlag.de/red/spps.

Editorial correspondence & manuscripts should be sent to: Dr. Andreas Umland, Department of Political Science, Kyiv-Mohyla Academy, vul. Voloska 8/5, UA-04070 Kyiv, UKRAINE; andreas.umland@cantab.net

Business correspondence & review copy requests should be sent to: *ibidem* Press, Leuschnerstr. 40, 30457 Hannover, Germany; tel.: +49 511 2622200; fax: +49 511 2622201; spps@ibidem.eu.

Authors, reviewers, referees, and editors for (as well as all other persons sympathetic to) SPPS are invited to join its networks at www.facebook.com/group.php?gid=52638198614
www.linkedin.com/groups?about=&gid=103012
www.xing.com/net/spps-ibidem-verlag/

Recent Volumes

231 *Anna Kutkina*
Between Lenin and Bandera
Decommunization and Multivocality in Post-Euromaidan Ukraine
With a foreword by Juri Mykkänen
ISBN 978-3-8382-1506-8

232 *Lincoln E. Flake*
Defending the Faith
The Russian Orthodox Church and the Demise of Religious Pluralism
With a foreword by Peter Martland
ISBN 978-3-8382-1378-1

233 *Nikoloz Samkharadze*
Russia's Recognition of the Independence of Abkhazia and South Ossetia
Analysis of a Deviant Case in Moscow's Foreign Policy Behavior
With a foreword by Neil MacFarlane
ISBN 978-3-8382-1414-6

234 *Arve Hansen*
Urban Protest
A Spatial Perspective on Kyiv, Minsk, and Moscow
With a foreword by Julie Wilhelmsen
ISBN 978-3-8382-1495-5

235 *Eleonora Narvselius, Julie Fedor (Eds.)*
Diversity in the East-Central European Borderlands
Memories, Cityscapes, People
ISBN 978-3-8382-1523-5

236 *Regina Elsner*
The Russian Orthodox Church and Modernity
A Historical and Theological Investigation into Eastern Christianity between Unity and Plurality
With a foreword by Mikhail Suslov
ISBN 978-3-8382-1568-6

237 *Bo Petersson*
The Putin Predicament
Problems of Legitimacy and Succession in Russia
With a foreword by J. Paul Goode
ISBN 978-3-8382-1050-6

238 *Jonathan Otto Pohl*
The Years of Great Silence
The Deportation, Special Settlement, and Mobilization into the Labor Army of Ethnic Germans in the USSR, 1941–1955
ISBN 978-3-8382-1630-0

239 *Mykhailo Minakov (Ed.)*
Inventing Majorities
Ideological Creativity in Post-Soviet Societies
ISBN 978-3-8382-1641-6

*For
F.L.*

Contents

Contents 7

List of Tables 9

List of Abbreviations 10

Acknowledgments 11

Foreword by *Roger E. Kanet* 15

1   Snapshot of Soviet Foreign Trade with the Third World in the Mid-1970s 27

2   East–South Relations at UNCTAD: Global Political Economy and the CMEA 61

3   Economic Issues in East–South Relations 95

4   The Political Economy of East–South Military Transfers 115

5   East–South Relations in Global Perspective 169

Index 193

List of Tables

1-1. Foreign trade of leading countries, 1975 28
1-2. Soviet trade turnover by principal countries, 1976 29
1-3. Soviet economic credits and grants extended to less developed countries, 1954–1975, in millions of U.S. dollars 42
1-4. Major recipients of Soviet economic aid, 1954–1975 and 1973–1975, in percents of total 44
3-1. Soviet schools of thought on global economic relations ... 102
4-1. Soviet deliveries of major weapon systems to the Third World 120
4-2. Soviet arms sales and hard-currency receipts (figures in millions of current U.S. dollars) 126
4-3. Hard-currency sources for the Soviet Union (figures in millions of current U.S. dollars) 127
4-4. Arms exports to the less-developed countries as a burden on the Soviet economy (figures in billions of current rubles) 130
4-5. Military and nonmilitary technicians from USSR and Eastern Europe in LDCs 140
5-1. Thematic and temporal distribution of chapters in this book 182

List of Abbreviations

CIA	Central Intelligence Agency
CMEA	Council of Mutual Economic Assistance
CP	Communist Party
EEC	European Economic Community
G77	Group of Seventy-seven
GATT	General Agreements on Tariffs and Trade
GDR	German Democratic Republic
GSP	Generalized System of Preferences
IBEC	International Bank for Economic Cooperation
IBRD	International Bank for Reconstruction and Development
IIB	International Investment Bank
ILC	International Law Commission
IMF	International Monetary Fund
ITO	International Trade Organization
LDC	less-developed country
MFN	most-favored nation
MPLA	People's Movement for the Liberation of Angola
NATO	North Atlantic Treaty Organization
NIC	newly industrializing country
NIEO	New International Economic Order
OPEC	Organization of Petroleum Exporting Countries
RBP	restrictive business practice
SIPRI	Stockholm International Peace Research Institute
TIC	tripartite industrial cooperation
UNCITRAL	United Nations Commission on International Trade Law
UNCTAD	United Nations Conference on Trade and Development
USSR	Union of Soviet Socialist Republics
WEFA	Wharton Econometric Forecasting Associates
WTO	Warsaw Treaty Organization

Acknowledgments

I thank Andreas Umland for his encouragement and Valerie Lange, Jana Dävers, and the staff of Ibidem Verlag for their assistance. The Acknowledgments below incorporate acknowledgments in any previously published works. I have converted any original bibliographic footnotes into inline citations with Lists of References at the end of each chapter. Substantive footnotes have been incorporated into the texts proper. About one-third of the material in this volume has never been published before. Brief details follow here.

Foreword. I thank Roger E. Kanet for his generosity of time and effort in framing and introducing these works, as well as for his patience in awaiting publication.

Chapter 1. The chapter "Snapshot of Soviet Foreign Trade with the Third World in Late 1970s" compiles extracts on East–South trade from the chapter, "Trade, Aid, and International Relations," which I co-authored with Paul E. Lydolph in his *Geography of the USSR: Topical Analysis*, 2nd ed. (Elkhart Lake, Wisc.: Misty Valley Publishing, 1979), 479–510. The publisher was wholly owned by Professor Lydolph. I have made every possible effort in good faith to locate his widow, children, or other relatives, but without success. I would ask them to contact me if they see this notice, so that appropriate arrangements may be made.

Chapter 2. The chapter "East–South Relations at UNCTAD: Global Political Economy and the CMEA" was first published as an article under the same title in *International Organization* 37, no. 1 (Winter 1983): 121–142. I thank MIT Press for permission to reprint the article. The research could not have been executed without support from the FERIS Foundation of America, sponsor of the Albert Gallatin Fellowship in International Affairs, Graduate Institute of International Studies (now Graduate Institute of International and Development Studies), Geneva. Members of the Institute's faculty who kindly shared their expertise and time are too numerous to mention. I must thank Urs Luterbacher and his colleagues for their hospitality, which greatly facilitated all my work. Harish Kapur and Marlis Steinert helped to shape this study's broad contours within their Working Group on EEC-Third World relations, where an early version was presented. Their suggestions greatly aided its revision. Comments by the editor of *International Organization* led me to reformulate some important points, which Catherine Mannick helped to clarify. A multitude of international civil servants and national representatives at the United Nations in Geneva accorded me confidential interviews. About 10 percent of this chapter is previously unpublished, integrating material from the original seminar paper, excluded for reasons of concision of argument from the published text.

Chapter 3. The chapter "Economic Issues in East-South Relations" was first published as an article under the same title in *Problems of Communism* 33, no. 4 (July-August 1984): 73-80. This academic journal is a US Government document and therefore, as I have confirmed, no permission for reprinting is required. I nevertheless wish now to thank David E. Albright, its erstwhile editor, for facilitating the original publication. About 10 percent of this chapter is new material that integrates passages from an unpublished draft, excluded for reasons of concision from the published text.

Chapter 4. The chapter "The Political Economy of East-South Military Transfers" was first published as an article under the same title in *International Studies Quarterly* 31, no. 3 (September 1987): 273-299. I thank the International Studies Association for permission to reprint the article in this volume. I was principal co-author with Laure Després and Aaron Karp, whom I thank for their agreement that it is republished here. The research could not have been executed without the support of the Scientific Research Council (University of Nantes), the National Center for Scientific Research (Paris), the Economic and Social Science Council (London), and the Swedish Council for Research in Social and Human Sciences (Stockholm); as well as the assistance International Institute for Strategic Studies and the Stockholm International Peace Research Institute, and also Robert Tartarin, Thomas Ohlson, and Michael Brzoska. A preliminary version was presented to the Research Committee on the Evolving International Economic Order at the Thirteenth World Congress of the International Political Science Association (Paris,

July 1985). About 30 percent of this chapter is previously unpublished, integrating passages from that paper which were excluded for reasons of length from the published text.

Chapter 5. The chapter "East–South Relations in Global Perspective" is a revision of an unpublished paper of the same title, presented to the Twenty-first Annual Conference of the Northeast Political Science Association (Philadelphia, November 1989). It is published here for the first time.

Foreword
Four Decades of Soviet Policy in the Developing World

Roger E. Kanet

The Soviet Union was one of two global superpowers for nearly a half-century until its final implosion at the end of 1991. Its competition with the United States for power and influence led to its engagement around the world with nearly all other states. Initially, the Soviet Union and the United States faced one another across what Winston Churchill called the Iron Curtain in Central Europe. Soon, however, the emergence of a host of new states from the decolonization of West European empires in Asia and Africa created new platforms for competition between the superpowers (Namikas 2016). The USSR and the United States inevitably expanded their competition to the Third World, where each viewed it in zero-sum terms.

This Foreword provides the historical context required for an adequate understanding of the place and importance of Robert Cutler's work on the economic and military instruments behind Soviet-bloc influence in the Third World. I thank him for encouraging me to cite liberally from my own work, which he considers to be characterized by the general evolution of such studies over the decades concerned.

1 Emergence of Soviet Policy in the Developing World

Prior to Stalin's death in 1953, the USSR had virtually no direct relations what later would be termed the developing world (Kanet 1974), except for various links established through relations with Communist Parties of "the East," such as the Communist Party of India and the Chinese Communist Party. Both of these were established in the first half of the 1920s and members of the Communist

International. There were relatively few independent states, in areas of what came to known as the Third World, with which to have state-to-state relations. The priorities of the Soviet Union and of the other states concerned anyway lay mainly elsewhere.

From the mid-1950s through the early 1980s, however, the Soviet Union, and Soviet bloc more broadly, established significant political, economic, and military relations with the new states that emerged from the West European colonial system. This new direction of Soviet foreign policy in the Third World represented perhaps the most significant global expansion of U.S.–Soviet competition. Across the West, specialists in Soviet foreign policy sought to make sense of those developments and to determine their implications. After the Arab oil embargo in 1973–74, international economic relations took on a higher profile on the general world political agenda, and so also on the research agendas of international-relations researchers. The smaller East European members of the Soviet bloc increased their exposure to world markets. Likewise, in the early 1970s, the Non-Aligned Movement began its push for the normative policy it called the New International Economic Order, couched in terms of a "North–South" divide or dialogue.

However, the "North–South" concept failed to distinguish between East and West; indeed, the Soviet bloc denied any responsibility for the economic difficulties of Third World countries, attributing them to inheritances from the old colonial system. "North" meant, in fact, the West. However, observers and analysts of the communist systems, noting the growing economic and trade profile of the smaller Soviet-bloc countries, as well as the USSR, in the Third World, found it natural to begin to distinguish, investigate, and write about "East–South" relations.

Among the important academic members of the group studying this phenomenon, starting at the end of the 1970s, was Robert M. Cutler. His "East–South Relations at UNCTAD" (chapter 2, below) was the first double-blind peer-reviewed article on East–South relations to appear in a major English-language, mainstream political-science journal. Much of his analysis of East–South relations during the 1980s focused on the economic relationship between the USSR and Third World states. Always putting contemporary events into historical context, he sought to assess the expansion of the USSR's global role and influence by focusing on the economic aspects of Soviet-bloc relations with the developing countries.

The study of "East–South relations" started to attract scholarly attention in the late 1970s. It explicitly put economic, financial, and commercial relations on an equal footing with military relations and the ideological issues. It sought to go beyond the analytical framework of bilateral Soviet foreign relations that typified "Soviet–Third World" studies up until then. Studies in that framework had focused exclusively on the Soviet Union, ignoring the foreign relations of other communist countries (and their distinctive aspects), and predominantly on the military and ideological aspects of the relationship (although often including Soviet foreign aid). Cutler's chapter 1 below, "Snapshot of Soviet Foreign Trade with the Third World in the Late 1970s," is a comprehensive and balanced treatment of the emergence and development of Soviet economic relations with Third World countries and their place in overall Soviet policy from their beginnings under Khrushchev through the late 1970s.

By the mid-1960s, Western colonial empires had collapsed, and many anti-Western regimes had taken root throughout Asia and Africa (Kanet 1981). Yet the USSR's new friends and allies in the Third World were generally among the weakest and most institutionally challenged states in the world. Initially the Soviets focused on Africa.

By the end of the 1960s they had extended this interest to the Middle East, especially including the Israeli–Arab conflict. Military and political support was a central and growing element of Soviet policy in this region, as Cutler makes evident in chapter 4, "The Political Economy of East–South Military Transfers," which still remains one of the best and most comprehensive article-length treatments of its subject. Cutler discusses quite extensively in several chapters here (previously mentioned chapters 2 and 4, and also chapter 5 "East–South Relations in Global Perspective") how the Soviets were extensively involved throughout the entire Third World by the beginning of the 1970s. Moreover, they had developed an entire theoretical apparatus, based on categories of "creative Marxism-Leninism," for analyzing developments there. This apparatus was wedded to an evolving ideology about how they played into the assumed eventual success of communism on the international level (Kanet 1972).

Indeed, by the early 1970s, the mainstream Soviet view (Inozemtsev 1972) was that the Conference on Security and Cooperation in Europe ("Helsinki Conference," 1972-1975) would confirm the shift of the European balance toward the Soviets. What they called the "changing international correlation of forces" would lead to a transition: the "socialist world-system" would predominate over the "capitalist world-system" on the global level, eventually overcoming and replacing it. Throughout the 1970s, the USSR and the Soviet bloc (including Cuba) provided substantial support to selected Third World governments and political movements. Economic and military assistance was the primary vehicle for establishing and maintaining such relations (Kanet 1989). Chapters 2 and 4 in this volume give extensive treatment to this topic. By the 1980s, however, internal Soviet weaknesses vitiated the Soviet leadership's confidence, leading them even to question the USSR's superpower status. The overcommitment of Soviet resources to support allies and clients across the entire globe was coming home to roost.

The final years of the Soviet system witnessed attempts by the leadership to reform the very structures of the Soviet state. These began with economic reform, but soon expanded to encompass the entire political system. The state's foreign and security policy framework was inevitably implicated in this attempted transformation. The Soviet leadership initiated fundamental changes in foreign policy. These changes included dramatically scaling back the global confrontation with the United States and reducing Soviet military and political involvement in regional conflicts around the world. Not only did all Soviet efforts at domestic reform fail; their unintended consequence was, moreover, to bring down the entire economic and political structure undergirding the extended Soviet-bloc system from Central Europe to the Chinese border.

The 1970s were arguably the high-point of Soviet and Soviet-bloc involvement with the developing world. (See chapter 1.) As noted above, during that decade the Soviets were extremely optimistic about the prospects for increasing their influence in the international system. Their policy instruments were principally economic and military support for the ruling regimes in the South. The U.S.-Soviet détente of the early and mid-1970s gave the Soviets the opportunity to take advantage of Third World conflicts. In Angola, Ethiopia, and Southeast Asia, for example, they helped favorable regimes consolidate power. (For detailed exposition from which the following is drawn, see Kanet 1989.) Soviet preoccupations with NATO and with China, nevertheless, ranked Europe and Asia higher in absolute importance for Soviet security. The USSR made major efforts to reduce its conflicts with the United States, partly to diminish American responses to Soviet involvement in the Third World. The Soviet Union's influence in the developing world during the decade benefited, in the end, as much from the incoherence of Western policy in Asia and Africa as from its own strength there.

By the early 1980s, despite their optimism and the good reasons for it, the Soviets found themselves increasingly on the defensive internationally. Détente with the United States had collapsed under the weight of Soviet adventurism in Africa and military intervention in Afghanistan. The USSR confronted new embargoes, higher American and Japanese military spending, and NATO's decision to deploy intermediate range nuclear weapons in Europe. Moreover, the Soviets discovered that the political appeal of their socio-economic policies had weakened significantly: they were now losing what they called the "ideological struggle."

2 From Retrenchment to Collapse of the Soviet State

After assuming political leadership in Moscow in spring 1985, Mikhail Gorbachev publicly described the problems facing the Soviet Union, calling for a reorientation of domestic and foreign policy. His main argument consisted of three points. First, the economic problems faced by the Soviets, including their growing technology gap with the West, augured poorly for the future. Second, economic reform (*perestroika*, meaning "restructuring") within the state-socialist framework was essential to overcome these problems and provide a foundation for future economic growth. Third, a more open political system, based on *glasnost'* (openness/transparency) and *demokratizatsiia* (democratization), was necessary to overcome entrenched political interests and to carry through the required reforms.

The rate of Soviet economic growth had been declining. In Gorbachev's (1987) words, economic growth had "fallen to a level close to economic stagnation." His primary economic advisor, Abel Aganbegyan (1988), even argued that overall economic growth had actually ceased. Overall, Brezhnev's successors confronted a situation filled with contradictions and challenges. The USSR remained a global superpower, but could use its military capabilities for political gains only with difficulty. Gorbachev's proposals were therefore, in part, based also on his concern about the future position and role of the USSR in the international system. He called for "new political thinking" to reform Soviet foreign policy.

That initiative complemented the increasing Soviet pessimism over developments in the global South. It soon led to important changes in actual policy and to a remarkable improvement in relations with the U.S. and the West in general, with Japan and China, and with the less radical developing countries. Gorbachev recognized that the Soviets, by the middle of the 1980s, had effectively been frozen out of influence in many key situations of global significance. His new policy in Europe, Asia, and the Third World was based on recognizing that the expansion of Soviet military power had not brought comparable political gains. This retrenchment of Soviet foreign policy did not signify, however, the abandonment of gains already made or the renunciation of the goal of expanding Soviet influence in the future.

Early in the Gorbachev era, "new political thinking" comprised three main policy elements (Kanet with Katner 1992). First was a rejection of the rigidity and aggressiveness of the Brezhnev years, complemented by an effort at revitalization by reducing the role of ideology in foreign policy making. Second was the addition of "global problems" to the Soviet foreign policy agenda, signifying that capitalists were no longer to be blamed for every injustice and that communists could cooperate with them to ameliorate the human condition. Third was the recognition that the existence of nuclear weapons made international security mutual in nature.

By 1986 Moscow's decision to reduce commitments to Third World states was evident. Besides reacting to the growing cost of supporting allies, some Soviet analysts questioned the long-term viability of some of their allies. Gorbachev (1987 173-4, 187) himself argued "that regional conflicts in Asia, Africa and Latin America are spawned by the colonial past, new social processes, or reoccurrences of predating policy, or by all three." The goal was to find political solutions to these problems. Moreover, every country had the right to its own solutions and neither superpower should intervene in these conflicts.

For three decades the Soviets optimistically expanded their involvement in Asia and Africa. The 1980s represented a period of reassessment and retrenchment in Soviet policy toward the global South even before the Soviet state began to collapse. They did remain, however, politically, economically, and militarily active in developments across Asia, Africa and Latin America. By the mid-1980s it was clear even to the Soviet leadership that their involvement in the Third World was costing more and more, and that their increasingly scarce resources were ever more strained. One American study of the cost of the Soviet empire — including growing subsidies to Eastern Europe, Cuba, and Vietnam — estimated it at between $35 and $46 billion per year by 1980 (Machowski and Schultz 1987).

Soviet views were changing. (See Valkenier 1983, reviewed below in chapter 3, "Economic Issues in East–South Relations"; also Valkenier 1987.) Official statements no longer focused on imminent progress by "radical" states or on the "invincible" nature of the supposed alliance between the USSR and national liberation movements. Prominent Soviet analysts (for example, Bovin 1984) began openly to question the optimism of the 1970s concerning likely developments in the Third World. (For comprehensive treatments of changes in Soviet views of Third World developments, see: Hough 1986; Papp 1985.)

Challenges to Soviet hegemony had emerged even in Eastern Europe by the beginning of the 1980s. Most important was the challenge to the orthodox communist regime in Poland. When Soviet leader Leonid Brezhnev died in 1982, Moscow was significantly involved in the developing world. Yet a reassessment of that policy had already begun. Many governments that the Soviets supported faced serious challenges and required continued Soviet support, not least Afghanistan. The Soviets had been instrumental in the 1979 coup in Afghanistan, for example, but they were soon involved in supporting the new government against internal military challengers. The costs of Soviet commitments to Third World clients were beginning to drain the Soviet economy itself. Soviet international-affairs experts in Moscow understood that the USSR's early successes in the Third World states did not create stable political and economic systems in those countries.

At the very same time, in the early 1980s, relations with the United States were continuing to deteriorate. The Reagan Administration, which came to power in January 1981, viewed Soviet behavior as an aggressive challenge to U.S. interests in the developing world and undertook a more assertive policy than its predecessor. By the time Brezhnev died in November 1982, the Soviet role in the developing world had greatly expanded in comparison with three decades earlier; yet its power and influence remained limited. The immediate post-Brezhnev leadership, first with Yuri Andropov (November 1982–February 1984) and then Konstantin Chernenko (February 1984–March 1985) at the head, still did not make any major policy shifts in that policy; if anything, it even increased its involvement in the Third World. It was only with the leadership of Mikhail Gorbachev after Chernenko's death that the policy changes noted earlier were introduced,

Thus, by the end of the 1980s and shortly before the demise of the USSR itself, "new thinking," as it applied to policy toward the developing world implied the demilitarization of regional conflicts and the search for political solutions to them; the removal of ideology from interstate relations; and restraint from interference in the domestic politics of other states. The impact of this "new thinking" for Soviet policy in the Third World became evident when the

Soviets began to withdraw their military forces from Afghanistan in 1988, reduced their troops in Angola and pushed for a ceasefire there in 1989, and announced in 1991 their intention to reduce their role in the civil war in Ethiopia. In other words, in the years and months leading up to the implosion of the Soviet Union in the fall of 1991 the government in Moscow was disengaging from many of its policies in the Third World, and elsewhere, that it had pursued for the previous four decades. Yet, consensus on foreign policy broke down as many in the party and state apparatus opposed the changes in both domestic and foreign policy being implemented by Gorbachev and his supporters.

Before December 1991 it had become evident that future Soviet policy toward the developing world (and the rest of the world more broadly) was unclear. Overall, any future Soviet commitments to revolutionary Third World movements would not be as extensive as they had been, but that support for existing Leninist regimes (e.g., Vietnam, Afghanistan, Ethiopia) would continue, perhaps on a reduced level.

3 Conclusion: East–South Relations in the Later Cold War

This Foreword has discussed East–South relations in the years leading up to the end of the Cold War, in order to set the stage for Robert Cutler's works published here. His analyses of Soviet and Soviet-bloc policy, focusing on economic factors of trade and aid, along with military assistance, hold up very well more than 30 years after they were first executed. Some of the items are expanded from their original publication, with the addition of previously unpublished material. The last chapter has never been published before.

Cutler's works here provide an important historical assessment of an extremely significant aspect of Soviet foreign policy and Soviet-bloc international relations in the last decades of the USSR's existence. They are of continuing value, and much of the analysis that they contain remains authoritative today, not only on their own merits but also for perspective and insight as the Soviet Union's major successor state, the Russian Federation, attempts to extend its role in global affairs.

References

AGANBEGYAN, Abel. 1988. *The Economic Challenge of Perestroika*. Bloomington: Indiana University Press.

BOVIN, Aleksandr. 1984. "The Difficult Roads of Freedom." *Izvestiia*, 12 November, p. 5. Translated in *Current Digest of the Soviet Press* 36, no. 48 (26 December 1984): 48.

GORBACHEV, Mikhail. 1987. *Perestroika: New Thinking for Our Country and the World*. New York: Harper and Row.

HOUGH, Jerry. 1986. *The Struggle for the Third World: Soviet Debates American Options*. Washington, D.C.: Brookings Institution.

INOZEMTSEV, N. N. 1972. "Les relations internationales en Europe dans les années 1970." In *Europe 1980: The Future of Intra-European Relations; Reports presented at the Conference of Directors and Representatives of European Institutes of International Relations*, 121-136. Foreword by Jacques Freymond. Collection de Relations Internationales 1. Leiden: Sijthoff; Geneva: Institut Universitaire de Hautes Études Internationales, 1972.

KANET, Roger E. 1972. "Changing Soviet Attitudes Toward the Developing Countries." In *On the Road to Communism: Essays on Soviet Domestic and Foreign Politics*, edited by Roger E. Kanet and Ivan Volgyes, 142-157. Lawrence: University Press of Kansas.

—. 1974. "The Soviet Union and the Colonial Question, 1917-1953." In *The Soviet Union and the Developing Nations*, edited by Roger E. Kanet, 1-26. Baltimore: Johns Hopkins University Press.

—. 1981. "Patterns of Eastern European Economic Involvement in the Third World." In *Eastern Europe and the Third World*, edited by Michael Radu, 303-322. New York: Praeger Publishers.

—. 1989. "The Evolution of Soviet Policy toward the Developing World: From Stalin to Brezhnev." In *The Limits of Soviet Power in the Developing World*, 36-61, edited by Edward A. Kolodziej and Roger E. Kanet. Baltimore: Johns Hopkins University Press.

—, with Garth T. KATNER. 1992. "From New Thinking to The Fragmentation of Consensus in Foreign Policy: Soviet Policy in the Third World." In *Soviet Foreign Policy in Transition*, edited by Roger E. Kanet, Deborah Nutter Miner, and Tamara J. Resler, 121-144. Cambridge: Cambridge University Press.

MACHOWSKI, Heinrich, and Siegfried SCHULTZ. 1987. "Soviet Economic Policy in the Third World." In *The Soviet Union, Eastern Europe and the Developing States*, edited by Roger E. Kanet, 117–140. Cambridge: Cambridge University Press.

NAMIKAS, Lisa. 2016. *Battleground Africa: Cold War in the Congo, 1960–1965*. Stanford: Stanford University Press.

PAPP, Daniel S. 1985. *Soviet Perceptions of the Developing World in the 1980s: The Ideological Basis*. Lexington: Lexington Books.

VALKENIER, Elizabeth Kridl. 1983. *The Soviet Union and the Third World: An Economic Bind*. New York: Praeger Publishers.

—. 1987. "Revolutionary Change in the Third World: Recent Soviet Reassessments." In *The Soviet Union, Eastern Europe and the Third World*, edited by Roger E. Kanet, 23–41. Cambridge: Cambridge University Press.

Roger E. Kanet is Professor Emeritus of Political Science at both the University of Illinois at Urbana–Champaign (since 1997) and the University of Miami (since 2019) after 53 years of university teaching, research, and administration. He holds both a Ph.D. (1966) and an A.M. (1965) in Politics from Princeton University, an M.A. in International Relations from Lehigh University (1963), an A.B. from Xavier University (1961), and a Ph.B. from Berchmanskolleg in Pullach-bei-München, Germany (1960). He began his teaching career at the University of Kansas, where he was also Director of Undergraduate Studies and Associate Chair in the Political Science Department. He spent almost a quarter-century (1973–97) at the University of Illinois at Urbana–Champaign, where he was Director of Graduate Studies, Head of the Political Science Department, and later Associate Vice Chancellor for Academic Affairs. At the University of Miami (1997–2019), he was first Dean of the School of International Studies, then Director of Graduate Studies in the Department of International Studies, and finally Professor of Political Science. Earlier in his career, he held post-doctoral fellowships at Columbia University, the University of Warsaw, and the Bundesinstitut für ostwissenschaftliche und internationale Studien (Cologne). He has published more than 240 scholarly articles and book chapters and has edited and contributed to 35 books, primarily on topics of Soviet and Russian foreign policy. The most recent of these are *The Routledge Handbook of Russian Security* (2019) and, with Dina Moulioukova, *Russia and the World in the Putin Era: From Theory to Reality in Russian Global Strategy* (Routledge, 2021).

1   Snapshot of Soviet Foreign Trade with the Third World in the Mid-1970s

> *The Soviet Union's trade with the Third World expanded significantly in the early and mid-1970s. Outside the communist world, its economic aid has been very small but its military aid has often been the most productive of its goals. The Soviets have helped with projects that Western countries did not aid due to political reasons. In both trade and aid, they have mainly emphasized countries in Asia and north Africa, in a belt extending from the western Mediterranean to the borders of China. Asia and north Africa received 80 percent of Soviet aid from the mid-1950s to the mid-1970s. Sub-Saharan Africa and Latin America have received relatively very little attention.*

Keywords: Soviet, trade, aid, developing, Third World, Africa, Asia

Soviet trade is in the midst of a period of expansion, under the aegis of détente and peaceful coexistence. Soviet leaders seem to have decided to attempt to increase the country's rate of industrial growth by importing huge amounts of advanced Western technology, while at the same time providing its citizens with incentives to work more effectively by importing Western consumer goods. The value of Soviet trade during the five years 1971–75 was 87 percent above its level during the five years 1966–70. Trade turnover increased more than 28 percent from 1974 to 1975 and more than 12 percent from 1975 to 1976. Some of this increase in value can naturally be attributed to general global inflation, which had particular affected petroleum products and gold, the two main Soviet exports to hard-currency countries. Even in terms of fixed prices, however, Soviet trade turnover in 1975 was 232 percent that of 1965.

In spite of this recent rapid increase, Soviet trade is still well below what one might expect of an economy the size of that of the Soviet Union. In 1975 the USSR ranked seventh globally in total trade turnover, but was nowhere near a leading trading country on a per capita basis. (See Table 1-1.) It has been estimated that Soviet trade would be about 3.5 times its current size if it had a market economy. It remains to be seen whether the current rise in trade volume is another crash effort to catch up technologically with the West, followed by a diminution of trade, or whether it marks the start of a Soviet program to maintain foreign exchanges at a level commensurate with the size of the country's economy.

Table 1-1. Foreign trade of leading countries, 1975.

Country	Imports (million current USD)	Exports (million current USD)	Total turnover (million current USD)	Trade turnover per capita (current USD)
United States	102,984	106,157	209,141	979
Fed. Rep. of Germany	74,208	90,021	164,229	2,656
Japan	57,881	55,844	113,725	1,025
France	54,247	52,214	106,461	2,017
United Kingdom	53,262	43,760	97,022	1,734
Italy	38,366	34,821	73,187	1,311
U.S.S.R.	36,969	33,310	70,279	276
Netherlands	34,573	35,075	69,648	5,101
Canada	34,306	31,881	66,187	2,899

Source: Compiled from data in United Nations, *1976 Statistical Yearbook* (New York: United Nations, 1977).

1.1 Recent Changes in the Structure of Trade

Significant changes in the structure of Soviet trade have occurred during the postwar period, particularly during the last decade of rapid growth. The number of trading partners has greatly increased, and the proportions of trade among primary trading partners have shifted. Commodities have also shifted in relative importance, and the Soviets have begun to import more than they export, particularly from hard currency developed and developing countries. To cover their debts, the Soviets have been extended long-term credits by those countries.

By 1976 Soviet trade had grown to 56.8 billion rubles, with 117 countries, of which 55.6 percent with other socialist countries and 50.8 percent was with other members of the Council for Mutual Economic Assistance (CMEA): Bulgaria, Cuba, Czechoslovakia, German Democratic Republic, Hungary, Mongolia, Poland, and Romania. Almost a third of Soviet trade was conducted with industrialized capitalist countries, and 11.5 percent with developing countries. (See Table 1-2.) During the last decade, Soviet trade has grown most rapidly with the United States, Japan, and West

European partners, at the expense of trade with other communist countries and with less developed countries (LDCs).

Table 1–2. Soviet Trade Turnover by Principal Countries, 1976.

	Millions of Rubles	Percent of Total
TOTAL	56,755	100.0
Socialist Countries	31,552	55.6
German Dem. Rep.	5,997	10.6
Poland	5,235	9.2
Czechoslovakia	4,543	8.0
Bulgaria	4,466	7.9
Hungary	3,492	6.2
Cuba	2,872	5.1
Yugoslavia	1,821	3.3
Romania	1,600	2.9
Mongolia	615	1.1
China	314	0.6
North Korea	301	0.5
Vietnam	296	0.5
Indust. Capitalist Countries	18,658	32.9
Fed. Rep. of Germany	3,009	5.3
United States	2,205	3.9
Japan	2,121	3.7
Finland	1,979	3.5
Italy	1,778	3.1
France	1,697	3.0
Great Britain	1,233	2.2
Other (19 countries)	4,636	8.2
Developing Countries	6,545	11.5
Iraq	715	1.3
India	648	1.1
Egypt	531	0.9
Brazil	446	0.8
Iran	445	0.8
Syria	235	0.4
Algeria	190	0.3
Other (69 countries)	3,335	5.9

Source: Computed from Ministerstvo vneshnei torgovli, *Vneshniaia torgovlia SSSR v 1976 g.* [USSR Foreign Trade in 1976] (Moscow: Statistika, 1977).

Soviet trade with most countries of the world has continued to increase slowly in absolute terms. Between 1965 and 1976, the fraction of total Soviet trade with the Industrialized West increased from 19 percent to 31 percent, while that conducted with Eastern Europe fell from 57 percent to 48 percent. Soviet trade with the developing world fell from 12 percent to 11.5 percent over the period, after having increased to 15 percent in 1973 and 1974. The two Germanys have emerged as the largest Soviet trading partners, each within its respective bloc.

Although the Soviets have had some success in selling manufactured goods on the world market, they have had a hard time finding ready markets in industrialized countries for what usually have been inferior consumer products. Consequently, the 1970s have seen an expansion of the export of fuels, electricity, ores, and metals, as prices for these items have skyrocketed. In recent years there has been renewed emphasis on an export profile that maximizes raw materials at the expense of consumer goods, while the portion of industrial goods remains essentially constant. In 1976 fuels, electric power, ores, and metals accounted for 49.5 percent of Soviet exports; wood and paper goods and raw materials of animal origin accounted for 8.5 percent; machinery and equipment accounted for 19.4 percent; and consumer goods accounted for 6 percent. Other types of exports accounted for the remaining 16.6 percent.

Soviet exports to the developing countries since 1960 have emphasized machinery and equipment—although not to the degree evident during the 1930s—and consumer goods, which now constitute their highest portion of total imports ever. In 1976 the composition of Soviet imports was: machinery and equipment, 36.3 percent; consumer goods, 35.4 percent; metals, ores, and fuels, 14.7 percent; wood and paper products and raw materials of animal origin, 4.1 percent; and other goods, 9.5 percent.

The structure and quantity of Soviet trade are determined by Soviet planners' priorities for bolstering the domestic economy. On the one hand, they are looking for advanced technology to improve their industrial productivity; on the other hand, they are looking for special types of consumer goods to satisfy the Soviet citizen. Most of the advanced technology has to be purchased from the industrialized capitalist countries, whereas consumer goods are purchased wherever they may be, often being taken in exchange as payment for Soviet aid projects in developing countries. In years of poor harvests, the Soviet Union has had to go to the West to purchase grain. This has become a continuing import item, and the Soviets signed in the early 1970s an agreement with the United States to purchase at least six million tons of grain per year.

Like the foreign trade of all-powerful countries, Soviet foreign trade has political overtones. After the Second World War, the Soviets swung the bulk of their trade for the first time to the countries of Eastern Europe and in 1949 established the CMEA in an attempt to consolidate their political and economic gains in that area. In the mid-1950s, the Soviets began granting aid to developing countries in the Near and Middle East and North Africa, as well as to emerging new nations in sub-Saharan Africa and to politically critical areas such as Korea, Vietnam, and Cuba. In many countries a great deal of this aid was military aid, for which statistics are frequently unavailable save by assuming that payments by these countries of consumer goods and raw materials to the Soviet Union represent reimbursement therefor.

The countries with which the Soviet Union maintains trade and diplomatic relations can be divided into several categories roughly on the basis of geographic area. Those categories organize the following discussion.

1.2 Eastern Europe

In the process of defeating Nazi Germany, Soviet troops came to occupy territory westward beyond Berlin and southward beyond the Danube River. The various countries in this area were characterized to different degrees by discontinuities in political institutions, by physical destruction from war, and by class tensions. Immediately after the war, Soviet objectives in Eastern Europe were basically three: to deny the area to other powers, to use the area to promote Soviet economic recovery from the war, and to prevent anti-Soviet elements from coming to power there. By February 1948, Poland, Romania, Bulgaria, Hungary, Czechoslovakia, and Yugoslavia all had communist governments. The Communist Parties (CPs) in the first four countries had limited indigenous support and promoted themselves by advocating nationalism (especially regarding territorial issues), by introducing popular social and economic reforms (especially land reform where there had been none in the interwar period), by expropriating private industry, and by undermining generally the legal opposition.

In Czechoslovakia the Communists had strong domestic roots and soon became the leading party. The head of the Czechoslovak CP became the country's premier in 1946, and the party thereafter consolidated its influence generally by legitimate means, though the final takeover in 1948 came on the eve of national elections. In Yugoslavia the communist revolution was the outcome of a civil war that raged simultaneously with World War II. As early as November 1945 a single slate of candidates had been presented to the Yugoslav electorate. The Yugoslav CP had extensive indigenous support and was thus able to introduce reforms faster than any other CP in Eastern Europe.

After the war was over, the USSR concluded reparations agreements with these East European states for alleged "collaborationist" behavior. These agreements allowed it to extract as much as $20 billion from that region in 1945–46. Beginning in 1948, the Soviet Union concluded a series of long-term bilateral foreign trade agreements with these states, even though national economic reconstruction had barely begun there. These agreements became a basic element of that reconstruction process: by 1950 these countries conducted the majority of their trade with USSR and with each other; the extremes were Poland (58 percent of total trade turnover) and Bulgaria (90 percent).

In January 1949, in response to the Marshall Plan, the Soviet Union, Poland, Czechoslovakia, Hungary, Romania, Bulgaria, and Mongolia created the CMEA. East Germany and Albania joined in 1950. Yugoslavia remained aloof and was rewarded with an embargo. Although the CMEA's purpose was said to be the promotion of economic development in the member-states, its major function was to coordinate their trade. In 1950 the ruble became the standard currency of CMEA transactions, making the Soviet Union the ultimate arbiter of rates of exchange.

CMEA remained relatively dormant until 1955, when it was revived in response to the formation in the preceding year of the

North Atlantic Treaty Organization (NATO). NATO also resulted in the creation of the Warsaw Treaty Organization (WTO, also called the Warsaw Pact). Until 1955 resources flowed primarily from Eastern Europe to the USSR, but Stalin's death in 1953 had opened the way for reforms in CMEA's organization. The strain in the Stalinist system of post-war political and economic relations in Eastern Europe had become unbearable, and the East Berlin uprising of 1953 and the Hungarian and Polish revolts in 1956 demonstrated drastic needs for reform. Such events induced the Soviets to extend credit to these national regimes in late 1956 and 1957. The purposes of CMEA were redefined to include (1) the facilitation of mutual exchanges of experiences and techniques, (2) the promotion of an international division of labor and of specialization in industrial production, and (3) the coordination of investment in the subsequent five-year plans. By 1958, the year after Khrushchev's consolidation of his power, genuine economic integration had become Soviet and CMEA policy in the region. The existing price system, which favored the Soviets heavily, was reformed in 1963, and the International Bank for Economic Cooperation (IBEC) was created for the purpose of multilateralizing trade within the bloc.

However, the notion of economic integration began to take on disquieting supranational tones, and Romania opposed the Soviet plan for integration during the CMEA sessions in 1962. With the support of East Germany and Czechoslovakia, the two most industrially developed East European states, Romania declared that international economic efficiency within the world Communist system would mean not only that the less industrialized countries (such as Romania) would develop more slowly, but also that they would have to provide raw materials and agricultural support for the further expansion of already industrialized national economies. The Soviets could not effectively threaten the Romanians with an economic boycott, because Western Europe could offer them alternative trade arrangements. Furthermore, China was using the issue in its dispute with the Soviets, which by then had become an open polemic. The argument raged for three years, the Romanians becoming ever more defiant and independent. In the end, shorter-term bilateral agreements once again became the preferred economic instrument throughout the CMEA. Only with changes in leadership upon the death of the Romanian leader Gheorghe Gheorghiu-Dej in 1965 and the ouster of Khrushchev in 1964, was the Soviet Union able to mollify its discontented ally.

Trade among East European countries themselves increased markedly from 1966 to 1968. IBEC failed to multilateralize the trade behavior of the CMEA members, but bilateral ties excluding the Soviet Union proliferated. They even collaborated with each other and without the Soviets on joint-stock enterprises. Khrushchev's heirs were still interested in integrating the CMEA members with one another, but the invasion of Czechoslovakia in 1968 had the side effect of quelling renewed moves to confer supranational economic power on CMEA, while also halting any incipient disintegration of the organization.

In the late 1960s, the Soviet Union still supplied most of Eastern Europe's raw-materials imports. In return, it purchased a large fraction of the latter's total machinery exports. As raw materials became more valuable in the world market and hard currency became more desirable, the USSR grew dissatisfied with this commodity structure of trade among the CMEA countries. As the 1970s began, the Soviet Union started asking other CMEA member-states to purchase more Soviet machinery and to deliver more consumer goods to the USSR.

In 1971, just in time for Cuba's entrance into CMEA in the following year, CMEA adopted a Comprehensive Program of Socialist Economic Integration, i.e., international economic cooperation. But it was only a set of proposals and contains few suggestions for their implementation. The Comprehensive Program was sought to address, over a time frame of 15 to 20 years, an enormous array of problems concerning coordination of programs to increase the international division of labor, foreign trade flows, and joint investment projects. The increased activity of IBEC and the creation of a new International Investment Bank (IIB) were two major attempts to realize those goals.

The CMEA Council instituted two further structural changes in 1974, against what is believed to be strong opposition by the East European states: the principle of unanimity was eliminated as a requirement for certain actions, in order to prevent Romania's opposition from holding up certain projects; and CMEA constituted itself a single legal entity, so as better to deal directly with the European Economic Community in Western Europe and with the United States. The latter move drew especially strong opposition from the East European countries, because it limited their independence in matters of trade and cooperation with the West. Two further proposals to promote integration were pressed in 1975. The first revised intra-CMEA pricing policies to Soviet advantage and initiated monetary reforms. The second altered planning procedures and provided for the investment by the East European countries of up to 10 billion rubles in extractive and primary manufacturing projects on the USSR. In spite of these measures, the individual countries of CMEA (including the USSR) have over the last 10 years turned more and more towards developed Western economies for commodities that the CMEA countries cannot supply to each other, in particular sophisticated industrial technology and training. Indicative of this trend is the statistic that the East European share of total Soviet trade declined from 57 percent to 48 percent between 1965 and 1976.

The Soviet Union continues to export mainly raw materials and energy to CMEA partners, although the amount of machinery and equipment is increasing. In the mid-1970s, more than a quarter of all Soviet exports to other socialist countries were fuels and electrical energy, about a fifth were ores and concentrates, and between a fifth and a quarter were machinery and equipment. Exports of oil, natural gas, and electricity to the east European countries have been facilitated by construction of the Druzhba (Friendship) oil pipeline, the Bratstvo (Fraternity) gas pipeline, and a number of other high-voltage electrical transmission lines including the Mir (Peace) line across the western Soviet border. These will be enhanced in the near future by the Orenburg natural gas pipeline, which will connect the newly discovered large gas fields of Orenburg Oblast in the southern Urals with several East European countries. During the mid-1970s, half of all Soviet oil and oil products went to Poland, Czechoslovakia, Bulgaria, Hungary, and the German Democratic Republic. Romania had its own oil supplies.

Soviet imports from Eastern Europe consist of consumer goods, machinery, and equipment. During the mid-1970s, about one-fifth of all Soviet imports from Eastern Europe were food products, another fifth manufactured consumer goods, and two-fifths machinery and equipment. During the mid-1970s Eastern Europe supplied close to 60 percent of all the machinery and equipment imports by the Soviet Union. This statistic is down from levels it had attained before the Soviet Union began substantial imports from West Germany, the United States, Japan, and other capitalist countries. East Germany supplies by far the largest proportion of machinery and equipment exports to the Soviet Union; Czechoslovakia and Poland are next in importance among East European countries, but now both of these have been surpassed in absolute figures by West Germany.

Rapidly rising world market prices for energy and raw materials during the first half of the 1970s caught the Soviet Union by surprise, as its customary trade relations with CMEA countries stipulated that prices be set only every five years. When the price of crude oil on the world market, for example, more than quadrupled between 1972 and 1974, the Soviet Union was caught between its desire to export more oil to the industrialized West in return for hard currency on the one hand and, on the other hand, its commitment to sell the oil to its CMEA partners near the old price.

This experience, combined with declining rates of economic growth in the USSR and exceedingly poor harvests in 1972 and 1975, convinced the Soviets to revise intra-CMEA pricing policies to their own advantage. Intra-CMEA prices were increased ahead of schedule, and the countries involved agreed to set intrabloc oil prices annually at a level equivalent to the average market price over the three most recent years. The Soviet Union still sold oil to the CMEA countries at a price lower than the world market, but it raised the price of oil appreciably and avoided major economic and political dislocation in the countries concerned.

Although the Soviets have encouraged the East European countries to look elsewhere for oil, they have decided to meet the bulk of CMEA's energy requirements at least during the current (1976–1980) Five-Year Plan, because any significant energy shortfall in Eastern Europe would create a severe, possibly insurmountable, balance of payments problem hampering future economic development. In return for supplying Eastern Europe with fuels and other raw materials at favorable prices, the Soviet Union has convinced the East European countries to increase significantly their investment in Soviet extractive industries. Various East European countries have agreed to help construct the Orenburg gas pipeline, the Ust-Ilim cellulose factory, an iron and steel complex at Kursk, the Kiembai asbestos plant, and a plant to produce ferro-alloys. For these projects the East Europeans have already promised 9 billion transferable rubles (over $13 billion dollars equivalent). They are extending this credit at the low interest rate of about 2 percent per year. The East Europeans countries are effectively subsidizing Soviet industry. They will be repaid over a period of about 20 years in the form of products produced by the projects for which they are now supplying equipment, machinery, and personnel.

Over the years, the primary concerns of the Soviet Union with regard to Eastern Europe seem to have been: (1) stability of economic and political relations, (2) quality and mix of products that can be supplied to the Soviet Union, and (3) favorable terms of trade for the Soviet Union. More recently, to these have been added: (4) good economic performance by the planned economies of Eastern Europe, (5) modernization of the Soviet and other CMEA economies, and (6) insulation from capitalist business cycles. Through the years, the Soviets have been faced with the difficult task of assuring the stability of supplies from the East European countries while helping them modernize and attain high product quality. It now appears that joint ventures, such as the ones just mentioned, might help resolve this dilemma. The Soviets want to continue to promote integration of the East European national economies with their own, and it appears that the joint ventures may be the way to do so without causing political upsets. In practice, however, the process is proceeding very slowly.

1.3 Other Socialist Countries

1.3.1 China

For the first decade of the existence of the People's Republic of China, through the late 1950s, the USSR rendered it fraternal socialist aid. However, ideological conflict between the two appeared. Khrushchev's famous 1956 "secret speech," which began his de-Stalinization campaign, made the break irrevocable. As interparty relations worsened, interstate relations became likewise strained. By 1960 Khrushchev had recalled to the USSR all Soviet technicians in China and terminated all economic aid, leaving factories half-built and tractors idle for want of spare parts.

The polemics between the Chinese and the Russians are not now as vituperous as they were in the 1960s. While interparty relations remain poor, the interstate relations have improved. Most stable in this regard is the establishment of a navigation commission to govern traffic on the Ussuri River, where Chinese and Soviet troops clashed in 1968. The underlying territorial questions, however, have not been resolved. The Chinese still claim much land now under the Soviet flag, north of the Amur River and east of the Ussuri River in the Far East, as well as along the international border of the former East Turkestan. The Soviets maintain a considerable troop buildup along their Chinese border, although at present the Chinese are not pushing these claims vigorously. China also continues to compete with the Soviet Union for influence in many Third World regions, particularly in Africa and southern Asia, and occasionally even in Eastern Europe and Cuba.

Trade between China and the Soviet Union has declined ever since the peak of over $2 billion in 1959. Now it barely exceeds Soviet trade with North Korea or Vietnam. In 1976 China accounted for only 0.6 percent of Soviet trade. Primary exports from the Soviet Union to China are machinery and energy resources, whereas primary exports from China to the Soviet Union are consumer goods, especially items of clothing and food.

1.3.2 North Korea and Vietnam

The Soviet Union has had experiences in Korea and Vietnam similar to those of United States: much involvement and little result. As early as 1964 North Korea changed its allegiance from the Soviet Union to China and shortly thereafter set out on a course independent from both of them. During recent years, North Korean government officials seem to have been engaging in questionable international monetary maneuvers in an attempt to pull themselves out of the hole of a large hard currency debt. An interesting episode occurred in December 1976, when nearly a third of the North Korean embassy personnel in Moscow were expelled in the wake of a scandal involving black marketeering in Scandinavia.

The Soviets created a steel industry in North Korea, just as the United States did in South Korea, and Soviet imports from North Korea include large amounts of steel, other metal products, ores, and machinery. Most Soviet exports to North Korea are also products of heavy industry. However, this trade is small in relative terms. In 1976, North Korea accounted for only 0.5 percent of total Soviet trade turnover.

Since the fall of the Thieu regime in South Vietnam, relations between the Soviet Union and the unified Vietnam have rapidly cooled. The Soviets no longer supply massive amounts of equipment to Vietnam, and the trade has dwindled to even less than that with the North Korea. What trade remains is still much more Soviet exports to Vietnam than vice versa. In June 1978, Vietnam became a member of CMEA. Trade with the Soviet Union could expand rapidly as a result.

1.3.3 Cuba

The USSR has subsidized the Cuban economy for many years by purchasing huge amounts of raw sugar, often above the world market price. However, the absolute value of this trade has not historically been high. In 1972, however, Cuba joined the CMEA and Soviet–Cuban trade has increased significantly since then, to such an extent that in 1976 Cuba accounted for 5.1 percent of Soviet trade. This was a higher portion of total Soviet trade than some of the East

European CMEA members and was almost as much as the share of West Germany, the top western trader with the Soviet Union. The Soviets generally import more from Cuba than they export, possibly indicating that the Soviet Union continues to supply Cuba with significant amounts of military aid. Almost all Soviet imports from Cuba remain raw sugar, some of which is eventually re-exported after it has been refined in the Soviet Union. Soviet exports to Cuba are primarily machinery of various sorts and petroleum.

1.4 Less-Developed Countries

The Soviet Union has always conducted some trade with the "Third World," mainly to purchase certain consumer commodities that are not produced at all, or not produced in sufficient quantities, in the Soviet Union, particularly luxury fruits and beverages such as cocoa, tea, oranges, and so on. Before the mid-1950s, this trade was never very large nor very vital to the Soviet Union, but some of it had political overtones that were important to the Soviets in the strip of countries along their southern margins stretching from the eastern Mediterranean to India.

In 1954, Khrushchev's government began an aid program, both civil and military. It has expanded and become intertwined with increasing trade and political aspirations in the various countries of the Third World, stimulating Soviet trade in these countries to the point where during recent years it has represented around 11–12 percent of total Soviet trade.

In many cases Soviet trade and aid agreements take the form of credit to LDCs. The purpose is to finance development projects that the Soviets largely construct and equip. The Soviets are usually repaid in kind with export products from recipient countries, often products of the aid projects themselves. Such projects have included mining and other raw material extraction, and the construction of major dams and other hydro-works, steel mills, roads and other transport facilities. The Soviets try to fit the type of project undertaken to the stage of development in each country and to take into account both the major needs of the economy of the recipient country and the level of skills of its labor force. Thus, in India the

Soviets have helped build steel mills, oil refineries, and other sophisticated industries. In Afghanistan they have emphasized such things as construction of highways into remote parts of the country, in order to open up these areas to trade and communication with the rest of the country.

Such development projects have involved the presence of Soviet engineers and other skilled workers and technical advisors. They first set up the projects and then remain to train their counterparts in recipient countries to run and maintain the equipment. By 1975 the number of Soviet technicians in LDCs had risen to about 18,000. By 1975 Moscow had trained about 23,000 technical personnel from various countries in the Soviet Union and about 450,000 on the job within the countries themselves. A scholarship program has brought the bright young elite from many countries of Asia and Africa to institutions of higher learning in Soviet Union.

Military aid has often been the most productive aspect of Soviet aid insofar as Soviet political aims are concerned, The Soviets frequently have entered into areas of political and military chaos at critical moments when crumbling local regimes were grasping for aid from any quarter, and have offered credits to buy sophisticated, costly military equipment that would become obsolete very rapidly. This strategy ties up exports from recipient countries for years to come, starting them down the road of unending purchases of new military equipment, as well as retraining of personnel as military equipment becomes more and more sophisticated each year.

Over the years, Soviet aid to LDCs has not amounted to more than 1 percent of the total world aid to them. While the Soviets have devoted 0.05 percent of their GNP to aid, Western industrialized countries have devoted an average of 0.3 percent of their GNP to aid. In many cases, Soviet aid has had disproportionate propaganda value because the aid has been concentrated in a few countries on a few large visible construction projects, always in the public sector. By contrast, aid from the United States, which is incomparably larger in total value than Soviet aid, has often been diffused into human welfare programs such as food relief, which have no lasting concrete edifices, or has been infused into developing countries through local privately owned concerns.

Another difference is that the Soviets have provided very few grants. Aid is usually extended in the form of credits to be paid back, typically over a period of 12 years, with export products from the developing countries. The interest rates have been about 2.5 percent, though they have been increasing recently. In contrast, much aid from the United States has been outright grants.

Table 1-3. Soviet economic credits and grants extended to less developed countries, 1954-1975, in millions of U.S. dollars.

TOTAL	10,859	EAST ASIA	156
AFRICA	1,435	Burma	16
Algeria	425	Cambodia	25
Cameroon	8	Indonesia	114
Central Afr. Republic	2	Laos	1
Chad	10	LATIN AMERICA	602
Congo	14	Argentina	245
Equatorial Guinea	1	Bolivia	31
Ethiopia	104	Brazil	30
Ghana	93	Chile	238
Guinea	200	Colombia	10
Guinea Bissau	1	Peru	28
Kenya	48	Uruguay	20
Mali	86	NEAR EAST & S. ASIA	8,666
Mauritania	4	Afghanistan	1,263
Morocco	98	Bangladesh	300
Niger	2	Egypt	1,300
Nigeria	7	Greece	84
Rwanda	1	India	1,943
Senegal	9	Iran	750
Sierra Leone	28	Iraq	549
Somalia	153	Nepal	20
Sudan	64	Pakistan	652
Tanzania	20	Sri Lanka	95
Tunisia	34	Syria	417
Uganda	16	Turkey	1,180
Upper Volta	1	Yemen (Aden)	15
Zambia	6	Yemen (Sanaa)	98

Source: Orah Cooper, "Soviet Economic Aid to the Third World," in United States Congress, Joint Economic Committee, *Soviet Economy in a New Perspective* (Washington, D.C.: U.S. Government Printing Office, 1976), p. 194.

Strangely enough, the low-interest loans from the Soviet Union seem to have impressed many of the less developed countries more than gifts have. Loans appear to convey a sense of dignity to the debtor country, allowing it to pay its own way rather than accepting charity. Also, in cases Western countries grant credit, interest rates have typically been much more than the Soviets have charged. This has given the Soviets opportunities to criticize Western countries as usurious.

Aid costs the Soviets very little in the end, since most of it will eventually be paid back. In fact, LDC payments to the USSR on earlier loans are already largely counterbalancing new Soviet loans being made to the LDCs. Over the entire period of Soviet aid, repayments have equaled about 40 percent of deliveries, and this percentage has risen over time. Repayments of principal and interest to the Soviet Union in 1975 approached $300 million while aid deliveries to the LDCs reached $400 million; the net aid transfer in 1975 was thus only about $100 million. Veteran recipients of Soviet aid already pay more to service their debts than they receive in new aid: e.g. India since 1969, and Iran and Iraq since 1975.

The Soviets have frequently assisted with projects that Western countries have declined to aid due to political reasons. An outstanding example is Egypt's Aswan Dam, for which the United States and other Western countries withdrew financing after Nasser nationalized the Suez Canal in 1956. The Soviets then stepped in to aid the Egyptians. Another example is the creation of a national oil industry in India after Western oil companies had told India it had no petroleum resources. The Indians later realized that the Western oil companies had not given them accurate information on Indian oil deposits, because these companies wanted to continue selling oil to India. Still another example is Soviet participation in developing India's iron and steel industry, a project Western corporations and governments refused to aid because the Indian government wished to make it a public, not private, enterprise.

The USSR pledged about $11 billion to the Third World in economic assistance between 1954 and 1975, but only about $6 billion of this aid has been delivered. Deliveries have lagged behind commitments by an average of seven years. Although Soviet foreign aid was a creation of Khrushchev and received much propaganda during his regime, commitments and deliveries of Soviet aid have been growing quietly throughout the current Brezhnev regime, so that annual deliveries are now nearly three times what they were under Khrushchev. Soviet trade with LDCs, however, has been increasing at a rapid rate. The share of aid deliveries in total Soviet exchange with LDCs has decreased from about 50 percent in 1953 to about 25 percent in 1974. The countries that have received the most Soviet aid—Egypt, India, Iran, and Iraq—have become the largest Soviet trading partners among the LDCs. During the first half of the 1970s these four countries accounted for between one-third and one-half of all Soviet-LDC trade.

Soviet aid has emphasized its neighbors in Asia and north Africa, in a belt extending from the western Mediterranean to the borders of China. (See Table 1-3.) Over the entire period, 1954-75, these countries have received 80 percent of Soviet aid. The remainder has gone in scattered amounts to 40 other LDCs of varying location and political persuasion. Sub-Saharan Africa has received about 8 percent of Soviet aid, Latin America a little more than 5 percent.

Table 1-4. Major recipients of Soviet economic aid, 1954-1975 and 1973-1975, in percents of total.

Country	1954-1975	1973-1975
India	18	14
Afghanistan	12	18
Egypt	12	—
Turkey	11	26
Iran	7	—
Pakistan	6	11
Algeria	4	—
Other	30	31

Source: Orah Cooper, "Soviet Economic Aid to the Third World," in United States Congress, Joint Economic Committee, *Soviet Economy in a New Perspective* (Washington, D.C.: U.S. Government Printing Office, 1976), p. 195.

The geographical distribution of aid to the belt of Afro-Asian countries bordering the Soviet Union has shifted somewhat from year to year. Over the entire aid period India has received the most Soviet aid, 18 percent of total. Egypt has ranked second, with 12 percent. Both these countries are important regional powers in their parts of the world. Egypt has recently turned more and more toward the West, however, and Turkey has become more neutral, so Soviet aid has turned from Egypt to Turkey. During the years 1973–75, Turkey received 26 percent of all Soviet aid to LDCs. (See Table 1-4.)

The three political aims underlying Soviet aid to the LDCs are: (1) to extend influence among the newly independent countries of Africa and Asia at the expense of the West; (2) to protect Soviet interests in Countries bordering the USSR, presenting to them the Soviet model of economic development; and (3) to maintain a presence in uncommitted countries, playing a waiting game in the hope of alignment eventually on the side of the Soviet Union. The Soviets have often interjected themselves into uncertain political situations at or even before the independence of LDCs, hoping to exert great influence with little effort in fluid situations. Such actions have backfired on the Soviets as often as not. Although they have been fairly successful in establishing ongoing relations with many countries, they have gained only few if any significant conversions to communism. This has been particularly true in Africa where nationalistic young leaders have arisen in newly emerging countries. In the last decade, the Soviets have negotiated with these people on their own terms, even to the detriment of local CPs in these countries.

Of course, Soviet actions have been more politically motivated in countries nearer to their own borders or in strategic areas of the world where the Soviets are trying to establish a presence. Ancient rivalries with Persian, Turkic, Arabic, and Mongolian Empires still color relations between the Soviet Union and their neighbors to the south, and the desire for port facilities in the Mediterranean has had great influence on Soviet relations with Egypt and other north African countries. Their current ambition to establish a large naval presence in the Indian Ocean has greatly influenced their activities in countries around the Red Sea, the Persian Gulf, and Southeast Asia. In parts of the world remote to the Soviets, such as Latin America, their activities have been more economically motivated to gain certain much-needed commodities, for example in recent years corn from Argentina and Brazil. Because of the different motives and different forms of activity in different parts of the world, Soviet relations with the developing countries are discussed below in several groups.

1.4.1 Southern Neighbors

1.4.1.1 Arab States and Israel

Gamal Abdel Nasser bought some machine guns from Czechoslovakia in 1955, when the West refused to sell arms. Thus began Soviet military penetration of the Middle East. Since the end of the Second World War, Moscow's primary aim in the Middle East has been to remove Western influence from the area. Such was the Soviet goal when the United Kingdom had hegemony in the region; such remains its goal now that British influence has waned and American influence has grown.

Until 1970, the year of Nasser's death, Egypt received somewhere between one-third and two-fifths of all Soviet military aid to LDCs. Since then, the amount has declined drastically. Syria, by contrast, received about one-twentieth of all Soviet military aid to LDCs until 1970, since which time it has received about three-tenths of such aid, or about $430 million per year, more than any other country. Iraq is the third-largest recipient of Soviet military aid, following behind Egypt and Syria. These three countries together received over half of all Soviet military aid between 1955 and 1974, and more than two-thirds in recent years.

During the twenty years from 1955 to 1974, Egypt received about $3.1 billion worth of Soviet military aid. In the second decade, 1964–73, it received $2.3 billion, or 15 percent of total Soviet arms exports to all recipients, including the Warsaw Pact countries and North Vietnam. Moscow's policy with respect to Egypt has been heavy-handed: not only has it opposed Egyptian national interests, including Sadat's trip to Jerusalem to seek peace with Israel, but also it has also upon occasion interfered in domestic Egyptian affairs. The Soviet Union's insistence that its naval facilities at Alexandria be declared off limits to Egyptian personnel is one of the milder infringements on Egyptian sovereignty.

As a result of such tensions between the Soviet Union and post-Nasser Egypt, Sadat ordered all Soviet military advisors out of Egypt in 1972 and later, in 1976, abrogated the Treaty of Friendship and Cooperation signed in Cairo in 1971. The latter action particularly disturbed the Soviets in view of their having granted Egypt $1.3 billion in economic loans and credits over the 22-year period, or 12 percent of all Soviet foreign aid to LDCs. The most famous of these aid projects was the Aswan High Dam, begun in the late 1950s with Soviet help after the West retaliated against Nasser's nationalization of the Suez Canal by refusing Egypt economic aid. Soviet–Egyptian trade, however, remains high. As late as 1975, the total trade turnover between the two countries was the highest among all Soviet trade with the Third World, excluding socialist LDCs such as Cuba.

Soviet–Egyptian trade has decreased somewhat since then, but in 1976 Egypt still ranked third in total trade on the Soviet–LDC list, following Iraq and India. Half of all Soviet imports from Egypt are cotton fiber and cotton thread. Other major commodities are leather footwear, perfumes and cosmetic articles, rice, essential oils and natural fragrances, and fresh oranges. These Egyptian exports represent most of the trade now, as the Soviet Union is collecting for past aid on development projects.

In 1972 there were about 18,000 Soviet military men in Egypt: 4000 advisors, 12,000 members of regular units, and 2000 specialized technicians, including 100 Soviet MiG pilots sent to Egypt in air defense squadrons in 1970. When Sadat ordered them to leave, however, he indicated that Egypt would continue to provide the Soviet navy with refueling and refitting facilities at Egyptian ports and that Soviet civilian advisors engaged in industrial projects and electrification of the countryside would be permitted to remain. The USSR had about 100 development projects going on in Egypt at that time.

Thus, despite all the political backing and all the military and economic aid that the Soviets have extended to Egypt, it appears that the Soviet presence in Egypt for the foreseeable future will be minimal. The Soviet Union is playing no significant role at present in negotiations that are going on between Egypt and Israel, both sides now relying on the United States for mediation.

As their presence and influence on Egypt have waned, the Soviets have turned their attention increasingly to Syria. Since 1970 Syria has received about 30 percent of all Soviet military aid to LDCs, equivalent to about $430 million per year. Soviet economic aid to Syria between 1954 and 1975 amounted to only $47 million, or 4 percent of all Soviet aid to the Third World; most of Syria's economic aid has come from Saudi Arabia. However, Syria has consistently ranked fifth or sixth among developing countries trading with the Soviet Union. Soviet imports from Syria consist primarily of cotton, wool, silk, knitted fabrics, and synthetic fabrics.

Although the Soviets in the past have traded with and offered economic and military aid to other Arab countries, including Algeria, Morocco, Tunisia, Libya, Kuwait, Jordan, Saudi Arabia, Sudan, Lebanon, the Peoples' Democratic Republic of Yemen, and the Yemeni Arab Republic, most of this activity has been minimal in recent years. During the civil war in Yemen in the early 1960s, the Soviets attempted without success to establish a presence in the critical southwest corner of the Arabian Peninsula, which controls the southern approach to the Red Sea.

In recent years Morocco has been the main Soviet source of fresh oranges, a commodity that Soviet citizens are eager to buy. Trade with Morocco could expand significantly in the near future as a result of a 30-year agreement signed in 1974 providing for Soviet aid in prospecting and mining phosphate ores in Morocco for shipment to the USSR. Apparently, the Soviets are eager to insure a continuing adequate supply for their phosphate fertilizer industry in the event that Kola phosphate minerals become depleted.

Oil from the Middle East is important to the USSR for three reasons: (1) the rising costs of exploiting their own domestic preserves, (2) the rapidly rising oil consumption among CMEA states, and (3) the desire to obtain hard currency and technology from the West.

The Soviet approach with respect to oil matters in the Arab states has been politically circumspect, though guided by opportunism. During the oil crises of 1973–74, for instance, the Soviets encouraged the oil producing countries to impose sanctions on their customers. After this was done, however, the Soviet Union turned around and violated the embargo against the United States and the Netherlands, selling oil directly to those countries. It is estimated that this operation brought the Soviets a windfall profit of about $5 million.

Soviet attitudes toward Israel are affected by both external and internal factors. Israel is an international problem for the Soviets because although most Arab states unequivocally oppose the very existence of Israel, its destruction would vitiate much of Moscow's influence on the Arabs and in the Middle East generally. Domestically, Israel is a problem to the Soviet Union because it offers an alternative to Soviet Jews that entices many of them to apply for emigration permits. Since emigration is viewed by the Soviets as a condemnation of the Soviet system, they tend to view the more than 100,000 Jews who have emigrated from the Soviet Union to Israel since 1971 as a national disgrace. Attempts by Soviet authorities to deny this emigration have aroused worldwide indignation and resulted in such punitive measures against the Soviet Union as the Jackson–Vanik amendment attached to the U.S. Trade Act of 1974 which denies most-favored-nation status to any country practicing restrictive emigration policies. The Soviets have not traded with Israel since the June 1967 war in the Middle East.

1.4.1.2 Turkey

Turkey's relations with the Soviet Union have been historically uneasy and have developed over time only in an atmosphere of mutual suspicion. Relations between them since World War II have blown hot and cold; they seem to have settled by now into lukewarmth. Since Turkey is a member of NATO, it has not received any Soviet military aid, but it has received an increasing amount of economic aid in recent years. Between 1954 and 1975, Soviet aid to Turkey totaled of $1.2 billion, equivalent to 11 percent of all Soviet economic aid to LDCs during that period. In the years 1973–75, however, Turkey has received 26 percent of all Soviet economic aid to LDCs. In recent years, Turkey has in fact become the biggest recipient of Soviet aid. Nevertheless, the USSR has been unable to obtain Turkish permission for the Soviet fleet to pass freely from the Black Sea into the Mediterranean Sea, even though it is helping Turkey build a bridge over Bosporus.

1.4.1.3 Iraq and Iran

The Soviet Union has long been interested in the Persian Gulf. If Persia had been incorporated into the Russian Empire, the USSR could have had an outlet to warm seas via the Persian Gulf. Today the Soviets are interested in Middle Eastern oil, and the strong Western presence in Iran—first British and later American–has bothered them. The Soviets' interest in the area has increased in the last few years, because they now have the capability to establish a strong naval presence in the Indian Ocean.

During the last decade, Soviet opportunities have appeared in both Iran and Iraq, which have now assumed independent military stances. In Iraq in particular, a 1968 coup replaced a pro-Western government with one that is more open to cooperation with the Soviet Union. Both countries have been major recipients of Soviet military aid in recent years. Over the period 1954–75, Iran received about 7 percent of all Soviet aid to LDCs. The Soviets have helped Iran to construct an iron and steel works at Isfahan, a hydropower station, grain elevators, and a trans-Iranian gas pipeline which will facilitate exports to the [South] Caucasus region of the Soviet Union. At present, natural gas represents about 55 percent of all Iranian exports to the Soviet Union.

The Soviets signed a friendship and cooperation treaty with Iraq after the 1968 coup. That treaty laid the basis for rapidly expanding Soviet aid and trade. In 1976, Iraq shot into first place among LDCs in trade with the Soviet Union. Almost all Iraqi exports to the Soviet Union are crude oil. After the Iraqis nationalized their oil industry, they were eager to conclude barter deals with the USSR and Eastern Europe because of difficulties they encountered in marketing. However, in 1973 they announced that they would not pursue such deals in the future because they wanted to acquire hard currency.

1.4.1.4 Afghanistan

Although Afghanistan's economic significance to the Soviet Union is minimal, the USSR has propagandized its aid to that country as a model of Soviet benevolence to a smaller, less-developed neighbor. Afghanistan has received far more Soviet aid per capita than any other country in the world. Between 1954 and 1975, Afghanistan received 12 percent of all Soviet aid extended to LDCs, and during 1973–75 this portion increased to 18 percent. Although Afghanistan has received some aid from other countries, including the United States, its preponderant source has been the Soviet Union. Soviet aid has helped to construct highways and agricultural facilities such as grain elevators.

Trade between the two countries has been moderate, averaging only about 120 million rubles per year. Over half of all Afghanistan's exports to the Soviet Union is natural gas, piped into the Tajik Soviet Socialist Republic just across the border. Afghanistan also sends cotton, wool, fruits, berries, and raisins to the Soviet Union. In return, it receives machinery, transport equipment, and geological surveying equipment. The Soviet presence in Afghanistan has escalated rapidly since the pro-Soviet coup in Afghanistan in May 1978.

1.4.1.5 India, Pakistan, Bangladesh

The Indian subcontinent has a low per capita income and a great deal of human poverty, but the sheer size of its population gives it weight in world affairs. Major powers have consequently taken special notice of it. The Soviets currently hope that South Asia will remain neutral and not enter any regional alliances that would injure Soviet interests there. The USSR has in recent years acted as supplier of aid to the subcontinent and a mediator of political difficulties among the three states there, India, Pakistan, and Bangladesh. In the 1960s in particular, the Soviets successfully arbitrated the Indo-Pakistani border dispute over Kashmir, and during the 1971 war the Soviets abetted the creation of the independent state of Bangladesh (formerly East Pakistan) while the United States tilted with China toward the West Pakistanis, who failed to repress the grass-roots aspirations of their ethnically distinct coreligionists in the East. Soviet mediation of negotiations of the military situation on the subcontinent brought about an agreement between India and Pakistan in March 1972 on the non-use of armed force and withdrawal of troops from occupied areas.

India, by far the most populous of the three countries, has received the lion's share of Soviet aid and trade with the region. Between 1954 and 1975 India received 18 percent of all Soviet exports to LDCs, and Pakistan received 6 percent. In recent years, Soviet aid to India has decreased and that to Pakistan has risen. Between 1973 and 1975, for example, India received 14 percent of Soviet aid while Pakistan received 11 percent. On a per capita basis, therefore, Pakistan now receives considerably more aid than India. During those three years, however, Turkey and Afghanistan received significantly more than either India or Pakistan.

Over the years, Soviet aid to the Indian subcontinent has been far less than American aid has been, but once again the Soviets have generally derived more propaganda mileage from their aid by concentrating on such things as steel mills, oil prospecting and refining, thermal and hydropower stations, and plants for producing electrical equipment, pharmaceuticals and surgical instruments.

The Soviets have supplied a modest amount of military aid to India. During the Indian–Chinese border conflicts in 1962 and 1965, they supported the Indian efforts against the Chinese. India has traditionally been the Soviet Union's primary trading partner in the Third World, although Iraq edged it out of first place in 1976. Soviet exports to India consist mainly of machinery and equipment for Soviet-aided construction works, oil and oil products, nitrogenous fertilizers, and urea. In return, the Soviets receive tea, cashew nuts, jute, rawhides, tobacco, and cotton goods, as well as a fairly wide variety other consumer items. Soviet military aid to India has been modest.

In 1965, the Soviet Union signed an agreement with Pakistan committing it to assist the latter in the implementation of 30 major development projects over a five-year period. These projects were primarily for projects in the steel and power industries and for the construction of seaports and airfields. The Bangladesh crisis in 1971 severely strained relations between the two countries, but in March

1972 Pakistan and the Soviet Union agreed to restore and extend economic, scientific, technical, and cultural relations. In March 1973, Moscow released Pakistan from the obligation to pay debts incurred by East Pakistan before it gained its independence as Bangladesh in 1971. In 1973, the Soviets signed a three-year trade agreement with Pakistan. Although Soviet economic aid to Pakistan has been rather high during the last few years, trade between the two countries has remained quite low. In return for Soviet equipment for aid projects, Pakistan mainly exports cloth, fabrics, and leather products to the Soviet Union. Soviet military aid to Pakistan has been minimal.

The Soviet Union has offered aid to Bangladesh from the beginning in 1971 and had, through 1975, committed $300 million to assist in the construction of a thermal power station, a radio broadcasting station, and an electrical equipment plant, and for geological prospecting for oil and gas. Actual trade, however, has remained rather low. The minor exports from Bangladesh to the Soviet Union are mainly jute, leather, and tea.

1.4.2 Sub-Saharan Africa

During the 1960s, the Soviets envisioned great opportunities in sub-Saharan Africa as one new country after another emerged from the disintegrating Belgian, French, and British empires. Most of these emerging countries were in varying stages of political, military, and economic turmoil, and the Soviets tried to manipulate unstable situations in their own favor.

Despite economic and military aid to such countries as Guinea, the Congo, Ghana, Mali, and Ivory Coast, the Soviets' success in influencing their economic and political development has been marginal. More recently, the Soviets have turned their attention more to establishing a military presence bordering the Indian Ocean, either in newly independent East African states such as Mozambique or near the Gulf of Aden farther north.

In 1975, Somalia was the only major Soviet aid recipient in sub-Saharan Africa. At the time the USSR was building a naval base there at Berbera on the Indian Ocean. However, during the Somali-

Ethiopian war in 1977, the Soviets began giving military support to Ethiopia, a genuinely fascist regime masquerading as Marxist-Leninist. For this, the Soviets were kicked out of Somalia. It appears that the Soviets committed the main error of post-1945 American foreign policy: supporting a dictatorship because of its ideological garb.

In the final analysis, Soviet aid to sub-Saharan Africa has been minimal. The biggest recipients have been Guinea, Somalia, and Ethiopia, which between 1954 and 1975 respectively received $200 million, $153 million, and $104 million. In recent years Ethiopia, Somalia, and Angola have received the most military aid. Most Soviet aid to Guinea was extended during the 1960s, and Ghana and Mali also responded to Soviet attention at that time. However, during the mid- and late 1960s a large number of military coups in Africa surprised and chagrined the Soviets, particularly the ones in Mali, Ghana, and Guinea. Guinean authorities especially hurt the Soviets during the Cuban missile crisis in fall 1962, when they denied the Soviets the right to land planes bound for Cuba at the Conakry airport, which the Soviets had finished reconstructing only a few months before.

In most of their attempts to interject themselves into critical military and political situations in Africa, the Soviets have run head-on into competition with the Chinese, who, in East Africa at least, seem to have had some natural advantages. Since 1970, China has granted almost twice as much aid to Africa as the Soviets have.

Major Soviet trading partners in the region are at present Nigeria, Ghana, Cameroon, Guinea, and the Ivory Coast. Soviet imports typically account for 80 percent of all trade with these countries. Cocoa represents between 80 and 100 percent of all Soviet imports except for Guinea, where bauxite accounts for about 70 percent of imports. The Soviets are helping the Guineans develop bauxite mines, and they are taking bauxite in payment for the economic and technical assistance. This bauxite is shipped to a new alumina plant at Nikolaev on the north coast of the Black Sea. The Soviets are also becoming interested in aiding the development in Nigeria of iron, steel, and oil industries, which might supply products to the Soviet Union. But Soviet trade and aid in sub-Saharan

Africa remains low in comparison with their activities in the Mediterranean and the Middle East.

1.4.3 Latin America

If sub-Saharan Africa seems too far away for the Soviets to be very greatly interest in it, Latin America is yet further removed. Excluding Cuba as a socialist country, Soviet trade and aid in Latin America has been low indeed. From 1954 to 1975 Soviet aid to all countries of Latin America totaled only 5 percent of Soviet aid to the Third World.

Soviet imports from Brazil and Argentina have risen significantly over the last few years as the Soviet need to import grains and other foodstuffs has continued to increase. Corn and wheat make up more than 70 percent of Argentina's exports to the USSR, and wool and frozen meat make up almost all the remainder. Brazil ships corn, raw sugar, coffee, cocoa beans, and cocoa liqueur to the Soviet Union. Much farther down the line in quantitative terms, Guyana ranks third among Latin American exporters to the Soviet Union, sending primarily bauxite. There is also very minor Soviet trade with Uruguay, Ecuador, Bolivia, Jamaica (alumina), Colombia, Mexico, Costa Rica, Venezuela, and El Salvador.

1.5 Soviet Intentions toward the Sea

During the last 15 years the Soviets have made a major reorientation from a country that is primarily a land power to one that also aspires to sea power. They have been rapidly building up their navy, their merchant marine, their fishing fleet, and their oceanographic research fleet. They have been building some of the ships themselves, but they have also purchased many of them from such countries as East Germany, Poland, Finland, Sweden, West Germany, Japan, England, Denmark, and the Netherlands. As a result, the Soviets' merchant marine probably is now the largest and most modern in the world.

The naval power of the Soviet Union is essentially on a par with that of the United States, although varying in makeup. Its fishing fleet is certainly the largest and most modern in the world, as is their oceanographic research fleet. In general, most of their ships are more adaptable to multipurpose uses than are ships of other nations. This is particularly true of their merchant marine, which is primarily made up of general cargo vessels that can handle virtually any type of cargo and can operate in areas that lack port facilities and cargo-handling equipment. Such ships could easily be converted to military auxiliary vessels when necessary.

Soviet objectives in the use of the seas seem to be both to deny the U.S. strategic control of such constricted shipping lanes as the Suez Canal, the Straits of Malacca, the Panama Canal, and the Straits of Gibraltar, and to use the sea as a source of food and other materials. To achieve these purposes, ends they have expended much energy to secure footholds in the ports of the Arab world along the Mediterranean Sea and the ports of Men in South Yemen and Singapore in Malaysia.

The Soviets have spread their fishing activities all over the world, to such a degree that they now rank second in the world in total fish catch, after Japan. They see fish as a major source of protein which can augment their meat diet at home where they have chronic shortages of meat. They also look upon the sea as a future source of vegetable and mineral products and are, in addition, carrying on underwater explorations for oil and gas in shelf areas such as those around the Sakhalin Island and along the Arctic coast.

The merchant marine is also a source of hard currency for the Soviet economy. The Soviets now not only carry more than 60 percent of their own foreign commerce in their own bottoms but also are providing similar services to many other countries of the world. This is a complete reversal of the situation 15 years ago when most Soviet trade moved in foreign vessels, representing a drain on the national economy to pay for foreign transport services. To these ends, the Soviets are engaging in perhaps the most vigorous scientific exploration of the sea of any country in the world. Their modern and well-equipped research vessels are everywhere measuring bottom topography, sea currents, marine life, and other valuable information.

1.6 Current Trends and Prospects for the Future

During the last decade, the world situation seems to have settled down somewhat. The Second Indochina War has ended, there have been more serious diplomatic attempts to achieve peace in the Middle East, and the Soviet Union has entered more widely into trade and aid relationships with the industrialized West and the developing world. In recent years, the attention of Soviet leaders has turned more and more toward domestic economic problems, particularly decreasing growth rates, and the corresponding need to import advanced technology from the West and consumer goods for their people. Soviet concerns have thus seemed to become more economic and less political as the Soviet Union gains vested interests in world order and material prosperity over time.

The world is no longer polarized between the U.S. and the USSR, but Moscow continues to decline to recognize that a tripolar or multipolar system is arriving on the world scene. In Europe, the USSR has been more interested in influencing political changes than in institutionalizing military and strategic security. Its goal of making the political unification of the continent impossible has largely been achieved. Even Western Europe, though not as disarrayed as the Soviets might wish, is not without internal divisions. Soviet trade with the West will not decrease. Its economic relationships, coupled with political contracts and treaties, even appear to be assuming a momentum of their own, decreasing the probability that any post-Brezhnev regime may reverse them.

The Soviets see China as the only country that not only represents a direct threat to Soviet territory but also threatens Soviet ideological hegemony. However, Sino-Soviet relations seem to be in a more quiescent state now, and India, with its change of government, has become more strictly non-aligned. Thus, it appears that the more populous countries of the world are acting more independently and that their potential adversaries, accepting them as such, are not forcing political alignments on them. All this would seem to augur well for world order in the foreseeable future.

Soviet policy toward the Third World has over the last decade been based on supporting LDCs' control of their own natural resources and on encouraging regional integration outside the world capitalist economy. The USSR has especially concentrated its attention on its "southern neighbors," a band of countries stretching from North Africa to East Asia. However, it has not increased its influence even within this target area. Although its share of trade with these countries has increased, in most cases that share remains substantially smaller than their trade with the West. In the Middle East, Soviet influence remains limited. Its policy a series of reactions to events it largely cannot control or even influence. In Africa, it has refurbished its image as a partisan of national liberation movements, but its ability or even desire to control the policies of the regimes it helps to establish (with Cuban troops) is open to question.

Further Reading

ADOMEIT, Hannes. 1975. "Soviet Policy in the Middle East: Problems of Analysis." *Soviet Studies* 27, no. 2 (April): 288–305.

ALBRIGHT, David E. 1978. "[The USSR and Africa:] Soviet Policy." *Problems of Communism* 27, no. 1 (January–February): 20–39.

AN, Tai Sung. 1973. *The Sino-Soviet Territorial Dispute*. Philadelphia: Westminster.

BORISOV, O. B., and B. T. KOLOSKOV. 1975. *Soviet-Chinese Relations, 1945–1970*. Bloomington: Indiana University Press.

CENTER for Strategic and International Studies [CSIS], ed. 1969. *Soviet Sea Power*. Special Report Series 10. Washington: Georgetown University, CSIS.

CLINE, Ray S. 1977. *World Power Assessment, 1977: A Calculus of Strategic Drift*. Boulder: Westview Press.

COHN, Helen Desfosses. 1972. *Soviet Policy Toward Black Africa: The Focus on National Integration*. New York: Praeger Publishers.

COMECON: Progress and Prospects, Colloquium 1977. 1977. NATO Directorate of Economic Affairs Series 6. Brussels: NATO Directorate of Economic Affairs.

CZERWINSKI, E. J., and Jaroslaw PIEKALKEWICZ, eds. 1972. *The Soviet Invasion of Czechoslovakia: Its Effects on Eastern Europe*. New York: Praeger Publishers.

DIBB, Paul. 1972. *Siberia and the Pacific a Study of Economic Development and Trade Prospects*. New York: Praeger Publishers.

DONALDSON, Robert H. 1974. *Soviet Policy Toward India: Ideology and Strategy*. Cambridge: Harvard University Press.

FREEDMAN, Robert O. 1975. *Soviet Policy Toward the Middle East Since 1970.* New York: Praeger Publishers.

GITELMAN, Zvi. 1977. "The Jewish Question in the USSR Since 1964." In *Nationalism in the USSR and Eastern Europe in the Era of Brezhnev and Kosygin,* edited by George W. Simmonds, 324–334. Detroit: University of Detroit Press.

GLASSMAN, Jon D. 1975. *Arms for the Arabs: The Soviet Union and War in the Middle East.* Baltimore: Johns Hopkins University Press.

HOLZMAN, Franklyn D. 1976. *International Trade Under Communism: Politics and Economics.* New York: Basic Books.

JAIN, J.R. 1974. *Soviet Policy Towards Pakistan and Bangladesh.* New Delhi: Radiant.

JUKES, Geoffrey. 1973. *The Soviet Union in Asia.* Berkeley: University of California Press.

KANET, Roger E., ed. 1974. *The Soviet Union and the Developing Nations.* Baltimore: Johns Hopkins University Press.

— and Donna BAHRY, eds. 1975. *Soviet Economic and Political Relations with the Developing World.* New York: Praeger Publishers.

KULSKI, Wladyslaw W. 1973. *The Soviet Union in World Affairs: A Documented Analysis, 1964–1972.* Syracuse: Syracuse University Press.

LEDERER, Ivo J., and Wayne S. VUCINICH, eds. 1974. *The Soviet Union and the Middle East: The Post-World War II Era.* Stanford: Hoover Institution Press.

LÖWENTHAL, Richard. (1977) *Model or Ally: The Communist Powers and the Developing Countries.* London: Oxford University Press.

MARER, Paul. 1974. "Soviet Economic Policy in Eastern Europe." In *Reorientation and Commercial Relations of the Economies of Eastern Europe: A Compendium of Papers Submitted to the Joint Economic Committee, Congress of the United States,* edited by John P. Hardt, 135–163. Washington: US Government Printing Office, 1974.

MccGWIRE, Michael, and John McDONNELL, eds. 1977. *Soviet Naval Influence.* New York: Praeger Publishers.

McLANE, Charles. 1973–74. *Soviet–Third World Relations.* Vol. 1, *Soviet–Middle East Relations* [1973b]; vol. 2, *Soviet-Asian Relations* [1973a]; vol. 3, *Soviet-African Relations* [1974]. London: Central Asian Research Centre.

MITCHELL, Donald W. 1974. *A History of Russian and Soviet Sea Power.* New York: Macmillan.

NAIK, J. A. 1972. *India, Russia, China, and Bangla Desh.* New Delhi: S. Chand, 1972.

NATUFE, Omajuwa Igho. 1975. "Soviet Policy in Africa 1945-1970: A Study in Political History." Ph.D. diss., McGill University.

PARVIN, Manouchar. 1977. "The Political Economy of Soviet-Iranian Trade: An Overview of Theory and Practice." *Middle East Journal* 31, no. 1 (Winter): 31-43.

RUBINSTEIN, Alvin Z., ed. 1975. *Soviet and Chinese Influence in the Third World*. New York: Praeger Publishers.

SAVIN, V.A. 1974. "The Territorial Structure of Soviet Export Industries." *Soviet Geography: Review and Translation* 15, no. 1 (January): 29-34.

SCHAEFER, Henry Wilcox. 1972. *Comecon and the Politics of Integration*. New York: Praeger Publishers.

SCHWARTZ, Morton. 1973. "The USSR and Leftist Regimes in Less-Developed Countries." *Survey* 19, no. 2 (Spring): 209-244.

SEN GUPTA, Bhabani. 1976. *Soviet-Asian Relations in the 1970s and Beyond: An Interperceptional Study*. New York: Praeger Publishers.

SHATTAN, Joseph Jacob. 1977. "Soviet Military Aid and the Politics of Leverage: The Soviet-Egyptian Case." Ph.D. diss., Tufts University.

SMITH, Glen Alden. 1973. *Soviet Foreign Trade: Organization, Operations, and Policy, 1918-1971*. New York: Praeger Publishers.

STAAR, Richard F., ed. 1976. *Yearbook on International Communist Affairs, 1976*. Stanford: Hoover Institution Press.

STEVENS, Christopher. 1976. *The Soviet Union and Black Africa*. New York: Holmes & Meier.

SZPORLUK, Roman, ed. 1976. *The Influence of East Europe and the Soviet West on the USSR*. New York: Praeger Publishers.

ULAM, Adam B. 1974. *Expansion and Coexistence: Soviet Foreign Policy, 1917-1973*, 2nd ed. New York: Praeger Publishers.

WALTERS, Robert S. 1970. *American and Soviet Aid: A Comparative Analysis*. Pittsburgh: University of Pittsburgh Press.

WEINSTEIN, Warren, ed. 1975. *Chinese and Soviet Aid to Africa*. New York: Praeger Publishers.

WRIGHT, Arthur W. 1974. "The Soviet Union in World Energy Markets." In *The Energy Question: An International Failure of Policy*, edited by Edward W. Erickson and Leonard Wavennan, 85-99. Toronto: University of Toronto Press.

2 East–South Relations at UNCTAD
Global Political Economy and the CMEA

> *UNCTAD provides focus for examining collective Soviet-bloc (CMEA) negotiating behavior toward the developing countries (Group of Seventy-seven, G77) in response to the initiative for a New International Economic Order in the 1960s and 1970s. Case studies are commodities trade and the Common Fund, the Generalized System of Preferences, the Code of Conduct for Liner Conferences, and the Code of Conduct for Transfer of Technology. The Soviet bloc seeks to use UNCTAD to transform international economic relations while conserving their place in the existing system. CMEA–G77 coalitions are due more to common domestic structures of state trading than to ideology. Their disagreements are traceable to divergent situations within the international economy itself. Interesting contrasts between the CMEA and the EEC as international organizations are revealed as well.*

Keywords: Soviet, CMEA, South, trade, aid, multilateral, negotiations, UNCTAD

Systematic studies of recent behavior by the socialist countries of Eastern Europe in universal international organizations are hard to find. Only a few works, nearly two decades old, address the behavior of the USSR, let alone its smaller allies, and they were completed before the UNCTAD machinery was put into gear (Dallin 1962; Jacobson 1963; Rubinstein 1964; but see Lindell 1972; Schwartz 1972 deals largely with the 1948 Havana Charter). The one exception to this statement concerns specialized international organizations (Osakwe 1972).

UNCTAD is of interest, however, precisely because it "is less political, more functionally specific, and technically oriented" than "the political organs of the United Nations ... [while] at the same time it is less independent, more intensely political, more functionally diverse, and less technical" than the specialized agencies (Gosovic 1972, 265). Focusing on UNCTAD has the added advantage of permitting some comparisons, in a transnational context, between the collective behavior of the East European countries and that of the countries of the European Community (EEC) toward the Third World. Such comparisons are usually complicated by the fact that the intergovernmental economic organization of the East European countries—the Council for Mutual Economic Assistance

(CMEA) — has neither the juridical status nor the common foreign commercial policy that the EEC enjoys. A focus on UNCTAD avoids this difficulty, for the CMEA is incarnated at UNCTAD as an autonomous collective entity, "Group D."

Group D includes the member-states of the CMEA at the time of the foundation of UNCTAD in 1964: the German Democratic Republic, Bulgaria, Hungary, Mongolia, Poland, Romania, Czechoslovakia, and the USSR. Mongolia entered the CMEA in 1962; the LDCs that joined the CMEA later, such as Cuba and Vietnam, continued to be part of the Group of Seventy-seven (G77), but they sometimes associated themselves with joint statements made in the name of the East European socialist countries. ("Socialist countries of Eastern Europe," "CMEA countries," and "East European countries" are all used synonymously with this term, even though Romania calls itself a "developing socialist country" and became a member of the G77 in 1976.) UNCTAD puts together all the industrialized countries maintaining a market economy and designates them as Group B.

The particular features of UNCTAD thus provide an opportunity not only to compare CMEA and EEC behavior toward the Group of 77 (G77) but also to examine the behavior of the socialist countries of Eastern Europe as a group in a unique international organization. My purpose here is neither to analyze the relative influence of the socialist states of Eastern Europe on decisions in UNCTAD, nor to describe quantitatively their trade with the G77. I intend, rather, to understand the CMEA countries' response to the foundation of UNCTAD, behind which they were a motive force; to analyze how their behavior in the organization has been transformed; and to compare, within the focus provided by UNCTAD, the conduct of the CMEA with that of the EEC. The study suggests some basic characteristics of the East European CMEA countries' response to the New International Economic Order (NIEO).

2.1 The CMEA Countries and the Foundation of UNCTAD

During the 1950s the socialist countries of Eastern Europe had hardly any trade with the capitalist world. The organization of their foreign trade system did not dovetail with the system of commerce organized by the latter. The situation of the LDCs being little more favorable, they and the CMEA countries alike were outsiders to the world trade system. It is true that during the 1950s the USSR and other CMEA members attached greater priority to East–West trade than to East–South trade (as is still the case today), but a rapprochement between the LDCs and the CMEA countries was nonetheless logical and natural. The latter sought to satisfy their own material needs at the same time as the former tried to ameliorate their situation. This was accomplished chiefly through long-term agreements for the purchase of primary products at stable and fixed prices. The two groups of countries found themselves not only advocating but also practicing a mutual solidarity in order, first, to resist the capitalist world trade system and, second, to transform it. This arrangement guaranteed some stability to the LDCs' national incomes but also worked to their disadvantage if world market prices rose, leaving them committed to the previously negotiated, lower contractual prices.

Several times in the 1950s and early 1960s the socialist countries of Eastern Europe, led by the USSR, advocated establishing an International Trade Organization (ITO) that would have coordinated and overseen the activities of the United Nations, of its organs, and of every other international organization concerned with international trade (ECOSOC 1958a, 1958b, 1964a, 1964b). From the beginning of the 1960s Third World countries began to enter the United Nations in greater numbers, and they took up the CMEA countries' earlier initiative to reform the world trade system. They called for a conference on the subject to be convened, but they insisted that the world trade system to be established should respond to their own desires rather than those of the CMEA countries (UNGA 1962). The latter, denying any responsibility for the impoverishment of the former, supported their demands against the West. These developments led to the creation of UNCTAD.

The *raison d'être* that the Soviets favored giving for establishing an ITO—a proposal they made yet again at the discussions that were to culminate in the foundation of UNCTAD (Ogarev 1964; Ognev and Ogarev 1964)—was the need to oversee the multitude of international organizations concerned with world commerce. Various documents suggest, however, that the most important aspect of such an ITO from the Soviets' point of view would in fact have been its universality. (Soviet sources establish the position of Group D, because the member-states of Group D present uniform positions, and the USSR has the preponderant voice in the Group. For a summary of some later differences in nuance among the approaches of the CMEA countries to issues involving the Third World, see Despiney 1980, 104–110.) Their aim was to break Western control of existing international economic institutions, such as the General Agreement on Tariffs and Trade (GATT) and the International Monetary Fund (IMF), which excluded the USSR (see, for example, Khvoinik 1965). One of the two principal goals of the ITO, as the Soviets conceived it, would have been to increase the legitimacy of the Soviet state in the system of international trade and in the legal regime governing that system. The Soviet Union also hoped that an ITO would promote an increase in East–West trade.

This conception of the ITO was less important to the functionaries in the USSR Ministry of Foreign Trade, whose responsibility it would have been to negotiate the organization's foundation. The Ministry's official monthly journal never gave the idea much attention, and reports from the USSR's negotiators at Geneva, published while the 1964 Conference was still under way, do not mention an ITO at all; the Ministry journal's polemics were directed, rather, chiefly against the GATT. At Geneva, the Soviet Union and its allies concerned themselves with complaints against the West's embargo and trade discrimination. Soviet representatives at the Conference refused to accept responsibility for LDC poverty, but they backed LDC demands against the capitalist countries. The USSR, Czechoslovakia, Hungary, and Poland agreed to raise the level of their trade with the LDCs in general, and to increase their imports of primary products in particular (ECOSOC 1964c). Eventually, Soviet negotiators at Geneva (Spandar'ian 1964, for example, was a member of the Soviet delegation to Geneva and division head in the Ministry of Foreign Trade; see also *VT* 1964) dropped their own projects for an ITO in order to support the LDCs' resolution that foresaw the establishment of the UNCTAD institutions suggested by Raúl Prebisch (Gardner 1968, 104–5; Bykov 1964).

Against possible criticisms of such tactics by their colleagues, two researchers at the Institute of World Economics and International Relations in Moscow, who had been attached to the Soviet delegation in Geneva, asserted the importance of establishing the rules for transforming the world trade system. In particular, they wrote (Zorin and Ivanov 1964, 83):

> But moreover, many of the socialist countries' propositions addressed the character of international trade relations, the structure of the Trade and Development Council, technical assistance, etc., often while fighting the West's alternative propositions. Why did this happen so? Above all, because what is concerned is the socialist countries' fundamentally different approach from the imperialist camp, to the methods of developing world trade and to the establishment of those methods.

Although the ITO had not been established as originally conceived, Soviet specialists on foreign trade regarded the results of the Geneva Conference favorably. Several months after the end of the Geneva Conference, one such analyst concluded a monograph on UNCTAD by observing that the LDCs emphasized the "questions of establishing without delay an organ of a transitional type that would be responsible for overseeing the fulfillment of the Conference's decisions — including the question of founding a new international trade organization." According to this author the institutionalized UNCTAD, including its Council, was an organ "of a transitional type" — a phrase not without significance in the Marxist-Leninist lexicon (Pinegin 1966, 147).

At the same time the Soviet jurist Fomin (1966, 328) evaluated favorably the principles adopted at the 1964 Conference, which, he declared, affirmed and complemented those of the U.N. Charter. A different Fomin (1980, 7) later opined that the NIEO's projected "reconstruction of the entire system of international economic relations ... has a direct impact on the interests of the socialist community in its cooperation with the developing states" and summarized some general Soviet proposals for realizing the NIEO in the context of the Marxist-Leninist ideological analysis of world economic development.

2.2 Group D Negotiating Behavior at UNCTAD

The two principal questions with which UNCTAD dealt during the 1960s were trade in commodities and preferential tariffs. Negotiations on these two subjects continued into the 1970s, the former in the context of a Common Fund, the latter in the context of a Generalized System of Preferences (GSP).

During the 1970s, other questions were raised at UNCTAD. They came to be resolved by the elaboration of various Codes of Conduct, of which a number now exist, some already agreed upon and some still only in draft form. I discuss two of these Codes: the Code of Conduct for Liner Conferences, which was the first to be negotiated; and the Code of Conduct for the Transfer of Technology, over which deliberations still proceed. Four sets of negotiations are thus treated here.

2.2.1 Commodities Trade and the Common Fund

The CMEA countries' policy in UNCTAD on the issue of trade in commodities is constrained by the national instruments through which their general trade policies are executed. These instruments impose a structure of *trade bilateralism* on their international trade. The organizational imperative of trade bilateralism is that debits and credits be balanced individually with every trading partner, and this is the root of the CMEA countries' anxiety at the prospect of a multilateral system of oversight and control such as the Common Fund. Trade bilateralism is also responsible for the problems of the "transferable ruble" system, which at the time of its establishment foresaw the multilateralization of trade relations within the CMEA itself. (See Brainard 1978 for a brief explanation. McMillan 1974 uses trade statistics to demonstrate the transferable ruble's failure to multilateralize intra-CMEA trade relations.)

Under the regime of trade bilateralism, the East European CMEA countries habitually prefer barter arrangements in commodities trade with LDCs, even for long-term agreements. They would otherwise be required to pay for those products with convertible currencies (which they prefer to use for purchasing Western technology and for servicing debts to Western banks) or to reserve for the LDCs a quota of their own products destined for export. Because the CMEA countries cannot satisfy their needs even by long-term bilateral agreements, they cannot entirely ignore efforts to harmonize the structure of world trade. They are consequently obliged to participate not just in world markets but in international commodity agreements as well.

Politically powerless to transform the world markets in which their economic needs require them to participate, the countries of Eastern Europe are habitually insecure in matters of commodities trade. The evolution of their attitude toward the issue of international commodity agreements is instructive. The change in the position of the USSR, the most conservative country in the CMEA and frequently the spokesman for Group D, illustrates the point.

The Soviet delegate to the UNCTAD session in New Delhi (1968) declared that his country could support the idea of an integrated program for commodities only if the use of buffer stocks were recognized as "a temporary measure ... within the framework of wider commodity agreements" (UNCTAD 1968, 64, 156–58). Five years later an authoritative article in the official journal of the USSR Ministry of Foreign Trade attempted to circumvent the suggestion, made at the VII (Special) Session of the UNCTAD Committee on Commodities, that the GATT concern itself with questions of access to markets and of price determination (Denisov 1973, 26). It proposed that UNCTAD take charge of such matters instead. Then in 1976, at UNCTAD's Nairobi session, Group D finally came out clearly in favor of combining the creation of buffer stocks in the framework of a Common Fund with bilateral commodities trade in the framework of intergovernmentally-negotiated trade agreements (UNCTAD 1976, 11–12). In 1978, however, the Soviet delegate remarked that such agreements could not refer to commerce between member-states of the CMEA, which was "fundamentally different." Wishing to limit the effects that these multilateral arrangements might have on the USSR's national economy, and fearful to protect his country's national sovereignty, the Soviet delegate also stated (UNCTAD 1978) that the USSR could subscribe only to those elements of such an international commodity agreement that were compatible with the plans and programs of the country's economic system.

By the end of 1979, the USSR was participating in the agreements on coffee (negotiated outside UNCTAD), tin, sugar, wheat, and cocoa; and it had showed itself ready to take part in the talks on rubber. Soviet participation in these agreements was limited to levying a tariff, destined to finance buffer stocks, on the exports of producing countries. However, this very participation marked a significant political change: the negotiations in 1980 on the Common Fund finally ended the Group D countries' reluctance to finance buffer stocks with convertible currencies. Ignoring at the talks the question of principle — whether they should contribute scarce convertible currencies to the Common Fund — they became more concerned with questions of principal — what the level of their direct contribution would be to the capital subscribed by the signatory states, and how the level of their financial participation would affect the allocation of votes in the fund (UNCTAD 1980).

Soviet negotiators (Ivanov and Polezhaev 1977, 41) abandoned their previous insistence on linking the creation of the Common Fund with the establishment of control over the activities of transnational corporations, a move they had touted as promoting "progressive socio-economic transformations in the developing countries." (Compare Ivanov and Polezhaev 1976, written before the March 1977 Conference. Ivanov works in the Ministry of Foreign Trade, and Polezhaev is the Soviet representative at the UNCTAD Committee for Commodities.) But if their positions have become less ideological, then such ideological questions have found expression in the terms of international law, for the Soviets and their East European allies pursue issues of this sort within a framework of international law. They base their arguments on non-binding international documents, such as the Charter of the Economic Rights and Duties of States, as well as on legally binding deliberations, such as issue from the discussions at the United Nations Conference on International Trade Law on the activities of transnational corporations or at the International Law Commission (ILC) on the responsibility of states.

Being among the foremost champions of state sovereignty, Soviet jurists seek to limit the rights and obligations of international organizations under international law. They also work to minimize the capacity of international organizations to modify or to be modified by the international-legal framework in which they are situated. The Soviet delegate to the Sixth Committee of the UN General Assembly, for example, commenting on the ILC's work, suggested—perhaps with the CMEA particularly in mind—that international organizations should be able to invoke their own statutes in order to decline to fulfill an obligation or to decline to submit to any part of a treaty that they may have signed (UNGA 1973, 1974, 1977). Similarly, he opined that international organizations have only a "limited juridical personality" and that their competence to conclude international treaties is likewise "limited." The Soviet position thus received a setback when it was agreed that the Common Fund should possess "full juridical personality" and enjoy "the capacity to conclude international agreements with States and international organizations, to enter into contracts, to acquire and dispose of immovable and movable property, and to institute legal proceedings" (UNCTAD 1980, Art. 41).

2.2.2 The Generalized System of Preferences

The description of the Generalized System of Preferences as "a new type of preference in trade between developed capitalist and developing countries," in the subtitle of an article in a professional periodical internal to the USSR Ministry of Foreign Trade (Filimonova 1976), may suggest that it does not apply at all to the Group D countries. However, it is worth noting that the inclusion of agricultural products in the final framework of the Generalized System of Preferences is due at least in part to the efforts of Group D, the members of which have always protested the agricultural tariff (and nontariff) barriers between them and the members of the EEC.

For most of the 1960s, the CMEA countries construed the issue of trade preferences to mean East-West trade or, in UNCTAD's language, "relations between countries with different social and economic systems." During that decade, however, Group D became the target of demands from the G77. In this respect, the Cairo Declaration of the Developing Countries (1962) is the basic general document, and UNCTAD's session in New Delhi (1968) is the key forum. where the LDCs specified the means through which they believed their general goals could be attained. The reply of the Group D countries was twofold. First, they maintained that East-South trade differed structurally from West-South trade in that it was more dynamic; by this they meant the quantitative statistics were more impressive. In fact, the annual growth rate of East-South trade was larger than that of West-South trade, but not so great as Group D suggested: their statistical comparisons were biased by their choice of base year. Second, the CMEA countries held that an increase in East-West trade would benefit world trade generally, including East-South trade (Gosovic 1972, 166, n. 42). They never explained why this should be so, but it nevertheless turned out to be true. It is worthwhile to consider briefly the source of this serendipity.

As trade expanded between the two European blocs during the 1960s, the East European states discovered that trade organizations in the capitalist world would take into account the idiosyncrasies of their national economic structures and institutions, and adapt themselves to their particular features. Some member-states of Group D responded by reforming their own national systems of foreign trade (see Korbonski 1976 for the political aspects). The degree of reform differed with the country; Poland and Hungary seem to have derived the greatest advantage from this evolution (Matejka 1978, chap. 5, is an excellent treatment). These reforms enabled those countries to respond more liberally to LDC demands, not just by introducing new tariff schedules but also by decentralizing toward the enterprise level the processes of decision and funding. This latter reform was more significant and had greater practical effect. Czechoslovakia had tended in a similar direction until the Soviet military intervention there in 1968.

In 1970 the member-states of Group D issued a joint declaration (UNCTAD, 1970), since unchanged and still authoritative, on preferential tariffs with respect to the LDCs. It stated that those East European countries maintaining tariff barriers would give preferences (UNCTAD 1971, paras. 96–107; 1972a; 1972b). It also recalled (UNGA 1965) that the USSR had abolished all tariffs on imports from LDCs in 1965. Actually, these particular moves had little if any effect, because the consumption of goods in centrally planned national economies depends not on prices that are supposedly lower due to the absence of import tariffs, but rather on the level of imports foreseen in the plan. Thus it was more significant that Group D's 1970 statement declared a willingness to provide, in the construction of national economic plans, for increasing the level of imports of finished semi-finished, and agricultural products from the LDCs. The Group D countries said they would not only accept such imports as payment against credits but also give technical assistance in the construction of industrial enterprises. Furthermore, they would apply these measures to every LDC without prejudice to its social or economic system.

At the same time the socialist countries of Eastern Europe invoked, and they continue to invoke, the "principle of mutual advantage" and the "principle of the equality of rights and obligations" in an attempt to limit the advantages that the G77 can derive from measures that respond to their demands (Vel'iaminov 1972, 208–34; 1977; Buvalik 1977, 318–25). In particular, Group D specifies that its respect for preferences in favor of the G77 does not supersede its own desire that all trade be conducted "without discrimination." By this the G77 means that the measures taken by the LDCs to promote their trade with the capitalist countries in Group B should not weaken the positions of socialist countries as exporters (UNCTAD 1976, 15). Thus the CMEA countries insisted, as they made concessions to the LDCs, that the latter should introduce measures favoring exports from the Group D countries, especially by granting terms of trade as favorable as those granted to capitalist countries.

The argument of the East European countries concerning the "principles" of world trade is representative of what may be called the "socialist offensive" in international trade law. The Group D countries use international trade law as a tool for transforming the existing system of world trade through the organs of the United Nations. Although jurists who are members of the ILC participate as private individuals, it is not without interest to note that citizens of the East European countries have played a large role in the deliberations on the most-favored-nation (MFN) clause. The first Special Rapporteur of the ILC on the MFN clause was Hungarian, and his successor is Soviet. The question here is not whether nationals of the Group D countries tend to favor the interests of their states. The fact is that the similarity of these states' social and economic systems creates common interests among them.

The MFN clause, which the ILC took up following the agreement on the Vienna Convention on the Law of Treaties (1969), is inexorably bound to the question of trade preferences. The current Special Rapporteur to the ILC, who is Soviet, opined in 1978 that the "principles" of the GSP take precedence over any others. He adjudged the negotiations occurring under the aegis of the GATT, as well as the GATT's opinions on the ILC's deliberations, to be merely "supplementary" to GSP principles (UNGA 1978, 26–28). At the same time, he decided that the EEC is not an "international" organization but a "supranational" one: by virtue of which, he explained, it is unique, therefore having no substantive place in customary law nor any normative place in the law of treaties (UNGA 1978, 9).

The participation at the ILC of individuals trained in the academies of the socialist countries of Eastern Europe allows the introduction into such deliberations of what they call the "principles" of socialist international law. The case of trade preferences illustrates how the bias in favor of the state interests of the CMEA countries, found in socialist international law generally and trade law in particular, can exercise itself not only against developed capitalist countries but also against LDCs.

2.2.3 The Code of Conduct for Liner Conferences

The Code of Conduct for Liner Conferences was the first Code of Conduct to emerge from deliberations at UNCTAD. (Juda 1981 provides a broad study of shipping issues.) Two key issues figured in its negotiation: the conditions for the Code's entry into force and the rules of arbitration. When the G77 first proposed that arbitration be binding, Group D hesitated to accept the idea. They agreed with the G77 on most of the categories of disputes but made some reservations, most notably the determination of freight rates. Group B then proposed a new arbitration formula, called "mandatory reconciliation," that would be applicable to all categories of disputes. Mandatory reconciliation is a nonbinding method that also permits the parties to a dispute to agree to a form of arbitration other than mandatory reconciliation. This proposal was supported by Group D, whose members probably saw in it an opportunity to preserve state sovereignty (see Minkov 1974, 74–76).

The importance attached to the question of arbitration in this Code, and the novelty of such Codes generally, raise the question of the juridical status of Codes of Conduct. The Soviet jurist G. M. Vel'iaminov (1972, 109–14) devoted significant attention to determining the status of the resolutions of the quadrennial UNCTAD sessions. His analyses also speak to the question of the Codes. In a first article, Vel'iaminov (1970) tried to reconcile the dichotomy between nonbinding and legally binding norms with traditional Soviet doctrine on the capacity of international organizations to create norms of international law. (Averkin 1974 seeks to generalize the question.) Later, basing himself on the Soviet delegation's interpretation of Resolution 15(II) of the New Delhi session of UNCTAD (1968), which recommended increasing Group D's imports from the LDCs, Vel'iaminov (1972, 145) proposed a definition of a norm of international law that "includes the category of nonbinding norms" and which concerned the capacity of international organizations to create such norms.

Suggesting that international organizations play an increasing part in the elaboration of norms of international law, he observed (Vel'iaminov 1972, 134) that "many" of UNCTAD's resolutions that "do not have a direct effect on the creation of norms can have significance for international law *de lege ferenda* [with respect to law to be proposed], particularly by preparing drafts of international conventions but also by helping specific norms to take root as customary law." This position was in line with Soviet international-legal practice, which sought to codify customary international law into treaties. Although Soviet international-law practitioners sought in principle to systematize all the norms governing international affairs, they recognized the role of custom where no applicable treaty existed and they nevertheless accepted a given principle as universally binding (Erickson 1972, 62).

One requirement for the Code's entry into force is curious: not only must a minimum number of states ratify it, but also the ratifying states must represent at least 25 percent of world shipping tonnage. This clause, proposed by Group D and then supported by the member countries of Group B, would seem to contravene the principles of the "representativity" of UNCTAD and the "equality of rights" of states, which the USSR seems to value so highly. But the USSR, as the fifth largest power in world shipping, uses such radical rhetoric only to mask its essential conservatism in matters of transforming the existing regime. For example, at the UNCTAD sessions in Manila (1980), Group D did not support the resolution to eliminate flags of convenience; it only desired the links between the flag and the country to be more strictly controlled. The clause on the Code's entry into force thus in fact expresses the CMEA countries' insecurity in the face of the LDCs' desire to transform the system of maritime commerce. The USSR seeks a more formally legalized system that would provide it with the very security that such a transformation threatens. In this sense Group D's approach to the issue reflects the general attitude that the Soviets habitually adopt at UNCTAD: change without risk.

As the majority of West European countries decided *en masse* to ratify during the quinquennial conference on the Code, it will enter into force. This decision was taken principally because those West European countries that had hesitated to ratify the Code—the United Kingdom, for example—were convinced, in the end, that it would protect them against competition from the Soviet fleet in East–West trade. The Code will constrain the socialist countries of Eastern Europe to furnish maintenance services equitably to every vessel, regardless of its country of origin. This provision contravened the desires of some Western powers, particularly West

Germany, which had been negotiating such questions bilaterally with the USSR. Some questions, such as the status of ports in socialist countries—which in the view of some Western countries, notably the United Kingdom, are not managed on a "commercial basis"—remain unresolved. Doubts remain about the ability of future maritime conferences to resolve the numerous difficulties still existing. These doubts are not assuaged by the absence of a spirit of compromise from the convention that was charged with formulating the Code of Conduct in the first place (Schiering 1979, 188–90)

Despite some initial differences, the Group D countries and the LDCs have tended to reach agreement on the goals to be desired from negotiations. Group D's tendency to use UNCTAD as a forum for denouncing imperialist exploitation manifested itself in perorations on "invisible commerce," including the question of flags of convenience as well as that of insurance (Krasnov 1971, 7–96; Krasnov and Chekhutov 1972). Working to protect their own interests, the East European countries have nothing to lose in supporting claims such as these by the G77 against Group B. It is therefore probable, for instance, that Group D will, in the end, support the abolition of flags of convenience (Hall 1980).

2.2.4 The Code of Conduct for Transfer of Technology

Agreement on a Code of Conduct for Transfer of Technology has not been reached because of unresolved issues—the same issues that had complicated the negotiations on a Code of Conduct on Restrictive Business Practices (RBPs). Provisions for the transfer of technology were agreed upon during the talks on the RBP Code, but the LDCs have since hardened their position. They now oppose the insertion of those same articles into the draft of the Code for Transfer of Technology. The reason for this dissatisfaction has been the subject of speculation. Some Western participants had begun to question the vitality and utility of the multilateral negotiations at UNCTAD, which toward the end of the 1970s seemed to reach a general impasse. Thus it is possible that the RBP agreement resulted from a perception by the G77 that an accord on some issue was politically necessary. Having signed the Code of Conduct on

Restrictive Business Practices, the G77 would have felt free to revise its position during later negotiations.

The liveliest question at the talks on transfer of technology concerns the law applicable to the settlement of disputes. Group B desires that a choice be possible between the law of the country transferring the technology and that of the recipient state, while the G77 maintain that the recipient should unequivocally hold jurisdiction. The G77 act as a bloc in confronting the developed countries, but they are in fact not unanimous. The most highly developed LDCs are potential exporters of technology, and they find themselves in a position similar to that of the Group B countries. They sympathize privately with Group B but rally publicly to the G77, where the influence of the least developed LDCs is quite significant. The question of the settlement of disputes rejoins that of arbitration, concerning which the socialist countries of Eastern Europe "widely recognize the autonomy of the will of the parties in contractual matters" (Maire 1974, 95; see also Dessemontet 1977, 29–35). The silence of the Group D countries on the question of applicable law bespeaks their tacit agreement with the point of view of the Group B countries.

Arguments over the character of the Code in international law shine further light on the matter. The G77 has never supposed that transfer of technology could be regulated by anything but a legally binding Code; meanwhile, Group B has never stated that it would accept anything but a nonbinding Code (Touscoz 1977). The position taken by Group D on the Code's juridical character slowly approached that of the G77, and by the end of the 1970s this trend had culminated in the two Groups' agreement on the idea of a nonbinding instrument that would recognize "the principle of nondiscrimination according to the country's economic and social system" (Roffe 1980). In Group D's view such a Code, following its adoption at UNCTAD, would become part of the law of nations and would then need to be integrated into the various national systems of law. But the Group D countries have not committed themselves concerning the juridical character of the international institution foreseen to monitor the Code's application. They prefer to postpone the decision on this matter, and thereby share the position taken on the issue by Group B.

Technology transfer from the socialist countries of Eastern Europe to the developing countries occurs within the framework of bilateral intergovernmental agreements or joint ventures (Romer and DeSolère 1977). Hence the CMEA countries do not feel affected by the question of controlling transfers between a parent transnational corporation and its subsidiary based in a developing country. The objective position of the Group D countries vis-à-vis the international patent system is not very different from that of the developing countries, and of the developing socialist countries in particular. The socialist countries of Eastern Europe lose nothing, then, when they agree with the G77 that such transfers should be strictly regulated; moreover, since the Group D countries themselves import Western technology, they may benefit from the regulation of such transfers. They furthermore argue, according to the "principle of mutual advantage," that Western countries should grant them, the Group D countries, terms as favorable as those that the developing countries receive.

Two important issues still unresolved in the negotiations over the Code for Transfer of Technology are the establishment of a "rule of reason" and that of an "effects test." These involve finding agreement on a standard method for determining the positive and negative effects of a transferred technique on the recipient country. Lall (1977) has suggested that the political and economic system of a developing country may in general define the sort of techniques that are transferred to it. Although the question is complicated by the mixed character of the national economy of many LDCs, he appears to mean the absence or presence of state trading in the given economic sector. The least developed LDCs, which are the most intransigent toward Group B, most often have socialist systems. It seems impossible for any proposed rule of reason or effects test to be neutral to the relationship between the organization of a country's foreign trade system and the state itself; the resolution of the matter will probably require the participation of an intergovernmental group of experts. (UNCTAD 1975 discusses the problems that can result from the transfer of technology from a socialist country to a developing country.)

2.3 International Organization and CMEA Foreign Trade

2.3.1 UNCTAD and East-South Commerce

The national economies of the East European countries are developing and their domestic economic structures are diversifying. The populations of these countries are increasing but they do not in general have sufficient raw materials or foodstuffs. Salaries are rising but consumer goods are lacking. UNCTAD, on the other hand, can make available information that would tend to organize world markets more "rationally." Various expert groups on commodities have, for instance, written studies describing the structure of markets in raw materials for the UNCTAD Secretariat. It should be possible for the LDCs to establish direct links with CMEA countries for trade in raw materials and foodstuffs that the latter often buy at present through Western middlemen. UNCTAD's Division for Trade with Socialist Countries should be able to facilitate such contacts as well as to identify new arenas of potential cooperation.

Economic relations between a developing country and an East European country are based on a long-term bilateral "commercial, economic, scientific, and technical agreement." Such agreements habitually contain a forecast of the level of trade, but the means for realizing the projection are always left to be specified later. Often the levels foreseen are not attained. Since the reason for failure varies with the individual case, it is not possible to give a general explanation of the phenomenon; nevertheless, the East European countries have shown themselves to be advantageous markets for those LDCs that are able to penetrate them. Furthermore, once the barriers are overcome, the LDCs are automatically included in the others' annual economic plans.

Several key elements of the problem of how to increase East-South trade relate to the question of multilateralizing trade payments between socialist countries and LDCs. Multilateralizing the transferable-ruble system would not cure all the ills from which East–South trade suffers, but it could help increase that trade. The "transferable ruble" is an accounting unit now used only in trade between the USSR and other CMEA countries; it is not even used in trade between, for example, Poland and Hungary. It is possible that a regional East European institution could permit the CMEA countries to protect their national economies from the results of reforms that foreshadow a multilateralization of the transferable ruble. The 1980 proposal of two Polish economists (Klerr and Zacher 1980, 26) to facilitate the transfer of technology from East to South by creating "quasi-supranational socialist enterprises [that] ... would not be directly and continuously connected with the domestic economic plan" was made in this spirit. Such institutions could make it possible for LDCs to export, to one of the smaller CMEA countries, goods produced in the LDCs using Soviet techniques. Were that to happen, a multilateralized transferable-ruble system could improve, via a third country, the balance of payments between the USSR and other CMEA members.

A multilateralized system would thus have unequivocal advantages in comparison with the current system of bilateral clearing. But inasmuch as this multilateralization may lead to a limited convertibility of the transferable ruble (Matejka 1974, 179–85), the LDCs could profit from it: for example, by using the transferable ruble only in their trade with East-bloc countries and conserving their fully convertible currencies for other needs, as most CMEA countries now tend to do themselves (see Botos 1982). Moreover, a multilateralization of payments in transferable rubles, with respect to third countries, could encourage the sentiment, already present among several CMEA members, that favors such a multilateralization within the CMEA. The Soviets draw advantage from the present structure of intra-CMEA payments, and therefore hesitate to take any move that suggests multilateralization of the transferable-ruble system.

Although such a multilateralized system would hardly resolve all LDC demands directed at the Group D countries (see Despiney 1980, 116–17, for a balance-sheet of LDC demands addressed to the Group D countries in 1976 and replies), it would open the way to a broader cooperation. Because of internal difficulties, however, the CMEA will require greater encouragement from outside to take the financial and institutional steps that will further benefit the Third World. Western countries could promote such a development in their role as participants in the program of Tripartite Industrial Cooperation, organized by the United Nations Industrial Development Organization (reviewed in UNCTAD 1979). UNCTAD itself could serve as a forum for discussion and as an organ for elaborating appropriate financial methods, with a view toward their application.

2.3.2 The CMEA and the EEC: A Few Contrasts

The Treaty of Rome gives the EEC competence to conduct external relations, and it specifies the manner in and the means by which to do so; the CMEA, however, has no analogous well-defined competence. Thus the EEC itself grants nonreciprocal preferences to the LDCs but the CMEA does not. Rather, each of its member states grants such preferences, modifying in turn the tariff schedule established by its national system of foreign trade. With respect to the Common Fund, the member states of the EEC are known to have disagreed among themselves over the very issue of stabilizing commodity prices. The Netherlands favored the establishment of the Fund, for example, whereas the Federal Republic of Germany and the United Kingdom originally opposed it. The participation of the EEC itself in commodity negotiations varies with the commodity involved, because the competence of the Community depends upon the method through which the buffer stocks are financed. Were the Community to assume responsibility for financing them, it would be exclusively competent in the negotiations; it appears too that the European Parliament would have to ratify the negotiated agreement in such a case. However, if the member states of the EEC participate directly in financing the buffer stocks, then the EEC would be obliged to negotiate in concert with its member states. The position of the EEC vis-à-vis the Common Fund is still more curious: by grace of a special provision it can become a member of the Fund, but it has no voting rights in the Fund even if it contributes capital to finance the buffer stocks that the Fund establishes. The CMEA has no standing in respect of either international commodity agreements in general or the Common Fund in particular.

A group of experts within the EEC studied the issues involved in the technology transfer negotiations and their work contributed to the draft Code elaborated by Group B (Dessemontet 1977, 2, n. 6). The governments of the member states of the European Community, however, do not coordinate their negotiating positions on transfer of technology. This notwithstanding, the issue of technology transfer between a parent transnational corporation and its national subsidiaries divides the Community rather clearly from the United States. The disagreement—which reflects the EEC's resistance to expanding the geographical domain where American antitrust law is applicable—existed during the negotiations on the RBP Code as well; however, the Community agrees with the United States on the other principal points at issue in the negotiations on the Code for Transfer of Technology, the determination of the rule of reason and the effects test. So far as the choice of applicable law for settling disputes is concerned, the member states of the EEC desire, like the other members of Group B as well as the Group D countries, to leave this open to the parties concerned.

The CMEA countries share an integrated perspective on international law and on its use in the international system, but this is hardly characteristic of the member countries of the EEC. It is evident from the several case studies here that the Group D socialist countries at UNCTAD are motivated in part by desires to increase the penetration of socialist juridical forms into international law and to unify international trade law. (In this connection, see also Fink 1975; Rajski 1978.) But they are careful clearly to distinguish between, on the one hand, norms of international law that define the position of international organizations in the system of international relations and, on the other, rules that govern the creation of such norms. For example, Morozov (since 1970 the Soviet judge at the International Court of Justice) has differentiated between the field on which the battle is waged to establish "principles of commonly recognized international law" such as peaceful coexistence—principles of a general type that the USSR has introduced, and of which it is therefore entitled to give an authoritative interpretation—and the field on which the "normative-regulatory function of international law" operates, aided by "the juridical norms of the concrete sectors" of public and private international law. According to Morozov (1975, 50–51), the former field, which includes "that sphere of interstate interaction [*mezhgosudarstvennogo obshcheniia*] where the effect of international law is applicable," defines and delimits the latter field, on which international organizations themselves, "specific and limited subjects of international interaction [*mezhdunarodnogo obshcheniia*]" act. (See further: Morozov 1972, 56, 60–64; 1974, 27–87.)

Thus it is evident not only that the CMEA countries act in the context of their own systematically developed framework but also that the framework includes a clear conception of the role of international organizations. The contrast between the EEC's behavior at UNCTAD and that of the CMEA appears, then, to reflect a difference in their conceptions of their respective juridical personalities. These diverse conceptions hinder the extension of commercial relations between the EEC and the CMEA. The question, political as well as legal, of the CMEA's competence to negotiate trade agreements in the name of its members, or to oversee their foreign trade, is fundamental. De Fiumel (1976, 68–77), Rajski (1976), and Sárközy (1977) all provide interesting treatments of the question from the standpoint of institutions and law. Baumer and Jacobson (1980) review these factors in the context of the political and economic situation.

The EEC participates as a unified body in UNCTAD only rarely, when its member states agree that the question at issue falls within the Community's competence. The member countries of the CMEA, by contrast, coordinate their points of view before important sessions regardless of the question under discussion, and without exception they all present the same position. Nevertheless, the CMEA sends its own delegate to UNCTAD meetings only infrequently, whereas the EEC does so regularly.

The collective behavior of the CMEA countries at UNCTAD would seem to have nothing in common with that of EEC countries. The only similarity between the two groups appears to be attributive: both are composed of under a dozen states. The most evident organizational difference is that, whereas the European Community constitutes only a part of Group B, the East European CMEA countries constitute Group D in full. Influence on decision making in the EEC is not so concentrated as it is in Group D, where the USSR's weight is preponderant. Yet it would seem that common policy attitudes among the socialist countries of Eastern Europe are due at least as much to the similarity of their position in the structure of world trade, as to the essential similarity of their domestic political structures. The conjunctural positions of the member countries of the EEC are more varied, and the divergence resulting from this is accentuated — except in special instances such as parent–subsidiary technology transfer — by the heterogeneity of those states' domestic economic and political structures.

2.4 Conclusion

Although UN General Assembly Resolution 1995(XIX) established the permanent status of UNCTAD at the end of 1964, the organization's survival of internal disagreements was assured only at the end of 1965, with the approval of Resolution 19(II) by its Trade and Development Council. That Resolution excluded from UNCTAD's competence any minute examination of the developed countries' policies and so ended a West–South confrontation that had cast doubt on the institution's viability (UNCTAD 1966).

In those earliest years the Group D countries had worked to attain two goals: to found an International Trade Organization following the Soviet idea, and to polemicize the idea of increasing East–West trade. Subsequent changes in UNCTAD and in the transnational environment transmuted these two motivations. From 1966 into the early 1970s, UNCTAD had to create internal structures and external relations to sustain and legitimate its birth and existence. The Group D countries' wish to create an ITO led them to support the evolution of UNCTAD's internal structure by motivating the creation of new organizations and institutional forms affiliated to UNCTAD, such as its Division for Trade with Socialist Countries and various intergovernmental expert groups. They supported its extension of external relations by agreeing to create the

International Trade Centre (ITC) established in cooperation with the GATT. Likewise the Group D countries' desire to increase East-West trade led them, internally within UNCTAD, to advocate creation of a Committee for Trade between Countries with Different Economic and Social Systems, and also externally to push for the foundation of the United Nations Conference on International Trade Law (UNCITRAL), which was created following a Hungarian proposal to the General Assembly.

The Soviets chose the question of normative integration, which has a definite legal aspect, as the framework for seeking to resolve such problems of internal organizational adaptation, as well as purely political problems and those of intercultural communication within UNCTAD. But the Soviet approach to international law was always bedeviled by an internal contradiction. According to Marxist-Leninist doctrine, law is part of the "superstructure" of the state and is conditioned by the economic "base" represented by material life, in particular the social relations governed by the ownership of the means of production.

So how could norms of international law exist that would be binding both for a bourgeois states (where those means are privately owned under capitalism) and for socialist states (where they are owned by the state)? Tunkin, perhaps the dominant figure in Soviet studies of international law, gave the answer in the early post-Stalin period. As he later summarized it (Tunkin 1971, 26–27), norm-creation in international law was about state behavior, not about ideological questions; the legal system of a given State, and consequently its regime of economic ownership, affected their application. From this it followed that the "ideological struggle" with the capitalist system would not influence theoretical questions about the *form* of international law, but it would affect the application of the *content* of international law.

Within that general approach, Morozov (1972, 56, 60–64; 1975, 46–47) emphasized the formal distinction between the norms which define the position of international organizations in the system of international relations and the norms that govern the right to create international-legal norms. By cooperation and compromise, socialist diplomacy would influence the development of a single traditional system of customary law in the direction of a socialist international law (Erickson 1972, 15). As the ideological struggle received a new and important emphasis in both practice and theory following the Twenty-fourth Congress of the Communist Party of the Soviet Union in 1971, the relationship between "base" and "superstructure" was necessarily adulterated by the assertion the essence of law "is not situated either in the field of ideological problems or that of different social consciousnesses."

With this in mind, it is instructive to consider patterns of Group D behavior at UNCTAD in light of the Krasner's (1982) elaboration of the analytic utility of the concept of "regime." The praxis of the East European CMEA countries can be summarized in terms developed by him: Group D adopts a modified structural approach, positing the primacy of states, in order to preserve its members' prerogatives in what it sees as a Grotian world, where regimes are pervasive. The explicit codification of an implicit regime becomes a process harnessed to the service of state interests. Thus the Soviet delegate to the Sixth Committee of the General Assembly declared (Tumanov 1969, 64) that only states were able to create juridical norms, and that therefore the ILC should only attempt to formulate those tendencies in international law that states are likely to accept. Morozov (1972, 56) later admitted that some international organizations could play a role in norm-creation but did not go further. Vel'iaminov (1970, 160) had by the already asserted that "the Soviet delegation [to the Geneva Conference (1964) that established UNCTAD] considered the Conference's decisions as 'international norms'."

This perspective on changing the world also recognizes that the institutionalization of a regime is an opportunity for transforming it. The socialist countries' application of similar norms of international law (e.g., the similarity of their practice of international trade law, often codified into socialist treaty law) strengthens their argument for the integration into international regimes of those norms — which, even if technical in nature, tend to be influenced by the structure of the national economic systems they are designed to complement. They thereby reflect state interests. (One example is the influence of the 1968 CMEA General Conditions of Delivery of Goods on the UNCTAD negotiations concerning multimodal transport.) Furthermore, it is possible for institutions themselves to become instrumentalities for regime transformation. Thus, the Group D countries have emphasized the universally inclusive character of UNCTAD in order to attempt to substantiate their claim that it is superior in law over other international forums.

An editorial of the authoritative Soviet legal-policy journal highlighted the growing importance of forums such as UNCTAD in the eyes of the socialist countries of Eastern Europe, and recommended the "deeper study, from the point of view of international law, of the problems and questions" raised by multilateral diplomacy, particularly "the method of 'consensus,' which is relatively new but ever more widely adopted" (SGP 1973, 7). This method was so new and strange that the word "consensus" in the original text was enclosed within quotation marks and followed in parentheses, by way of explanation, by the Russian word for "agreement" (*soglasovanie*). Whenever a trade question falls within the competence of an international organization other than UNCTAD — such as the GATT, the IMF, or the International Bank for Reconstruction and Development (IBRD, "World Bank") — Group D will contend that it falls equally within UNCTAD's. The other organizations, the Group maintains, should therefore collaborate on the given topic with UNCTAD, which would fulfill the functions of coordination and oversight because its universality makes it more representative.

This analysis suggests an explanation of the dynamic of uncertain defensiveness that characterizes Group D's attitude toward LDC demands. On the one hand, the forces that bring Group D and the G77 closer together are based less on ideological considerations than on common domestic structures of state trading. (Kostecki 1978, 207, notes that "surprising little has been written by economists and other researchers on state trading in ... the developing countries.") For instance, when the G77 demanded that all developed countries annually contribute one percent of gross national product to financial development aid, Group D rejected the norm that the world may be divided into the rich (including both capitalist and socialist countries) and the poor. Group D cast responsibility for the LDCs' plight onto Group B, which includes former colonial powers; but the USSR and its allies in Group D support the LDCs' demands against Group B in matters of trade preferences and the regulation of technology transfer, demands from which they themselves may equally benefit.

On the other hand, the forces that drive apart the positions of the LDCs and the CMEA countries, whose divergence often reflects their respective positions in the world economy, derive from national (i.e., state) interest. Thus Third World demands for an increase in the level of East–South trade — which still is very low in comparison with that of West–South trade — for a time merely distracted the socialist countries of Eastern Europe from their preoccupation with their own complaints against the Western countries. Group D replied to those Third World demands for an increase in East–South trade not just by denying any and all responsibility for LDC poverty. It combined this tactic into its project of creating norms of international law. It did so by seeking, first, to transform the ideological bases of their own general world-economic analysis into such international-legal norms, and second, to move from there into the project of translating these norms into a generally accepted prescriptive program.

The socialist countries found more success in realizing the first than the second of those. This is very likely due to the fact that the economic position of the LDCs in the world economy somewhat resembled their own in some respects. This resemblance was more marked in the cases of the Common Fund and the GSP negotiations in the 1960s, than it was in those of the Liner Conferences and transfer of technology in the 1970s. (For example, Third World flag-of-convenience countries have state merchant marines like the Group D countries, but have generally opposed the latter's initiatives because their interests are conditioned by their being part of the world capitalist system.) At the same time, the Group D countries never hesitated to defend their particular economic interests, whether by trying to avoid the obligation to contribute convertible currencies to the Common Fund, or by protecting their merchant marines against possible assaults at a future Liner Conference.

The growth of East–West trade in during the 1960s led to the transformation of the system of the trade exchanges among the Group D countries themselves, that development led in its turn to a greater openness of the Eastern countries to the LDCs. The 1970s revealed that this development was a unique circumstance that did not manifest any universal law of social or political life. The particularity of Group D's interests, as distinct from those of the G77, became more evident and clearer after UNCTAD succeeded in legitimating itself as a self-standing organization in the early 1970s. That common goal had required more cooperation between the two groups. When Group D reasserted its own interests at UNCTAD, in East-West trade as against East-South trade, this development was partly a result of the success in institutionalizing UNCTAD as a self-standing organization.

The routinization of UNCTAD's activities, through its successful creation of internally adapted and differentiated organizational structures, led the Group D countries to lose faith that UNCTAD could transform the world economy through its regularized external functions. They therefore sought to change the values that UNCTAD itself incorporated and manifested, the better to enable the greater transformation for which they had hoped. International trade law and the theory of norm-creation in international law were their chosen vehicles for that. Thus for Group D, questions of normative integration came to prevail over, and to seek to subsume, those of politics, adaptation, and culture.

It is possible to discern from this research, using categories delineated by Krasner (1982, 194–204), the syntax of logic that the Group D countries use in the dialogue over the evolving international regimes for trade and development: *usage and custom*, recognized by *knowledge*, become established *norms and principles* or give rise to alternative ones), which *instrumental political power* harnesses to the service of the state's *egoistic self-interest* and rationalizes in terms of *cosmopolitan political power* (i.e., ideology). In the context of debates over the NIEO, this may well be the generative grammar of CMEA discourse.

References

AVERKIN, A. G. 1974. "K voprosu ob osobennostiiakh iuridicheskogo statusa IUNKTAD, IUNIDO, i PROON" [Towards the Question of Aspects of the Juridical Status of UNCTAD UNIDO and UNDP], *Vestnik Moskovskogo universiteta*, ser. 12, *Pravo* 29, no. 2 (March–April): 66–73.

BAUMER, Max, and Hanns-Dieter JACOBSEN. 1980. "EC and COMECON: Intricate Negotiations between the Two Integration Systems in Europe." In *Western Europe's Global Reach: Regional Cooperation and Worldwide Aspirations*, edited by Werner J. Feld, 110–124. Elmsford: Pergamon Press.

BOTOS, Katalin. 1982. "On the Further Development of the Currency and Financial System of the CMEA." *Soviet Studies* 34, no. 2 (April): 228–253.

BRAINARD, Lawrence J. 1978. Die sozialistische Wahrungsordnung in Bedragnis. *Neuer Zürcher Zeitung*, 10 February: 19.

BUVAILIK, G. E. 1977. *Pravovoe regulirovanie mezhdunarodnykh ekonomicheskikh otnoshenii* [The Legal Regulation of International Economic Relations]. Kiev: Naukova Dumka.

BYKOV, A. 1964. "Nastoiatel'noe trebovanie vremeni [An Urgent Demand of the Times]. *Vneshniaia torgovlia* 44, no. 5 (May): 3–6.

DALLIN, Alexander. 1962. *The Soviet Union at the United Nations*. New York: Praeger Publishers.

DE FIUMEL, Henryk. 1976. "The Council for Mutual Economic Assistance in International Relations." *Studies on International Relations* 7: 60–78.

DESPINEY, Barbara. 1980. "Pays socialistes et nouvel ordre économique international," in *Stratégies des pays socialistes dans l'échange international*, coordinated by Marie Lavigne, 103–118. Paris: Economica.

DESSEMONTET, François. 1977. "Transfer of Technology under UNCTAD and EEC Draft Codifications: A European View on Choice of Law in Licensing." *Journal of International Law and Economics* 12, no. 1 (March): 1–55.

ECOSOC. 1958a. United Nations, Economic and Social Council. "USSR Draft Resolution on the Establishment of an International Trading Organization." UN Document E/AC.6/L.216 (7 July).

—. 1958b. United Nations, Economic and Social Council. "USSR Draft Resolution for the Convening of a Second United Nations Conference on Trade and Employment." UN Document E/AC.6/L.217 (7 July).

—. 1964a. United Nations, Economic and Social Council. "Draft Resolution to Establish an International Trading Organization." UN Document E/CONF.46/50 (22 May).

—. 1964b. United Nations, Economic and Social Council. "Letter from the Delegation of the USSR." UN Document E/CONF.46/51 (5 February).

—. 1964c. United Nations, Economic and Social Council. "Possible Future Development of Trade between the Socialist Countries and the Developing Countries." UN Document E/CONF.46/L.17 (12 June).

ERICKSON, Richard J. 1972. *International Law and the Revolutionary State: A Case Study of the Soviet Union and International Customary Law.* Leiden: A.W. Sijthoff.

FILIMONOVA, T. V. 1976. "Preferentsii IUNKTAD: novyi tip preferentsii v torgovle mezhdu razvitymi kapitaliticheskimi i ravivaiushchimisia stranami [The UNCTAD Preferences: A New Type of Preference in Trade between Developed Capitalist and Developing Countries]." *Biulleten' inostrannoi kommercheskoi informatsii* 19, no. 5 (May): 3–19.

FINK, Karl Hermann. 1975. "L'arbitrage socialiste dans le commerce Est-Ouest." *Droit et pratique du commerce international* 1, no. 3 (September): 367–381.

FOMIN, B. S. 1980. "The New International Economic Order." In Laszlo and Kurtzman (1980), 1–17.

FOMIN, V. V. 1966. "OON i nekotorye pravovye voprosy mezhdunarodnoi torgovli [The UN and Some Legal Questions of International Trade]." *Sovetskii ezhegodnik mezhdunarodnogo prava, 1964–1965* [Soviet Yearbook of International Law, 1964–1965], edited by V.N. Avilin et al., chief editor N.A. Ushakov, 320–329. Moscow: Nauka.

GARDNER, Richard N. 1968. "The United Nations Conference on Trade and Development." *International Organization* 22, no. 1 (Winter): 99–130.

GOSOVIC, Branislav. 1972. *UNCTAD: Conflict and Compromise – The Third World's Quest for an Equitable World Economic Order through the United Nations.* Leiden: A.W. Sijthoff.

HALL, William. 1980. "UNCTAD's Plan to Transform World Shipping." *Financial Times* (18 January).

IVANOV, A., and V. POLEZHAEV. 1976. "Problemy mezhdunarodnoi torgovli syr'em: aktual'nost' poiski resheniia" [Problems of International Raw-Materials Trade: The Current Situation in Search of a Resolution], *Vneshniaia torgovlia* 57, no. 5 (May): 36–43.

JACOBSON, Harold K. 1963. *The USSR and the UN's Economic and Social Activities.* Notre Dame: University of Notre Dame Press.

JUDA, Lawrence. 1981. "World Shipping, UNCTAD, and the New International Economic Order." *International Organization* 35, no. 4 (Autumn): 493–516.

JUDET, Pierre, Philippe KAHN, A. C. KISS, and Jean TOUSCOZ. 1977. *Transfert de technologie et développement,* directed by Pierre Judet. Paris: Librairies techniques.

KHVOINIK, P. 1965. "Diktat ili ravnopravie" [Dictates or the Equality of Rights]. *Mirovaia ekonomika i mezhdunarodnye otnosheniia,* no. 12 (December): 15–26.

KLERR, Jerzy, and Lech ZACHER. 1980. "Technology Transfer from CMEA Countries to the Third World." In Laszlo and Kurtzman (1980), 18-31.

KORBONSKI, Andrzej. 1976. "Detente, East-West Trade, and the Future of Economic Integration in Eastern Europe." *World Politics* 28, no. 4 (July): 568-589.

KOSTECKI, M. M. 1978. "State Trading in Industrialized and Developing Countries." *Journal of World Trade Law* 12, no. 3 (May-June): 187-207.

KRASNER, Stephen D. 1982. "Structural Causes and Regime Consequences: Regimes as Intervening Variables." *International Organization* 36, no. 2 (Spring): 185-206.

KRASNOV, G. and A. CHEKHUTOV. 1972. *Developing Countries: Problems of Foreign Economic Relations*. Moscow: Novosti.

KRASNOV, G. A. 1971. *Torgovlia uslugami ili ekspluatatsiia?* [Trade in Services or Exploitation?]. Moscow: Mezhdunarodnye otnosheniia.

LALL, Sanjaya. 1976. "The Patent System and the Transfer of Technology to Less-Developed Countries." *Journal of World Trade Law* 10, no. 1 (January-February), 1-16.

LASZLO, Ervin, and Joel KURTZMAN, eds. (1980) *Eastern Europe and the New International Economic Order: Representative Samples of Socialist Perspectives*. New York: Pergamon Press.

LINDELL, John O. 1972. "The USSR in UNESCO." Ph.D. diss., New York University.

MAIRE, Jean-Paul. 1974. "Problèmes de qualification juridique et de détermination du droit applicable aux accords de coopération économique et industrielle." *Annales d'études internationales* 5: 93-103.

MATEJKA, Harriet. 1978. *Trade Control in Eastern Europe*. Geneva: Éditions Médecine et Hygiène.

McMILLAN, C. H. 1974. "The Bilateral Character of Soviet and East European Foreign Trade." *Journal of Common Market Studies* 13, no. 1 (September): 1-20.

MINAKOV, A. I. 1974. "O deistvitel'nosti arbitrazhnykh soglashenii" [On the Validity of Arbitration Agreements]. *Vestnik Moskovskogo universiteta*, ser. 12, *Pravo*, 29, no. 5 (September-October): 69-76.

MOROZOV, G. I. 1972. "O prave mezhdunarodnykh organizatsii" [Concerning the Law of International Organizations]. *Sovetskoe gosudarstvo i pravo*, no. 5 (May): 55-64.

—. 1974. *Mezhdunarodnye organizatsii: nekotorye voprosy teorii* [International Organizations: Some Problems of Theory], 2d ed. Moscow: Mysl'.

—. 1975. Mezhdunarodnoe pravo i mezhdunarodnye otnosheniia [International Law and International Relations]. *Mirovaia ekonomika i mezhdunarodnye otnosheniia*, no. 6 (June), 46-51.

OGAREV, Iu. 1964. "Sozdanie mezhdunarodnoi torgovoi organizatsii — nastoiatel'noe trebovanie zhizni" [Life Urgently Demands the Foundation of the International Trading Organization]. *Mirovaia ekonomika i mezhdunarodnye otnosheniia*, no. 2 (February): 82-94.

OGNEV, A., and Iu. OGAREV. 1964. "Sozdanie mezhdunarodnoi torgovoi organizatsii — vazhneishaia zadacha konferentsii" [The Conference's Most Important Task Is To Establish the International Trading Organization]. *Vneshniaia torgovlia*, 44, no. 2 (February): 1-19.

OSAKWE, Chris. 1972. *The Participation of the Soviet Union in Universal International Organizations: A Political and Legal Analysis of Soviet Strategies and Aspirations inside ILO, UNESCO, and WHO*. Leiden: A.W. Sijthoff.

PINEGIN, B. M. 1966. *Nasushchnye problemy mezhdunarodnoi torgovli* [Vital Problems of International Trade]. Moscow: Mezhdunarodnye otnosheniia.

RAJSKI, Jerzy. 1976. "Rozwój miedzynarodwych stosunków umownych RWPG z panstwami trzecimi" [The Development of the CMEA's International Contractual Relations with Third Countries]. *Panstwo i pravo* 31, no. 7 (July): 40-51.

—. 1978. "Basic Principles of International Trade Law of Certain European Socialist States and of East-West Trade Relations." *Droit et pratique du commerce international* 4, no. 1 (April): 9-28.

ROFFE, P. 1980. "UNCTAD: Code of Conduct for the Transfer of Technology — Progress and Issues under Negotiation." *Journal of World Trade Law* 14, no. 2 (March-April): 160-172.

ROMER, J.-Christophe, and Michel DESOLÈRE. (1977) "Accords conclus par les pays socialistes européens avec les pays en voie de développement." In Judet et al. 1977, 341-379.

RUBINSTEIN, Alvin Z. 1964. *The Soviets in International Organizations*. Princeton: Princeton University Press.

SÁRKÖZY, Tamas. 1977. "A KGST-országok nemzetközi gazdálkodó szervezetei intézményi rendszeréről" [On the Institutional System of International Trading Organizations in CMEA Member-Countries]. *Gazdaság* 11, no. 3 (September): 93-106.

SCHIERING, Wulf-Peter. 1979. "Liner Code und EG-Schiffahrtspolitik." *Aussenpolitik* 30, no. 2 (Summer): 182-191.

SCHWARTZ, Charles Anthony. 1972. "UNCTAD: Soviet Politics in the North-South Conflict." Ph.D. diss., University of Virginia.

SGP. (1973) Editorial board, *Sovetskoe gosudarstvo i pravo*. "Mir i sotrudnichestvo — trebovanie epokhi" [The Era Demands Peace and Cooperation]. *Sovetskoe gosudarstvo i pravo*, no. 9 (September): 5-11.

SPANDAR'IAN, V. 1964. "K itogam konferentsii OON po torgovle i razvitiiu" [Towards the Results of the U.N. Conference on Trade and Development]. *Vneshniaia torgovlia* 44:8 (August), 3–8.

TOUSCOZ, Jean. 1977. Le code international de conduite pour le transfert des techniques. In Judet et al. 1977, 197–225.

TUMANOV, V. A. 1969. "Sovremennyi antimarksizm i teoriia prava" [Contemporary Anti-Marxism and the Theory of Law]. *Sovetskoe gosudarstvo i pravo*, no. 4 (April): 57–66.

TUNKIN, G. 1971. "Mezhdunarodnoe pravo i ideologicheskaia bor'ba" [International Law and the Ideological Struggle]. *Mezhdunarodnaia zhizn'*, no. 11 (November): 26–38.

UNCTAD. 1966. United Nations Conference on Trade and Development. *Resolutions and Decisions*. UN Document TD/B/71, August. New York: United Nations.

— 1968. United Nations Conference on Trade and Development. *Official Records*. UN Documents TD/II/C.1/SR.7 (February 12); TD/II/C.1/SR.13, (19 February).

—. 1970. United Nations Conference on Trade and Development. *Report of the Special Committee on Preferences*. UN Document TD/B/329/Add.3 (9 October).

—. 1971. United Nations Conference on Trade and Development. *The Generalized System of Preferences: Report by the UNCTAD Secretariat*. UN Document TD/124 (12 November).

—. 1972a. United Nations Conference on Trade and Development. "[The Generalized System of Preferences:] Scheme of Bulgaria." UN Document TD/B/3781/ Add.1 (5 April).

—. 1972b. United Nations Conference on Trade and Development. "[The Generalized System of Preferences:] Scheme of Czechoslovakia." UN Document TD/B/378/Add.2 (5 April).

—. 1975. United Nations Conference on Trade and Development. *Major Issues Arising from the Transfer of Technology: A Case Study of Sri Lanka*. UN Document TD/B/C.6/6 (7 October).

—. 1976. United Nations Conference on Trade and Development. "Joint Declaration by Socialist Countries." UN Document TD/211 (28 May).

—. 1978. United Nations Conference on Trade and Development. "Press Release." Unofficial Document TAD/INF/935, 6 January.

—. 1979. United Nations Conference on Trade and Development. *Tripartite Industrial Cooperation and Cooperation in Third Countries*. UN Document TD/243/Supp.5 (20 April).

—. 1980. United Nations Conference on Trade and Development. *Agreement Establishing the Common Fund for Commodities*. UN Document TD/IPC/CF/CONF/24, 29 July.

UNGA. 1962. United Nations General Assembly. *The Cairo Declaration of the Developing Countries*. UN Document A/5162/Annex (16 August).

—. 1965a. United Nations General Assembly. *Letter from the Permanent Representative of the USSR to the United Nations, Addressed to the Secretary General*. UN Document A/5870/Rev.1 (5 February).

—. 1967. United Nations General Assembly. *Official Records*. UN Document A/C.6/SR.959 (2 October).

—. 1973. United Nations General Assembly. *Official Records*. UN Document A/C.6/SR.1403 (6 October).

—. 1974. United Nations General Assembly. *Official Records*. UN Document A/C6/SR.1489 (31 October).

—. 1977. United Nations General Assembly. *Official Records*. UN Document A/C.6/32/SR.38 (7 November).

—. 1978. United Nations General Assembly. *Report on the Most-Favored-Nation Clause, by Mr. Nikolai Ushakov, Special Rapporteur*. UN Documents A/CN.4/309 (11 April), A/CN.4/309/ADD.1 (12 April), A/CN.4/309/ADD.2 (10 May). In *Yearbook of the International Law Commission, 1978*, vol. 2, pt. 1: 1–30.

VEL'IAMINOV, G. M. 1970 "Konferentsiia OON po torgovle i razvitiiu i mezhdunarodnoe parvo" [The U.N. Conference on Trade and Development and International Law]. In *Sovetskii ezhegodnik mezhdunarodnogo prava, 1969* [Soviet Yearbook of International Law, 1969], edited by R.L. Bobrov et al., chief editor R.L. Bobrov, 157–161. Moscow: Nauka.

—. 1972. *Pravovoe uregulirovanie mezhdunarodnoi torgovli* [The Legal Regulation of International Trade]. Moscow: Mezhdunarodnye otnosheniia.

—. 1977. Mezhdunarodno-pravovye osnovy vneshnetorgovykh sviazei SSSR [The International Legal Bases of the USSR's Foreign Trade Ties]. *Vneshniaia torgovlia* 57, no. 10 (October): 48–57.

VT. (1964) Editorial board, *Vneshniaia torgovlia*. Na Zhenevskom forume [At the Geneva Forum]. *Vneshniaia torgovlia* 44, no. 5 (May): 7–10.

ZORIN, Val. and I. IVANOV. 1964. "Zheneva: nekotorye vyvody i uroki" [Geneva: Some Conclusions and Lessons], *Mirovaia ekonomika i mezhdunarodnye otnosheniia*, no. 8 (August), 78–92.

3   Economic Issues in East–South Relations

In the years following the 1973–1974 oil embargo, the international trading behavior of the East European members of the Council for Mutual Economic Assistance (CMEA) diverged more and more from that of the Soviet Union, especially in trade with the less-developed countries. This trend reflects not only different political, economic, and legal perspectives on relations between industrialized societies in the Third World, but also individual national efforts to gain practical advantage in an increasingly competitive world market. The present article reviews one American monograph (Valkenier 1983), three Soviet monographs (Danilov 1982; Obminskii 1982; Popov 1982), and three edited volumes multinationally produced with East European participation (Laszlo and Kurtzman 1980; Lavigne 1980; Saunders 1981) that address these themes.

Keywords: Soviet, CMEA, trade, aid, Third World, LDCs, Eastern Europe

DANILOV, E.A. *SEV i tret'i strany: Iuridicheskie predposylki i formy sotrudnichestva* [CMEA and Third Countries: Legal Premises and Forms of Cooperation]. Moscow, Nauka, 1982.

LASZLO, Ervin, and Joel KURTZMAN, eds. *Eastern Europe and the New International Economic Order: Representative Samples of Socialist Perspectives*. New York, Pergamon Press, 1980.

LAVIGNE, Marie, ed. *Stratégies des pays socialistes dans l'échange international*. Paris, Economica, 1980.

OBMINSKII. E.E. *Gruppa 77: Mnogostoronnaia ekonomicheskaia diplomatiia razvivaiushchikhsia stran* [The Group of 77: Multilateral Economic Diplomacy of Developing Countries]. Moscow, Nauka, 1982.

POPOV. V.D. *Ekonomicheskoe sotrudnichestvo stran SEV s razvivaiushchimisia gosudarstvami* [Economic Cooperation of CMEA Countries with Developing Countries]. Moscow, Ekonomika, 1982.

RADU, Michael, ed. *Eastern Europe and the Third World: East vs. South*. New York, Praeger Publishers, 1981.

SAUNDERS, Christopher T., ed. *East–West–South: Economic Interactions between Three Worlds*. New York, St. Martin's Press, 1981.

VALKENIER. Elizabeth Kridl. *The Soviet Union and the Third World: An Economic Bind*. New York, Praeger Publishers, 1983.

THE MEMBERS of the Council for Mutual Economic Assistance (CMEA) are playing an ever-larger role in the global economy. The complexity of their economic relations with the developing countries in particular is increasing. But the international trading behavior of the Council's six East European members over the past decade has diverged more and more from that of the USSR, reflecting quite different perspectives on West–South relations and on the world market. This article analyzes those differing approaches to economic relations with the less-developed countries (LDCs) from the standpoint of international political economy. Drawing on international law as well as politics and economics, this article also examines how East–South trade affects traditional Marxist-Leninist images of international affairs.

I follow here the standard usage of the terms "West," "South," and "East," which refer respectively to the advanced industrial democracies; to the Third World countries; and to Eastern Europe and the Soviet Union. The acronym "DCs," sometimes used for "developing countries," is more frequently used to mean "developed countries"; therefore, I use "LDCs" in this article. The use of "LDCs" to mean "least developed countries" — which in UN parlance are properly called the "least developed developing countries" or "LDDCs" — is likewise confusing and to be avoided. In the context of the United Nations, the LDC's are sometimes called the "Group of Seventy-seven" (G77), although they now number over 120), and the East European CMEA countries "Group D." Both these terms derive from usage in the United Nations Conference on Trade and Development (UNCTAD).

Although East–South trade constitutes only about 2 percent of total world trade, it is quite important to the East European countries: more important, in fact than it is to the developing countries. For example, whereas in 1982, the import and export shares of East–South trade in all international commerce of CMEA countries were 13.2 and 13.8 percent respectively, East–South trade for the LDCs in 1981 composed only 2.5 percent of imports and 5.3 percent of exports. The developing countries' participation in overall East–bloc trade rose strikingly throughout the 1970s. In the case of Romania, for example, exports to developing countries jumped from 9.6 to 28.1 percent of the country's total foreign trade between 1970 and 1981.

Too much research on this subject consists of descriptive analyses either of trade ties between LDCs as a single unit and individual CMEA members, or of trade and aid ties between CMEA members taken together and selected developing countries. However, most of the books reviewed here offer other perspectives, treating CMEA-LDC relations from the standpoints of international economics, law, and politics. Such perspectives surpass the usual scope of English-language analyses, which focus on military trade and aid from the CMEA countries to the LDCs (e.g.: Pajak 1981; Copper and Papp 1983; Gu 1983). They also shed light on recent developments in East-South trade and provide insights not obtainable from purely political or geostrategic approaches (e.g., Nötzold 1979; Gati 1980; Kostecki 1979; McMillan 1980; Berrios 1983).

Aside from selected chapters in Laszlo and Kurtzman (1980) and in Saunders (1981), only Radu's (1981c) book devotes considerable attention to the economic relations of individual CMEA members with the Third World. In his introduction, Radu (1981a) focuses on economic relations through a geopolitical lens, offering a four-fold classification of "Southern" countries and a six-fold classification of "Eastern" ones. This is a legitimate enterprise, but the lens is clouded with jargon. None of the contributors to the book makes use of these typologies, not even Radu himself (1981b) in his inconclusive chapter on Romanian relations with the Third World. Still less enlightening are the chapters on Yugoslavia (Milenkovitch 1981) and Albania (Biberaj 1981). Radu is not the only contributor who includes, in his chapter, tables to which the text does not refer.

Perhaps it is no coincidence that the quality of the analysis is roughly proportional to the degree to which economic considerations are integrated into strategic analysis. A case in point is Sodaro's (1981) solid and well-written survey of the German Democratic Republic's (GDR) relations with the Third World. Sodaro considers trade and aid within a general framework subsuming GDR-LDC economic relations under broader questions of the country's role in Soviet strategy. His conclusion on this point bears noting:

> The GDR's activities in the Third World may be viewed as fulfilling four functions: (1) assisting the Soviet Union's efforts to influence various Third

World states or liberation movements; (2) providing the GDR with necessary import goods and export markets; (3) enhancing the international visibility and prestige of the GDR, a goal which assumes special significance in view of East Germany's continuing rivalry with the Federal Republic; and (4) bolstering the internal legitimacy of the GDR. (Sodaro 1981, 134)

Still more demonstrative of the virtue of incorporating economic factors into political analysis is Vratislav Pechota's (1981) excellent chapter on Czechoslovakia. Pechota, who in 1966 chaired the Sixth (Legal) Committee of the United Nations General Assembly, makes good use of his background as an expert in international law and international organization. He judiciously traces the trends in Czechoslovak foreign trade over the last three decades and convincingly demonstrates the crippling effect that the 1968 Soviet invasion had on Czechoslovakia's capacity to undertake initiatives to ameliorate its foreign trade situation. Pechota also discusses the influence of legal aspects of commerce on Czechoslovakia's economic interaction with the Third World, particularly that involving technology transfer and joint stock companies. His chapter clearly illustrates how the fields of law and economics can make valuable contributions to the discussion of political relations between developing and socialist countries.

The concluding chapters in the Radu book, by Kanet (1981) and by Radvanyi (1981), discuss economic relations not between the Third World and individual CMEA members, but between the Third World and the CMEA countries taken together. Kanet's chapter is particularly rich and synthetic, demonstrating a breadth unfortunately absent in much other work on the subject. He rightly concludes (Kanet 1981, 325) that most East European states see the Third World as more important for stabilizing and strengthening their own national economies than for anything else; that they nevertheless continue to provide costly military and other support to Third World revolutionary movements and regimes backed by the Soviet Union; and that there is no contradiction in this approach since military-political support can lead to increased economic relations in the future.

Radvanyi provides an overview of patterns in the evolution over three decades of collective socialist foreign economic policy that tends to support Kanet's conclusions. He notes (Radvanyi 1981, 343) that individual CMEA members pursue "the search for new markets and commercial gains" in different ways and to different degrees. For example, Hungary prefers to use hard currency in its trade with LDCs, conducting nearly two-thirds of its Third World commerce this way. Other East European countries show this preference, though to lesser degrees. The USSR's heavy reliance on barter is an exception. Of course, countries that conduct trade with the Third World in hard currency can use any resulting trade surplus to help offset deficits in East–West trade. Although the amount of surplus varied from country to country, in 1982 the six East European members of CMEA together realized a surplus in their Third World trade equal to 72 percent of their deficit in trade with the West.

Diambou (1980) focuses on the LDC side of this issue. His analysis of the financial arrangements available to the developing countries for settling accounts in international trade with the CMEA countries touches on LDC use of multilateral devices to diversify payments. "Multilateralization" of payments refers to balancing accounts with an ensemble of trading partners rather than with any one particular country. For this, a commonly acceptable means of payment is necessary. The transferable ruble is a bilateral device because it is used to settle accounts only between the USSR and other parties. When Moscow is not one of the traders concerned, the device cannot be used to settle accounts, even if the partners involved also trade with the Soviet Union. The discussion of this problem by Ausch (1972) is especially good.

Diambou does not mention the transferable-ruble system, the multilateralization of which has long been debated within CMEA. The transferable-ruble system has not, however, lent itself to such operations in practice. It is not excluded that the transferable ruble may become more convertible into hard currencies through broader utilization. (On the relation between multilateralization and convertibility, see Matejka 1974, 1980.) However, in such a case, the LDCs might reserve it for trade with the East European countries, conserving their fully convertible currencies (as the socialist countries themselves now do) for purchasing Western technology and amortizing debts to Western banks.

It is no secret that certain smaller CMEA members would prefer to see the transferable ruble multilateralized, because the transferable-ruble system as now constituted favors the USSR; Moscow remains quite conservative on the question. At present the transferable ruble is used only in accounting between the USSR and other CMEA members; it is not used even for settling accounts between, for example, Poland and Hungary. (See Bién and Nosiadek 1980 on obstacles to its use as a means for payment between developing countries and East European countries.)

THE DIFFERENTIATION of the foreign trade patterns of the smaller CMEA countries from that of the Soviet Union reflects the evolution of diverse perspectives on global trade generally and on Eastern Europe's role in the world economy in particular. These perspectives arise from differing schools of thought on how to deal with the Third World. They animate discussion not only in the smaller CMEA countries but in the USSR as well. Principal among these different schools are the ones delineated by Elizabeth Valkenier in her excellent examination (1983) of Soviet perspectives on the world economy. Indeed, the most intriguing parts of her study are those where she treats the influence of East European thinking on Soviet views (1983, 59–62, 127–35), the evolution of Soviet views over the last 10 years (1983, 52–59, 62–69, 81–97, 111 –21, 147–50), and current Soviet policy concerning particular Third World development issues (1983, 97–103, 122–27, 135–43). Valkenier, demonstrating an impressive depth and breadth of knowledge of the Soviet literature, shows how Soviet views of the world economy have changed in response to economic realities, forcing the USSR to recognize the impossibility of exercising decisive leverage over the developing countries.

Valkenier distinguishes (1983, 148–49) three groups among Soviet decision-makers and political economists: ideologues, skeptical realists, and globalists. Ideologues, she contends, still believe that Soviet interests are best served by manipulating Third World resentments against the West. Skeptical realists make a different argument. They contend that the Soviet Union should base its policy more on cost-benefit analysis than on ideological precepts, since LDCs tend to act independently according to their perceived self-interests. Finally, the globalists argue against using the developing countries' problems as a lever for tilting the world correlation forces in the USSR's favor. They assert instead the need for broad cooperation among all advanced countries to help solve those problems — overpopulation, food shortages, backwardness — that would otherwise create unrest in the LDCs.

She distinguishes between "globalist" and "bifurcated" approaches in Soviet analyses of the world market. Advocates of the latter approach, in conformity with traditional Marxist-Leninist analysis, maintain that capitalist and socialist world markets exist independently and simultaneously side by side, whereas globalists assert that these markets are integrated. Valkenier also discusses schools of analysis in the Soviet Union regarding West-South relations. Participants in this debate are proponents either of the "economic liberation" (i.e., from neocolonialism) approach or of the "interdependence" (i.e., of advanced capitalist and less-developed countries) approach.

To Valkenier's three-fold classification we can add a fourth school of thought that seems to be emerging in most recent Soviet literature on the Third World. Obminskii's (1982) monograph is an example of it. This school of thought still sees Western exploitation, and the Third World's reaction to it, as the dominant development pattern among LDC. But this school urges opposition to such "neocolonialism" while recognizing the complexity of current international trade patterns. It is convenient to call its adherents "hortatory pragmatists," as clarified in Table 3-1.

In her analysis, Valkenier (1983, 183–84) calls Obminskii's earlier (1974) work the "first book to offer the new [globalist] interpretation of the international division of labor frankly admitted that the 'perfect' system of Soviet-Third World exchanges was not an operative but only a hypothetical situation." But Obminskii's more recent (1982) book, reviewed here, demonstrates how the constraint of ideology may rigidify the globalist viewpoint. The impact of such a constraint can be seen in the author's insistence on associating the economic program of the G77 with the political program of the Non-Aligned Movement. Thus, Obminskii attributes the growth of the influence of the G77 partly to its relations with the latter movement. Discussing various ongoing negotiations at the United Nations Conference on Trade and Development (UNCTAD) and summarizing the issues underlying them, Obminskii offers an ambivalent evaluation of the LDC program of "collective self-reliance." He interprets this program as comprising chiefly the UNCTAD-sponsored work on economic and technical cooperation among developing countries. Obminskii ignores the constructive efforts of the developing countries' regional organizations to establish inter-LDC cooperation. Instead, he deplores at length the effects of the "exacerbation of the world capitalist economic crisis" on the G77.

TABLE 3-1. Soviet schools of thought on global economic relations.

		Image of West–South Relations	
		Economic Liberation	Interdependence
Image of the World Market	Bifurcation	IDEOLOGUES	SKEPTICAL REALISTS
	Globalism	HORTATORY PRAGMATISTS	GLOBALISTS

Source: Constructed by the author, based on Valkenier (1983).

The emergence of the hortatory-pragmatist school seems to have paralleled a shift in the locus of decision-making in the international commerce bureaucracy in the Soviet Union. Indeed, in recent years the work of the various Soviet ministries involved in such activity has been increasingly supervised by the State Committee for Foreign Economic Relations and the State Committee for Science and Technology. This has reduced the ministries' relative autonomy in foreign trade decision-making and insinuated into Soviet foreign trade planning a conservative tendency that complements the hortatory-pragmatist school. For example, when Oleg Bogomolov, director of the Institute of the Economy of the World Socialist System in Moscow, had the opportunity to specify the nature of Soviet participation in realizing the New International Economic Order (NIEO), he offered only the prospect of intensifying existing East-South economic relations, not that of transforming them. In particular, he envisioned (Bogomolov 1981, 254; see also, Bogomolov 1983) continuing East-South economic cooperation in mineral prospecting, extracting and processing raw materials, industrial construction, and activities that would increase CMEA imports of labor-intensive manufactures and products of LDC national industries. These are typical features of the division of labor between North and South.

ONE OF THE most striking aspects of the evolution of East-South trade over the last 10 years is the CMEA countries' failure to establish strong commercial relations with the newly industrializing countries (NICs). As a result, imports by CMEA countries of manufactured goods from the Third World actually decreased in the 1970's. During this decade as well, the NICs were rapidly becoming the most dynamic manufactures market in the South. This was probably what Hungarian economist Szentes (1981) had in mind in his discussion of the question that Bogomolov shunted aside, namely, how new forms of technical cooperation might help not just quantitatively to redistribute economic goods along existing patterns, but instead qualitatively to restructure economic relations in general and the international division of labor in particular. Szentes, a true globalist according to the typology in Table 3-1, suggests, for example, that imports of primary products from LDCs could be linked with the development of those countries' manufacturing industries. According to him, the importing country could export appropriate machinery to the LDCs concerned, and then progressively increase its proportion of imports of finished or semi-finished products, as against raw materials, from that sector.

Hungary's trade with the developing countries is not only more varied and wide-ranging than that of any other CMEA member, but also more important to the country itself. Simai (1980) mentions the use of convertible currencies and the innovative incentive structure for encouraging foreign trade at the enterprise level (drawing on Dobozi 1978a; Szentes 1978). These features have enabled Hungary to engage in cooperation agreements with Western firms to construct "turnkey" plants in developing countries or to engage in joint ventures there. (A "turnkey" plant is one that the contractors agree to build and install to the point of readiness for operation, and then turn over to another party for occupancy; training of personnel is sometimes also part of the turnkey agreement.) In the late 1970s, the Hungarian firm Csepel agreed with the Swedish firm Volvo on the establishment of joint ventures in the automotive industry; the Hungarian firm Chemokomplex agreed with the Austrian firm Vereinigte Edelstahlwerke on turnkey plants; the Hungarian firm Babolina Agricultural Combinate agreed with the West German firm Protinas on turnkey farms and agricultural equipment; and so forth.

Of course, Hungary is not the only CMEA country to engage in tripartite cooperation. Indeed, every CMEA country has taken advantage of this new practice. Thus, CMEA members' growing reliance on transfer of technology to encourage foreign trade has increased the centrality of this issue in East–South trade relations. A comparative analysis of East–South and West–South technological transfer could help to clarify the future role of the CMEA countries in the emerging international economic order.

It would also be important to determine how successful recipient countries have been in controlling the social and economic effects of technologies transferred to them. If features of the technology transfer project are treated as independent variables, then economic and social structures in the recipient countries become dependent variables. In this framework, the developing country's machinery for controlling the effects of technology transfer projects is an intervening variable. Matched–case comparisons of East–South, West–South, and East–West–South ("tripartite") projects would be appropriate. Carefully framed research on this question could even touch on whether Eastern and Western technologies are ideology-free or whether they in fact motivate different social and economic changes in the recipient country. But research on the more general problem would certainly help clarify how various centrally planned economies may contribute to the development of the global economy, illuminating, in turn, the nature of their participation in it. (Portes 1979, expresses the dominant view; compare Pajestka and Kulig 1979; further, see UNCTAD 1980.)

Specialists in the CMEA countries disagree on what the nature of that participation should be. For example, Paszyński from Warsaw's Foreign Trade Research Institute differs with Dobozi and Inotai, from the Institute for World Economics in Budapest, over the basic role of foreign trade in socialist planning. For Paszyński (1981, 39), "the main function of exports in a socialist economy is not to provide for the most effective resource allocation and to optimize capacity but to secure revenue to cover indispensable import requirements." For Dobozi and Inotai (1981, 49), however, the merging of the CMEA countries "into the international division of labor [is] an essential precondition for the improvement of their economies' efficiency and viability." Both these perspectives are "interdependentist" in Valkenier's terms, but Paszyński appears locked in a bifurcationist approach to the world market, whereas Dobozi and Inotai emerge as globalists.

Such nuances of difference among the CMEA countries' approaches to issues of the strategies for Third World development are analyzed by Barbara Despiney. She also outlines (Despiney 1980, 116–17; compare Cutler 1983) the guarded responses of the CMEA countries to a series of demands made to them by the G77 at UNCTAD. In the same book, Decaye (1981) points up differences of interest between countries in the East and South, notably the increasing competition between these two parts of the world for Western markets for their manufactured goods. (See further: Robert 1983.) It is precisely in conditions of such increasing competition that the differences among national commercial policies of the individual CMEA countries become especially significant.

This East–South competition is becoming particularly acute in labor-intensive manufactured goods and material-intensive semi-manufactured products. Additional areas of competition include attempts to entice foreign firms (mainly Western transnationals) to invest in local manufacturing for export, and to attract Western capital. Tripartite industrial cooperation (TIC) constitutes an innovative possibility for surmounting some of this conflict. Patrick Gutman, who is probably the world's leading authority on TIC, defines that phenomenon (1981, 337) as "the joint construction by Eastern Europe and the West of industrial complexes in ... Third World countries." According to Zevin, from Moscow's Institute of Economics of the World Socialist System, TIC offers LDCs three advantages: it is coordinated by the developing country; it enables the developing country to overcome excessive reliance on the West for economic development; and it helps (Zevin 1981, 301) to oppose "the self-seeking activities of the transnational corporations." However, Gutman's empirical study of TIC involving French companies suggests that in reality these advantages may not be realized:

> It seems necessary to distinguish between the merits of TIC as a particularly appropriate means of international industrial marketing for the Eastern and Western partners and its real value for the development of third countries. In this respect current studies of TIC generally tend to treat it as an autonomous phenomenon, ... [but] TIC is at the same time a manifestation of the dynamics of the system—both East and West—and consequently one factor in the interplay of their competition and perpetuation. (Guttman 1981, 349)

Indeed, Gutman's analysis shows that in "France–East–South" TICs between 1965 and 1975, third-country firms did not even participate in the construction of two-thirds of the projects. Moreover, "the average share of the South in the work is less than 10 percent of the global value of the projects" (Gutman 1981, 343). Even Zurawicki's (1979, 176–77) otherwise hopeful projection for TIC in the long run envisions the South's inability to participate in other than a "residual" manner.

THE GROWTH of East–South cooperation, with or without the West's participation, is hampered by the absence of adequate institutional machinery. For example, technology transfer from the socialist countries of Eastern Europe to the developing countries occurs within the framework of bilateral intergovernmental agreements or joint ventures. However, despite increasingly frequent exchanges of trade delegations, contacts between ministries and enterprises in the respective countries have not been regularized. Here again one encounters the question of trade instruments, including means of payment.

Polish economists Klerr and Zacher (1980) suggest that the creation of a regional CMEA institution might help to surmount obstacles to the broader use of the transferable ruble by protecting its members' national economies from possible domestic effects of multilateralization. They contend (Klerr and Zacher 1980, 26) that "quasi-supranational socialist enterprises ... [that] would not be directly and continuously connected with the domestic economic plan" could facilitate East–South technology transfer through arrangements whereby LDCs use Soviet industrial techniques to manufacture products for export to the East European countries.

Not only could such a mechanism increase the level of East–South trade; it could also help to rectify chronic imbalances in payments between the USSR and other CMEA members. But under international law the status of such "quasi-supranational" enterprises would have to be defined; at present, even joint ventures involving two CMEA members in a third country are established under one of the national systems of law. CMEA lacks not only financial instruments for reconciling trade balances among countries but also institutions capable of reconciling divergent national aims and interests (Ausch 1972, 155–90; UNCTAD 1978).

Legal aspects of the CMEA countries' foreign economic activities have by and large been overlooked by Western scholars (Feldbrugge 1982). This is so because legal forms and formalities frequently seem removed from the actual practice of international affairs. Danilov's chapter (1982, 91–123) on "the participation of non-CMEA countries in the Council's work as observers" typifies this disjunction. After giving a general account of what observer status in international organizations means in light of the 1969 Vienna Convention on the Law of Treaties, he then asserts (Danilov 1982, 104) that the Convention does *not* regulate CMEA, since the, latter "is not an international organization of the universal type in the sense of the [Convention]." He further implies that while CMEA is not covered by treaty law, its practice nevertheless contributes to customary international law. As Tiraspolsky (1983) shows, observer status is anything but a halfway-house to full CMEA membership.

Danilov's commentary is entirely uninteresting, but his argument has significant implications. In particular, he argues that CMEA is not subject to the international law generally governing international organizations, because it lacks full juridical personality. Morozov (1974, 276-87), the Soviet judge at the International Court of Justice, is the authoritative voice on the Soviet doctrine of the law of international organizations. The Soviet position tends to limit the law applicable to CMEA to interstate treaty law, with the result that its member-states tend to become responsible for the organization's obligations. Indeed, the 1973 agreement between CMEA and Finland, a developed country, exhibits precisely this feature (Fiumel 1976; Butler 1981). CMEA is then left to enjoy the rights of being an international organization without responsibility for the concomitant duties.

In his discussion of CMEA institutional links with developing countries, Danilov never resolves the issue of bilateral intergovernmental agreements, because CMEA's executive organs are competent to sign agreements with third parties only when its member-states specifically empower it to do so, exclusively on a case-by-case basis. Danilov contends that this is in the nature of CMEA as an "interstate" organization that is not "supranational." His reasoning complements the Soviet claim that the European Economic Community (EEC) is unique as a "supranational" organization and that, being an exception, it cannot form the basis for any rule concerning the law of international organizations. In this he overlooks, as does the whole Soviet doctrine of international law, the actual existence of a body of EEC law that has evolved over time (on this, see further: Cutler 1983, reprinted in this volume).

However, this issue is addressed in Popov's (1982) series of essays on economic cooperation between LDCs and different CMEA members. Although the author's enumeration of the various agreements and projects is rather long (Popov 1982, 61-123) and quite unorganized, his specification of diverse types of economic arrangements — and of what those arrangements mean in practice for the terms on which such cooperation proceeds — is very useful. Parts of the book read like a handbook for negotiators from CMEA and Third World foreign trade ministries and for project directors in East-South industrial cooperation. The last essay (Popov 1982, 124-39) develops mathematical criteria for evaluating projects of East-South cooperation, particularly enterprise construction.

Popov (1982, 8-60) provides an excellent outline of the framework of international law in which East-South economic relations take place, including the relevant structure of international organizations. Legal issues will continue to play a role in the evolution of CMEA cooperation with developing countries, including tripartite industrial cooperation (Boguslavskii et al. 1982, 93-108, 285-88; Dobozi 1981). However, legal problems remain. Either these will be resolved, and East-South cooperation will expand; or the refusal to address them (including the payments problem) will further alienate the socialist countries' international-legal doctrines from the LDC experience with international commerce. This in turn will affect which of the four tendencies in Table 3-1 will predominate in the global trading behavior of the various CMEA member countries. Those behaviors differ so much from country to country that East European scholars may useful to develop the field of comparative CMEA law, the study of which does not exist at present.

There is in fact a transferable ruble fund within the CMEA, but no country uses it. The CMEA members experience difficulties and bottlenecks in forming inter-enterprise links. Hungary, Poland, and Czechoslovakia have the most developed institutional structures for promoting this, but any coordination remains strictly binational. A multilateralized transferable ruble system would not resolve all the claims directed at the Eastern countries by the developing countries, but it could open the way to broader cooperation.

The socialist countries of Eastern Europe continue to develop their national economies and diversify their domestic economic structures. They are good markets for the developing countries. Economic relations between countries of the East and South usually take place within the framework of a long-term bilateral "commercial, economic, scientific, and technical agreement." Trade does not always attain the levels projects in these general agreements, but there is no single explanation for this. Yet developing countries find themselves automatically included in the socialist countries' annual national economic plans, once they have overcome the difficulties involved in coordinating their production with the imports that the socialist countries intend.

IT IS USEFUL to conclude by asking what research program will encompass questions of international law and economics, as well as politics, within the scope of East–South trade and development relations. Viewing East–South economic relations as one leg of the East–West–South commercial triangle, we may enumerate a series of issue areas within the evolving international economic order. A rough list would have to include development financing, international trade, industrialization and technology transfer, food and natural resources, institutional and organizational policies, and social issues. Each of these areas may serve as a conceptual focus for elaborating an analysis of the prevailing international regime (or competing regimes). The implications of various development approaches ("self-reliance," "basic needs," "rural development") for those regimes could then be specified.

Any comprehensive assessment of the CMEA countries' place in international affairs must take account of the increasingly scarce and expensive labor force in the CMEA countries, growing East European imports of Third World natural resources and manufactures, the acute debt of the East European countries, and the increased politicization of East–West trade. The perspective of international political economy is particularly useful in research into trade and aid relations between CMEA and developing countries. It is complemented by international-law approaches, which provide a necessary point of reference in the study of so rapidly developing and diversifying a domain as East–South interactions.

Examination of data on military assistance, financial arrangements for settling debts, and legal doctrines affecting international trade may produce useful insights into such interactions. Political scientists, economists, and international lawyers, respectively, excel at analyzing those issues. But such analysts working together may also learn a great deal about such a significant topic as how Marxism-Leninism, as an ideology, influences the norms underlying the world trade system, or how clashes among the national commercial policies of CMEA members reflect the differentiation of their interests. After all, members of all three disciplines contend that they are concerned with the allocation of scarce resources.

References

AUSCH, Sándor. 1972. *Theory and Practice of CMEA Cooperation*. Budapest: Akadémiai kiadó.

BERRIOS, Ruben. 1983. "The Political Economy of East-South Relations." *Journal of Peace Research* 20, no. 3 (September): 239-252.

BIBERAJ, Elez. 1981. "Albania and the Third World: Ideological, Political, and Economic Aspects." In Radu (1981c), 55-76.

BIÉN, Andrzej, and Grzegorz NOSIADEK. 1980. "Improving the Function of the Transferable Ruble as an International Currency." *Soviet and East European Foreign Trade* 16 no. 2 (Summer): 26-47.

BOGOMOLOV, Oleg. (1981) The CMEA Countries and the New International Economic Order. In Saunders (1981), 246-256.

—. (1983) CMEA and Global Problems. *International Affairs* (Moscow), No. 5 (May), 21-31.

BOGUSLAVSKII, M. M., O. V. VOROB'EVA, and R. F. ZAKHAROVA. 1982. *Mezhdunarodnaia nauchno-tekhnicheskaia i proizvodstvennaia kooperatsiia: Pravovye aspekty* [International Scientific-Technical and Production Cooperation: Legal Aspects], editor-in-chief M. M. Boguslavskii. Moscow: Nauka.

BUTLER, William E. 1981. "COMECON and Third Countries." *Co-existence* 19, no. 1 (April): 41-52.

COPPER, John D., and Daniel S. PAPP, eds. 1983. *Communist Nations' Military Assistance*. Boulder: Westview Press.

CUTLER, Robert M. 1983. "East-South Relations at UNCTAD: Global Political Economy and the CMEA." *International Organization* 37, no. 1 (Winter): 121-142. [Reprinted in the present volume.]

DANILOV E.A. 1982. *SEV i tret'i strany: Iuridicheskie predposylki i formy sotrudnichestva* [CMEA and Third Countries: Legal Premises and Forms of Cooperation]. Moscow: Nauka.

DE FIUMEL, Henryk. 1976. The Council for Mutual Economic Assistance in International Relations." *Studies on International Relations* 7: 60-78.

DECAYE, Jocelyne. 1980. "La concurrence Est-Sud sur les marchés de l'Ouest : le cas des biens manufacturés." In Lavigne, 1980, 133-152.

DESPINEY, Barbara. (1980) Pays socialistes et nouvel ordre économique international. In Lavigne (1980), 103-118.

DIAMBOU, Jean. (1980) "Faiblesses et qualités des relations Est-Sud." In Lavigne, 1980, 119-132.

DOBOZI, István. (1978a) "Economic Cooperation Between Hungary and the Developing Countries." In Dobozi 1978b, 87-138.

—, ed. (1978b) *Economic Cooperation between Socialist and Developing Countries*. Budapest: Hungarian Scientific Council for World Economy.

—. 1983. "Technology Transfer between Developing Countries and Eastern Europe: Mechanisms, Obstacles and Prospects." In *Emerging Development Patterns: European Contributions*, edited by István Dobozi and Péter Mándi. Budapest: Hungarian Academy of Sciences, Research Institute of World Economy.

—, and András INOTAI. 1981. "Prospects for Economic Cooperation between CMEA Countries and Developing Countries." In Saunders 1981, 48–65.

FELDBRUGGE, F.J.M. 1982. "The Untapped Potential in the Study of Soviet and East European Law." *Studies in Comparative Communism* 15, no. 4 (Winter): 384–390.

GATI, Toby Trister. 1980. "The Soviet Union and the North–South Dialogue." *Orbis* 24, no. 2 (Summer): 241–270.

GU Guan-fu. 1983. "Soviet Aid to the Third World, an Analysis of Its Strategy." *Soviet Studies* 35, no. 1 (January): 71–89.

GUTMAN, Patrick. 1981. "Tripartite Industrial Cooperation and Third Countries." In Saunders 1981, 337–364.

KANET, Roger. 1981. "Patterns of Eastern European Economic Involvement in the Third World." In Radu 1981c, 305–332.

KLERR, Jerzy, and Lech ZACHER. 1980. "Technology Transfer from CMEA Countries to the Third World Countries." In Laszlo and Kurtzman 1980, 18–31.

KOSTECKI, Maciej. 1979. "L'U.R.S.S. face au système de commerce multilatéral." *Revue d'Études Comparatives Est–Ouest* 10, no. 3 (September)" 75–89.

LASZLO, Ervin, and Joel KURTZMAN, eds. 1980. *Eastern Europe and the New International Economic Order: Representative Samples of Socialist Perspectives.* New York: Pergamon.

LAVIGNE, Marie, coord. 1980. *Stratégies des pays socialistes dans l'échange international.* Paris: Economica.

MAGGS, Peter B. 1981. "The Legal Structure of Technology Transfer in Eastern Europe." In *Soviet and East European Law and the Scientific-Technical Revolution*, edited by Gordon B. Smith, Peter B. Maggs, and George Ginsburgs, 272–294. New York: Pergamon.

MATEJKA, Harriet. 1974. "Convertibility in East Europe." *Annales d'études internationales* 5: 175–190.

—. 1980. "Compensation, Convertibility and the Volume of East–West Trade." In *East–West Relations: Prospects for the 1980s*, edited by Giuseppe Schiavone, 33–46. New York: St. Martin's Press.

McMILLAN, Carl H. 1980. *The Political Economy of Tripartite (East–West–South) Cooperation*, East–West Commercial Relations Research Report 12. Ottawa: Carleton University, Institute of Soviet and East European Studies, January.

MILENKOVITCH, Michael M. 1981. "Yugoslavia and the Third World." In Radu, 1981c, 273–300.

MOROZOV, G.I. 1974. *Mezhdunarodnye organizatsii: nekotorye voprosy teorii* [International Organizations: Some Problems of Theory], 2d ed. Moscow: Mysl'.

NÖTZOLD, Jürgen. 1979. "Die RWG-Staaten und der Nord–Süd Dialog." *Aussenpolitik* 30:2 (Summer), 192–209.

OBMINSKII, E.E. 1974. *Razvivaiushchiesia strany i mezhdunarodnoe razdelenie truda* [The Developing Countries and the International Division of Labor]. Moscow: Mezhdunarodnye otnosheniia.

—. 1982. *Gruppa 77: Mnogostoronnaia ekonomicheskaia diplomatiia razvivaiushchikhsia stran* [The Group of 77: Multilateral Economic Diplomacy of Developing Countries]. Moscow: Nauka.

PAJAK, Roger F. 1981. "The Effectiveness of Soviet Arms Aid Diplomacy in the Third World." In *The Soviet Union in the Third World: Successes and Failures*, edited by Robert H. Donaldson, 384–408. Boulder: Westview Press.

PAJESTKA, Josef, and Jan KULIG. 1979. "The Socialist Countries of Eastern Europe and the New International Economic Order." *Trade and Development: An UNCTAD Review*, no. 1 (Spring): 78–81.

PASZYŃSKI, Marian. 1981. "The Economic Interest of the CMEA Countries in Relations with Developing Countries." In Saunders 1981, 33–47.

PECHOTA, Vratislav. 1981. "Czechoslovakia and the Third World." In Radu 1981c, 77–105.

POPOV, V.D. 1982. *Ekonomicheskoe sotrudnichestvo stran SEV s razvivaiushchimisia gosudarstvami* [Economic Cooperation of CMEA Countries with Developing Countries]. Moscow: Ekonomika.

PORTES, Richard. 1979. "Est, Ouest et Sud: le rôle des économies centralement planifiées dans l'économie internationale." *Revue d'études comparatives Est–Ouest* 10, no. 3 (September): 31–73.

RADU, Michael. 1981a. "East vs. South: The Neglected Side of the International System." In Radu 1981c, 3–51.

—. 1981b. "Romania and the Third World: The Dilemmas of a 'Free Rider'." In Radu 1981c, 235–272.

—, ed. 1981c. *Eastern Europe and the Third World: East vs. South*. New York: Praeger Publishers.

RADVANYI, Janos. 1981. "Policy Patterns of Eastern European Socialist Countries toward the Third World." In Radu 1981c, 333-344.

ROBERT, Annette. 1983. East-South Competition in the Western European Markets. In *Emerging Development Patterns: European Contributions*, edited by István Dobozi and Péter Mándi, 467-488. Budapest: Hungarian Academy of Sciences, Research Institute of World Economy.

SAUNDERS, Christopher T., ed. 1981. *East-West-South: Economic Interactions between Three Worlds*. New York: St. Martin's Press, 1981.

SIMAI, Mihaly. 1980. "Hungary and the Third World: A Case Study of Trends and Policies of Cooperation." In Laszlo and Kurtzman 1980, 64-83.

SODARO, Michael. 1981. "The GDR and the Third World: Supplicant and Surrogate." In Radu 1981c, 106-141.

SZENTES, Tamás. 1978. "The Development of Economic, Technical, and Scientific Relations Between Hungary and the Developing Countries." In Dobozi 1978b, 139-160.

—. 1981. "The New International Economic Order: Redistribution or Structuring." In Saunders 1981, 303-308.

TIRASPOLSKY, Anita. 1983. "Le CAEM et ses partenaires privilégiés du Tiers-Monde: Angola, Éthiopie, Mozambique, Yémen du Sud, Afghanistan." *Courrier des pays de l'Est*, no. 274 (June): 3-34.

UNCTAD. 1978. United Nations Conference on Trade and Development. *Multilateralization of Payments in Trade between Socialist Countries of Eastern Europe and Developing Countries: Selected Documents*. UN Document TD/B/703.

—. 1980 *United Nations Conference on Trade and Development. Legislation and Regulations on Technology Transfer: Empirical Analysis of Their Effects in Selected Countries*. UN Document TD/B/C.6/55 (28 August).

VALKENIER, Elizabeth Kridl. 1983. *The Soviet Union and the Third World: An Economic Bind*. New York: Praeger Publishers.

ZEVIN, Leon. 1981. "Concepts of Economic Development of the Developing Nations and Problems of Tripartite Cooperation." In Saunders 1981, 246-256.

ZURAWICKI, Leon. 1979. *Multinational Enterprises in the West and East*. Alphen aan den Rijn: Sijthoff & Noordhoff.

4 The Political Economy of East–South Military Transfers

This article analyzes, consecutively, arms transfers from the Union of Soviet Socialist Republics (USSR) and its East European allies to the developing countries (stressing the economic motives of buyers and sellers that influence the supply of and demand for those arms), the East Europeans' role in East–South military relations (particularly their contribution to technical assistance and personnel training), and the cooperation of the USSR and the East European countries in military production. The analysis demonstrates that the international political economy and world-system approaches complement one another, and the principle for their reconciliation is established. Conclusions are drawn from the analysis concerning Eastern Europe's military relations with the Soviet Union, which are reconceptualized on the basis of the empirical work presented. The significance of changes in those relations for the future course of global military-industrial development is briefly explored.

Keywords: Soviet, Warsaw Pact, WTO, military, aid, Third World, developing

East–South economic relations are only one leg of the East–West–South commercial triangle. A comprehensive assessment of those relations consequently entails consideration of such diverse phenomena as the increased politicization of East–West trade, the acute debt of the East European countries, growing East European imports of Third World natural resources and manufactures, and the increasingly scarce and expensive labor force in the member countries of the Council of Mutual Economic Assistance (CMEA). This list of phenomena makes clear the need to take into account analyses emerging not only from the discipline of international politics, but also from those of international economics and international law. A rough list of general issue areas within the evolving international economic order provides an approach to the problem of defining the scope of this short paper, which cannot compass all those numerous and complex issues. That list would necessarily include development financing, international trade, industrialization and technology transfer, food and natural resources, institutional and organizational policies, and social issues. (For a more comprehensive list, developed in further detail, see Makiyama 1980.)

Analysts might use the various rubrics of the evolving international economic order, listed above, as conceptual foci for elaborating analyses of competing international regimes within a given issue area (for example, see Rothstein 1984b). The implications of those regimes for various approaches to economic development — such as "self-reliance," "basic needs," and "rural development" — could then be specified (along the lines of Rothstein 1984a). The approach to our subject through international political economy here rejoins the established perspective of international law within the context of international relations as understood by political scientists. Within this group of issue areas, East–South military relations are informed first and most directly by the category of international trade, second by that of industrialization and technology transfer (because the Eastern bloc licenses arms production only in exceptional instances), and third by that of social issues.

Most work on military assistance given by the Union of Soviet Socialist Republics (USSR) and its East European allies to the less-developed countries (LDCs) approaches the subject from the standpoint of global strategy, either through studies of bilateral military relations (e.g., Soviet arms exports to a given Third World country) or through the compilation of aggregated arms-trade statistics. This article adopts a perspective grounded in the evolution of the international economic order. It investigates the specifically economic factors that affect Soviet arms trade with the Third World and that explain why Eastern Europe's military assistance to the Third World has shifted from arms transfers to technical assistance. The analysis illuminates how changes in Soviet–East European military cooperation have affected East European competitiveness in the global arms market.

Traditional scholarship on Soviet–East European relations can be divided into two major schools of thought, the hierarchical and bargaining models. Each of these presents a different interpretation of conventional arms production and trade by Eastern Europe. The hierarchical model views the Warsaw Treaty Organization (WTO) and the Council of Mutual Economic Assistance (CMEA) as instruments of Soviet control and alliance management, enabling the USSR to ensure the execution of its policies and the efficient mobilization of East European military resources for that purpose. According to this model (implicit in Remington, 1971; Checinski, 1975; Hutchings, 1983), Moscow needs East European arms production to maximize the size of WTO forces but restrains its allies from acquiring any significant independent capabilities. Military procurement in the Soviet bloc, in this view, is strictly standardized, and production is based on an alliance-wide division of labor. Arms transfers occur exclusively at Soviet behest and principally for Soviet purposes. Any benefits to Eastern Europe are only incidental.

According to the bargaining model, on the other hand, the WTO behaves much like the North Atlantic Treaty Organization (NATO). East European countries vie with the Soviets and one another to maximize their political opportunities and economic welfare. They compete for sales both within the WTO and in the Third World, where they compete with Western suppliers as well. According to this model (implicit in Wolfe, 1965; Erickson, 1982; Campbell, 1984), the governments of the East European countries bargain explicitly as well as tacitly with Moscow over the size of their militaries, the sophistication of their arsenals, and the output of their military industries. The East Europeans use arms exports to promote a variety of national interests, including the health of their domestic arms industries, while striving at the same time to maximize imports of Soviet and Western military-industrial technology that they can then use to develop the widest possible range of their own indigenous weapon systems.

Both the hierarchical and bargaining models offer important insights into Soviet–East European relations. The analysis that follows will show that the bargaining model is more appropriate for explaining arms production in the East European countries, while East European arms transfers correspond more closely with the hierarchical expectations of Soviet initiative and guidance. But neither of these traditional models adequately explains recent developments in either arms production or arms transfers. A unified explanation must be sought elsewhere. A perspective that emphasizes universally applicable economic principles such as comparative advantage can bridge the gap that prevents the hierarchical and bargaining models from providing a comprehensive explanation of these contemporary developments.

The first three parts of this article illustrate three levels at which economic phenomena can be analyzed in the study of world politics. The first part considers the behavior of a single state actor, the Soviet Union, invoking the tradition of classical economics through an analysis of supply and demand to explain variations over time in Soviet arms trade with the Third World. The second part of the article shifts the discussion to the East European countries and their participation in military transfers to the Third World, including technical assistance and arms. This part of the analysis treats overall patterns of relations between the East European countries on the one hand and the Third World countries on the other. It draws implicitly on the *world-system* analytical perspective by considering each group principally as an aggregate entity, though noting their internal differentiation where appropriate.

The analysis of differences within the WTO bloc comes to the fore in the third part of the article, which analyzes Soviet–East European coordination of military production. This analysis delineates basic elements in Soviet–East European relations that motivate patterns of Soviet behavior, exposited in part one, and of patterns of East European behavior, exposited in part two. It pays special attention to differences in behavior between the Soviet Union and its East European allies, and among the latter individually. As such, it focuses on sources of change (see Krasner, 1982b: 186–89) in the region-specific international regime that governs the intra-WTO division of labor concerning military exports and technical assistance to the Third World. The third part of the article concentrates on how that regime explains differences among the East European countries' patterns of military transfers and the differences in those patterns over time. It thus illustrates the application of the *international political economy* approach to the analytical task at hand.

Part four of the article evaluates the research from the standpoint of the "international political economy" approach and the "world-system" approach. These are often contrasted with one another. Each of them has a prodigious literature but they are, for different reasons, of relatively limited assistance for the study of East-

South relations. The long-standing "international institutions" approach, through which it would be possible to treat East–South issues, has in recent years suffered from neglect, although it is used in some recent work (Cutler 1983; Despiney 1980, 1984). It has in fact been swamped by, and to a degree absorbed into, the international political economy approach, which does not hesitate to claim all transnational phenomena, including international institutions, as subject within its domain.

The fifth and concluding part of the article summarizes the findings and addresses related issues such as the Soviet and East European roles in the world economy, both in general and in military production, as well as directions for further research.

4.1 Economic Determinants of Soviet Arms Exports

4.1.1 Determinants of Third World Demand for Soviet Arms

The vast growth of the international arms trade during the 1950s and 1960s can be explained first of all by the decolonization of Western empires, which created a large number of potential new consumers. Beginning in 1956, the USSR entered the market as an important provider of arms. (For a review and evaluation of the various available data sets on Soviet and East European arms transfers, see Després 1985.) At first every producer furnished arms principally to its political clients, but the developing countries quickly learned how to take advantage of rivalries between the two superpowers and their allies. There are numerous instances of an LDC turning to the USSR after being refused a particular arms system or not being granted a given condition of sale by the United States, the United Kingdom, or France (Chari 1979, 233). This happened in India in the early 1960s, in Egypt in the mid-1950s (Kamoff-Nicolsky 1980, 1), and also more recently in Zambia in 1979 and Jordan in 1981.

This led to a certain "banalization" of the USSR as an arms supplier; if during the 1960s arms purchases from the USSR were a clear sign of an LDC's opposition to Western countries, by the 1970s they were no longer systematically associated with support for

Soviet foreign policy. Numerous countries, such as Peru and Jordan, purchase Soviet armaments but accept only a minimum number of Soviet military advisors on their soil. Their votes in international forums do not seem to be influenced by their arms supplier. (For a detailed comparative analysis, see Schrodt 1983.)

Table 4-1. Soviet deliveries of major weapon systems to the Third World.[a]

Year	Total USSR deliveries to Third World (millions of 1975 USD)	OPEC + Syria percent share of USSR deliveries to Middle East + N. Africa	OPEC + Syria percent share of USSR deliveries to Third World	USSR percent share of global deliveries to Middle East + N. Africa
1970	1,136	27	16	43
1971	1,515	33	19	47
1972	1,225	26	11	42
1973	1,537	52	42	54
1974	1,930	99	78	50
1975	2,160	76	66	44
1976[b]	1,554	102	63	21
1977	2,156	100	39	14
1978	3,526	100	44	29
1979	4,565	89	62	55
1980	5,265	83	58	56
1981	2,785	95	69	39
1982[c]	2,904	97	65	26
1983[c]	2,372	93	50	40
1984[c]	2,856	98	58	n.a.
1985[c]	2,651	99	52	n.a.

[a] All figures based on unrounded data. Sources unless otherwise specified: Brzoska and Ohlson (1986, 356–57); SIPRI (1984a).
[b] "Share of OPEC+Syria in USSR deliveries to the Middle East and North Africa" is over 100 percent due to Nigeria, an OPEC member not in the Middle East-North Africa region.
[c] Source for "Share of OPEC+Syria in USSR deliveries to the Middle East and North Africa" and "Share of OPEC+Syria in USSR deliveries to the Third World": SIPRI (1986a).

Clients' arms dependence on their single patrons declined during the 1970s, in large part because the number of arms suppliers on the international market had increased. However stricter terms of sale—such as the demand for cash payment rather than the extension of loans or outright grants as in the past—also

POLITICAL ECONOMY OF EAST–SOUTH MILITARY TRANSFERS   121

encouraged clients to shop around. European producers and the new arms producers in the Third World, as well as the USSR, took advantage of President Carter's decision to restrain American arms sales to the Third World, thereby breaching America's domination of the market (Laird 1983, 30–31). A seller's market has been transformed into a buyer's market (Mallmann 1979; Laird 1983, 27–28), and this transformation has been so thoroughgoing that even traditional Soviet clients have not hesitated to seek negotiations with other suppliers. In a general sense, arms clients sought to diversify their sources of supply (Pierre 1982, 18) in order to reduce their political or military dependence. As a result, the Soviets have had to become more flexible and competitive in setting the conditions of their sales.

The rise in the price of oil in the 1970s and the increased oil revenues of the OPEC countries influenced the growth in demand for Soviet arms during that decade. (See Table 4–1.) Some such buyers were already traditional Soviet clients—Algeria, Iraq, Libya, and Nigeria, for example—although their purchases were traditionally in small amounts. In 1975, following normal delivery delays, the overall volume of arms purchases by OPEC countries from the USSR suddenly increased to 15 times the average of the five preceding years. Since 1974 OPEC, plus Syria, have represented the lion's share of sales by the USSR to the Mideast/North Africa region—usually over 95 percent. Purchases from the USSR by countries in this region generally amount to less than half their total purchases from all arms producers; only 1973–74 and 1979–80 have been exceptions, when these were slightly over half (SIPRI, 1984b, 212–13; 1985).

After a hiatus in 1976–77, the increase in Soviet arms deliveries to the OPEC countries and Syria continued without interruption until 1980. Since then, OPEC (plus Syrian) purchases from the USSR have declined significantly: average deliveries for 1981–83 amounted to only 68 percent of total deliveries of major weapon systems in 1980. Since 1982, deliveries have stagnated at this same level. Given the usual delay between arms orders and arms deliveries, this development may be explained as the result of stagnating revenues after the drop in the price of oil in 1979. Half of the overall decline in Soviet arms sales to the less-developed countries since 1980 is due to a drop in demand by the OPEC countries and Syria, whose arms purchases are largely funded by the OPEC states.

The other half of the decline in Soviet arms sales to the Third World since 1980 is attributable to the non-oil-exporting LDCs, which suffer increasingly from over-indebtedness; as a result, they must restrain their imports generally, including arms imports in particular. In this perspective, the USSR's situation is similar to that of other arms producers, all of whom are faced with the recent decline in global demand. But the Soviet Union has not defended its share of the Third World arms market very well: in 1979-80 that share was about 45 percent, in 1981-82 it was 32 percent, and by 1983-84 it had dropped to about 27 percent. The West European countries, whose market share together was less than 20 percent before 1980, reached a peak of 28 percent in 1981 but then declined, leveling off at 23 percent in 1983-84. This is still a larger market share than that of the United States. After President Carter's policy of self-restraint led to a sharp drop in the U.S. market share, from 55 percent in 1976 to 24 in 1979 and 22 percent in 1981, the figure rebounded to 30 percent in 1983, only to fall back again to 21 percent in 1984 (Grimmett 1982, 16; 1984, 22). The newer arms producers, like the West Europeans, have also increased their Third World market shares.

The principal Western arms producers frequently sell licenses for military production to their privileged clients, but the USSR has until now been extremely reluctant to do this, despite repeated requests by certain LDCs, Iraq in particular, for the transfer of arms-production technology. Among all LDCs, only India has obtained the right to produce major Soviet weapon systems under license. Since the beginning of the 1960s, the USSR has constructed two factories in India to make MiG-21 engines and airframes as well as a factory for electronic equipment. In 1978 — largely in an unsuccessful bid to dissuade India from purchasing Anglo-French jaguar airplanes — the USSR agreed to permit India to co-produce MiG-23/27s. More recent agreements license Indian co-production of T-72 tanks and MiG-29 aircraft (Laird 1983; Lewis 1985).

The Indians seem generally satisfied with this cooperation in the field of production. Their goal was to achieve a degree of self-sufficiency. During the first phase, 1966–67, the MiGs were assembled from imported parts. In 1972, 60 percent of the airplane was locally produced, and since then a factory for subsystems has been built in order to increase this fraction still further. Despite their success, the Indian military complain about Soviet reticence to furnish technical information, this being a reflection of the latter's general penchant for secrecy. Such difficulties have not developed into major differences largely because of the political oversight that leaders of the two countries have exercised over their respective military bureaucracies (Chari 1979, 236–40).

Soviet arms transfers to the Third World result from more than Soviet foreign policy objectives. The foregoing analysis, for example, demonstrates that the difficult economic and financial situation of many Third World countries explains much of the drop in Soviet arms sales to them. Not only national economic objectives but also technological imperatives and the international economic order come into play here. What incentives, then, from the Soviet Union's point of view — over and above well-known strategic and political advantages — motivate Soviet trade with the Third World in military commodities?

4.1.2 Determinants of the Supply of Soviet Arms to the Third World

Three economic arguments are frequently offered to explain East-bloc arms sales to the LDCs: economies of scale, comparative advantage, and hard-currency exchange. According to the first argument, the unit cost of a product decreases when the number to be produced increases. For example, Roberts (1983, 159) notes that the proportion of Soviet combat aircraft exported to the number produced, between 1978 and 1981, was 35 percent; for tanks and self-propelled guns, 42 percent; and for helicopters, 29 percent. Similarly, from 1977 to 1981, 40 percent of all surface-to-air missiles produced were exported (see Laird 1983, 21, 27). These estimates are close to those given by Ofer (1976, 231) for the 1967–75 period. But because a large proportion of exported arms is produced during a previous period and hence does not influence the current cost of production, such estimates can be only very approximate. Some analysts therefore feel that economies of scale do not help to explain Soviet arms exports. Indeed, Papp (1983: 7) indicates that the most recent models are exported in only small quantities. And the increase in the production run that he attributes to exports — 13 percent for the MiG-23 and 17 percent for the MiG-25 — would not have a significant effect on the production costs. (See also Pierre 1982, 79, on this point.)

The second economic argument is in the tradition of analysis of international specialization. It suggests that when the USSR exports arms, it is only exploiting a comparative advantage with respect to this particular economic good. According to this line of reasoning, the Soviets do not produce much else of great interest to the developing countries. That being so, and the Soviets being unable to compete with the West in economic, industrial, commercial, or ideological affairs, they quite rationally compete instead with their most efficiently manufactured products (Laird 1983, 8; Pierre 1982, 73; Ofer 1976, 236).

However, the most important economic factor in explaining Soviet arms sales is incontestably the hard-currency gains that are realized. CIA analysts have published two estimates of the hard-currency receipts that the USSR gains from arms to the developing countries (CIA 1978; Zoeter 1982). These two series are very different from one another. Moreover, the 1978 series assumes that the LDCs paid hard cash for 10 percent of the arms they bought before 1973 and 43 percent after 1973, whereas the 1982 series assumes that these percentages vary annually and recalculates them. These latter percentages were calculated by Zoeter (1982) from an unidentified series of data on arms deliveries that differs greatly from the series published at the same time by the U.S. Department of State (1982). Ericson and Miller (1979), on the other hand, use the first CIA series.

If we use the Department of State series to calculate the percentages of arms sold for hard currency, then we obtain lower and more greatly fluctuating figures. These figures rise from 40 percent in 1970 to 74 percent in 1975, remaining thereafter between 60 and 70 percent except for a drop to 51 percent in 1979. This drop can very probably be attributed, first of all to the OPEC countries' financial difficulties resulting from the fall in the price of oil, and second to the fact that deliveries to noncommunist developing countries in 1979 rose only very slightly whereas those to Vietnam that year rose sharply only to fall to their previous level in the following year.

The most recently published CIA data (Zoeter 1982) assumed that the percentage of arms deliveries paid in hard currency had risen monotonically from 52 percent in 1970 to 96 percent in 1978 and fallen slightly thereafter to 85 percent in 1981. This drop resulted from the OPEC countries' financial difficulties caused by the fall in the price of oil and from a spike in arms deliveries to Vietnam in 1979. On the other hand, Wharton Associates estimate that since 1980 about three-quarters of Soviet arms sales have been made for hard currency but only one-quarter of that being paid in cash, the remainder being financed by hard-currency credits from the Soviet Union to its Third World clients. (See Table 4–2.)

What fraction of total hard-currency receipts do arms sales represent? Zoeter estimates an average proportion of 16 percent from 1971 to 1981, with highs near 20 percent in several years. During this period the USSR would have gained about twice as much hard currency from arms sales as from gold sales, but only about 40 percent as much as from oil and natural gas sales. Comparison of the hard-currency gains due to arms sales (about $27 billion between 1971 and 1981) with the hard-currency debt of the USSR (about $12.5 billion at the end of 1981) (Zoeter 1982) reveals that this debt would have been three times as large in the absence of arms sales, assuming that the Soviets would not have changed their purchasing strategy and that they would have taken loans from Western banks in order to pay for imports that they settle in hard currency.

Table 4-2. Soviet arms sales and hard-currency receipts (figures in millions of current U.S. dollars).[a]

Year	Arms sales to LDCs	Hard currency sales (percent of total sales)	Hard currency sales on credit (percent of hard currency sales)	Net USSR hard-currency debt[b]	Cash hard currency gain as percent of net hard currency debt
1980	5,631	4,265 (76)	3,065 (72)	9720	12
1981	6,687	4,918 (74)	3,885 (79)	12,520	8
1982	8,353	6,157 (74)	3,448 (56)	9,990	27
1983	8,264	5,966 (72)	4,534 (76)	9,577	15
1984[c]	7,547	5,585 (74)	4,189 (75)	8,960	47
1985[c]	5,873	4,346 (74)	3,260 (75)	13,664	24

[a] Sources: WEFA 1984, 14; 1986a, 15; 1986b: 10.
[b] Includes only assets of banks reporting to the Bank for International Settlements. The CIA (1986, 74) estimates for net USSR hard-currency debt in millions of current U.S. dollars are: for 1980, 9,200; for 1981, 12,500; for 1982, 10,000; for 1983, 10,900; for 1984, 10,200; and for 1985, 14,400.
[c] Estimates for "Sales for hard currency and as a percent of total sales," "Hard-currency sales on credit and as percent of hard-currency sales," and "Net USSR hard-currency debt" generated on the assumption that ratios of hard-currency sales to total sales, and of hard-currency sales on credit to all hard-currency sales, will be comparable with those of the recent past.

A study published by Wharton Associates (Laird 1983, 24–25) furnishes still another estimate, that Soviet arms sales paid in hard currency are fixed at 40 percent for the period 1971–73, rising to 75 percent after 1973. This estimate of 40 percent for the years 1971–73 is lower than both Zoeter's estimate and the U.S. Department of State's (1982) estimate. Yet all these estimates are closer and more compatible if absolute values rather than percentages are compared. For example, Laird estimates that from 1971 to 1980 the USSR gained $21.1 billion in hard currency out of total sales of $32.4 billion, grants excluded. The equivalent CIA data, which include grants evaluated at par to selling prices, are $22.7 and $37 billion. Given problems of data comparability, the difference is remarkably small. Laird (1983, 26) estimates that between 1971 and 1980 about 88 percent of the Soviets' $21.1 billion total hard-currency gain from arms sales was used to purchase products from the developing countries, leaving only $2.6 billion to cover — and only in part — the commercial deficit with the West.

POLITICAL ECONOMY OF EAST–SOUTH MILITARY TRANSFERS   127

One's confidence in these calculations, of course, depends upon one's faith in the accuracy of the magnitude of the CIA and Wharton estimates. And the two series exhibit rather close orders of magnitude concerning arms sales, confirmed moreover by the SIPRI data. The CIA and SIPRI register declines respectively in 1979 and in 1980, whereas the Wharton Associates estimate that those sales continued to rise through 1982, falling only in 1983. There is no contradiction here, since the CIA and SIPRI measure actual deliveries and not sales for future delivery. From 1982 to 1985, the gain in hard-currency cash may be estimated (according to the Wharton methodology and assuming that the past tendencies will continue) at a total of about $6.6 billion of net hard-currency debt at the end of 1985. (See Table 4–2.)

Table 4–3. The USSR's hard-currency sources (millions of current U.S. dollars).

Year	Hard-currency gains[a]	Net sales of fuels[b]	Gold sales[c]	Hard-currency arms sales (including those on credit)[d]	Hard-currency arms as percent of hard-currency gains
1980	30,264	17,977	1,580	4,257	14
1981	31,678	18,580	2,700	4,918	16
1982	34,177	20,208	2,150	6,157	18
1983	34,278	20,120	750	5,960	17
1984[e]	33,826	19,353	1,300	5,585	17
1985[e]	29,695	16,031	2,000	4,346	5

[a] Source: CIA (1986, 74), comprising estimates of exports plus invisibles (such as tourism and merchant shipping) plus gold sales.
[b] Source: CIA (1986, 74), including oil, gas, coke, and coal exports, minus imports from non-socialist countries, according to Soviet statistics.
[c] Source: WEFA (1986a, 14; 1986b, 10–13). CIA (1986, 74) estimates are: for 1980, 1,580; for 1981, 2,700; for 1982, 2,150; for 1983, 750; for 1984, 1,000; and for 1985, 1,800.
[d] Source: WEFA (1986a, 14; 1986b: 10–13).
[e] Estimates for "Hard-currency arms sales (including those on credit)" and "Hard-currency arms sales as a percent of hard-currency gains" generated on the assumption that ratios of hard-currency sales to total sales, and of hard-currency sales on credit to all hard-currency sales, will be comparable with those of the recent past (see Table 4–2).

For the last six years available, from 1980 to 1985, hard-currency arms sales (including those on credit) represent about three times the volume of gold sales, which is also slightly less than 30 percent of the net sales of fuels. (See Table 4-3.)

Estimating the USSR's hard-currency receipts and hard-currency debt is a very delicate and uncertain enterprise; the methods are not revealed, and as is known, the financial aspects of the transactions are extremely difficult to uncover. It is therefore noteworthy that the Wharton and CIA estimates nearly agree, even though the Wharton analysts do not reveal the same evolution of the phenomenon over the entire period as do the CIA analysts. One can nevertheless conclude that arms sales to the Third World are indeed one of the major sources of hard currency for the Soviet Union and that both the decline in the overall volume of those sales and the decrease in oil prices explain the 1985 increase of the Soviet net hard-currency debt from $9 billion to $13.7 billion.

If the Soviet Union seeks to sell the maximum quantity of arms in order to obtain the maximum amount of precious hard currency, then it must at the same time expend its own precious raw materials for this purpose and use production capacity and skilled labor that could be allocated to other production. Consequently, and in this sense, it is possible to pose the question of whether arms exports represent a significant burden on the Soviet economy.

The value of the USSR's arms exports as a percentage of its gross social product is extremely low — on the order of several parts per thousand — but it has constantly grown during the period studied. Because military products and production goods are relatively substitutable (Melman 1982, 73–83; Bond 1983, 183–91; Cohn 1983, 199; Mosley 1984, 32–34, 65–66; Dussauge 1985, 120–22), we can interpret those exports as a fraction of overall total investment, or of the gross machinery production. These percentages are clearly higher: Table 4-4 shows them increasing steadily from 0.8 and 1.1 percent respectively in 1971 to 3.8 and 3.4 percent in 1982, decreasing thereafter to 2.7 and 2.2 percent in 1985 as a consequence of the decrease in arms sales themselves.

It follows that the USSR's arms exports to the developing countries are neither a large nor a negligible burden on the country's productive capacity. (The USSR's exports to developing countries represent a relatively low fraction of its exports: 13.2 percent in 1985, for which year its total exports to all countries were 72.5 billion rubles, or about 5 percent of that year's gross social product.) The question remains, how to explain fluctuations in the USSR's arms sales to developing countries. The very nature of these transactions could explain the absence of a regular and constant flow; Libya alone could strongly influence the total quantity of arms sold in any given year.

But more fundamental and structural reasons relative to the nature and the functioning of the Soviet planning system have been invoked to explain these fluctuations. Hutchings (1978) notes that the USSR's arms sales to developing countries followed the same pattern during the Sixth, Seventh, and Eighth Five-Year Plans, rising at the beginning and the end of the plan and falling from the second through fourth years. He offers several explanations for this. First, the length of time needed to develop major arms systems seems to average about six years. If research and testing begin with the first year of a given five-year plan, then production would start during the first year of the following five-year plan. This new production would reach a regular rhythm during the third year of the plan, and exports to the Third World would begin two years thereafter, following the arms' first distribution to the Warsaw Pact. This would cause an increase of arms exports during the first and second years of the plan, which is what is observed (see also Checinski 1977). Second, Hutchings remarks that the socialist countries concentrate their imports toward the last years of the plan. Consequently, the Soviet Union would tend to concentrate its exports to those countries during these years, augmenting its exports to the Third World only toward the beginning of the plan. Third, Hutchings mentions a positive correlation between the USSR's military spending and its arms exports.

However well these reasons may explain regular fluctuations of the USSR's arms sales to the Third World during the 1950s and 1960s, the last 15 years exhibit regularities that are wholly different.

Table 4-4. Arms exports to the less-developed countries as a burden on the Soviet economy (figures in billions of current rubles).[a]

Year	Arms sales to LDCs[a]	Gross social product[b]	Arms exports as percent of gross social product	Global investment[c]	Arms exports as percent of global investment	Gross machinery production[d]	Arms exports as percent of gross machinery production
1970		643.5		79.5		54.8	
1971	0.703	685.3	0.1	86.2	0.8	61.5	1.1
1972	1.335	717.4	0.2	93.4	1.4	69.5	1.9
1973	1.714	770.9	0.2	98.7	1.7	78.8	2.2
1974	1.666	816.4	0.1	107.0	1.6	88.8	1.9
1975	1.602	862.6	0.2	115.6	1.4	100.3	1.6
1976	2.008	903.9	0.2	122.2	1.6	110.7	1.8
1977	3.312	946.9	0.3	128.2	2.6	122.0	2.7
1978	3.674	995.7	0.4	137.5	2.7	134.0	2.7
1979	3.674	1,028.1	0.4	140.0	2.6	145.7	2.5
1980	3.654	1,078.5	0.3	144.9	2.5	156.5	2.3
1981	4.807	1122.8	0.4	152.1	3.2	167.3	2.9
1982	6.066	1,236.0	0.5	159.3	3.8	177.3	3.4
1983	6.140	1,292.7	0.5	159.3	3.8	177.3	3.4
1984	6.161	1,345.8	0.5	174.3	3.5	205.7	3.0
1985	4.842	1,382.5	0.4	181.3	2.7	222.3	2.2

[a] Sources: WEFA (1982, 1986b), converted from current dollars using the following rates of exchange (in dollars per ruble): 1971, $1.11; 1972, $1.21; 1973, $1.36; 1974, $1.32; 1975, $1.39; 1976, $1.33; 1977, $1.36; 1978, $1.46; 1979, $1.52; 1980, $1.541; 1981, $1.391; 1982, $1.377; 1983, $1.346; 1984, $1.225; 1972, $1.213.

[b] Sources: TsSU (1974, 57; 1975, 58; 1980, 54; 1982, 45; 1985, 59; 1986, 45).

[c] Sources: TsSU (1975, 520; 1980, 363; 1984, 355; 1986, 365), converted from constant to current rubles under the assumption of a constant 1 percent annual increase in prices.

Arms sales to the Third World drop at the beginning of these plans and then increase from the second through fifth years. This modification of the planning system's behavior could result from the fact that the USSR is under greater compulsion to obtain hard currency;

such a condition could alter its arms sales behavior. An alternative explanation, equally speculative, would note the customary practice of "storming" at the end of the plan: storming this time to maximize hard-currency revenues. Whichever is the case, it is clear that not just external factors but also Soviet domestic constraints are an important influence on Soviet arms trade patterns.

4.1.3 Past and Future of Soviet-LDC Military Cooperation and Sales

Military cooperation between the USSR and the LDCs assumes varied forms, and there is no transparent correlation between simple military cooperation and economic cooperation. Iran, Turkey, and Morocco — three of the six largest recipients of Soviet economic aid between 1954 and 1981 (U.S. Department of State 1983, 17–18) — have no military cooperation with the USSR. The same is the case for Brazil, which is third in the amount of economic aid received from the East European countries, and for Iran, which is fifth. Nor is there any correlation between a country's annual arms orders and the number of trainees sent to the USSR, although one might think that there should be a causal link between the two, since trained personnel would be needed to operate the military commodities transferred (CIA 1978, 4). Any hypothesized causal link would have to control the level of technological sophistication of the recipient country: the higher that level, the lower the number of trainees. (By contrast, the relationship between the level of development and need for technical assistance among countries importing Western arms is a U-shaped curve. This is because newly industrializing countries, for instance, have the technical skills to use Soviet arms, whereas the most advanced Western arms remain too sophisticated for them to handle alone.) Finally, there is no simple relation between the number of trainees that an LDC sends to the USSR or Eastern Europe and the number of military advisors from these countries in the LDC.

The particular situation of any developing country involves civilian as well as military cooperation, not to mention commercial relations. At one extreme of this spectrum is Turkey, whose civilian cooperation with the USSR is very high but whose military cooperation with and arms purchases from the USSR are nonexistent. Afghanistan has a high level of military cooperation and a significant civilian cooperation, but its arms purchases in recent years have been very low. India, which until 1980 sent almost no military trainees to the USSR or Eastern Europe and received very few technicians either military or civilian (150 and 1,625 respectively in 1981), is an important trading partner of the USSR, one of its largest arms-sales clients, and, moreover, benefits from military cooperation agreements. Recently these agreements have been extended to include the production of the most modern Soviet weapon systems, which is probably why since 1980 India has sent about 1,800 trainees to Warsaw Pact countries and in 1985 hosted as many as 500 military technicians from those countries. Finally, Libya represents another extreme case. It exhibits a high level of arms imports, relatively low general commerce, and a large number of trainees and military personnel (3,300 military technicians and 44,000 civilian personnel from the Eastern bloc, and this for a country with a population of 2.5 million).

Even if we introduce into the analysis different categories of LDCs that the Soviets themselves distinguish—for example, a first group of countries of socialist orientation (Afghanistan, Ethiopia, Angola, South Yemen, Mozambique), a second group also of socialist orientation but less closely tied (Iraq, Syria, Algeria, Guinea, Congo, Madagascar, Tanzania, Burma, Benin), and then a third group comprising all other LDCs—there still remains no homogeneous cooperation policy even for each of these groups. To be sure, military relations are significant for both groups of socialist-oriented LDCs, but this is the case for other LDCs as well, such as Libya and India. Moreover, such countries as Mali and Nigeria, and above all Zambia, have in the past purchased at least as many arms and received at least as much military cooperation as the sub-Saharan countries in the second group of socialist-oriented LDCs.

What lies ahead for Soviet arms sales? Will the stabilization in evidence since 1980, following a sharp decline, continue, or will the long-term trend since 1956 reassert itself? From a strategic and military point of view, the Soviet leadership does not seem about to adopt a policy of self-restraint in arms sales. Nor do other major exporters manifest any sign of self-restraint; the case is rather the contrary. Moreover, the LDCs themselves consistently oppose any discussion of this subject at the UN (Mallmann 1979, 304-5). Wherever one turns, there appears to be no political will that would limit the global arms race by controlling arms sales. The decline in arms sales to the Third World—and there has been a decline—results only from the increasingly heavy economic constraints on the purchasers.

It thus emerges that the USSR follows no ideal-typical policy of military and economic cooperation in its relations with LDCs. General economic factors certainly impel the USSR, like all other arms producers, to export the maximum quantity. In the Soviet case, the hard-currency factor is decisive. We must conclude that Soviet arms sales will continue to fall only to the extent that the LDCs continue to suffer from the lack of dynamism in the global economy and that at the first signs either of their economic recovery or of the alleviation of their debts (which itself seems improbable in the short or even the intermediate run), purchases by LDCs would cause Soviet arms sales, and those of other producers, to rise once more.

4.2 Eastern Europe's Role in East–South Military Transfers

4.2.1 Arms Sales

The East European countries also have important military relations with the Third World. Their arms transfers, for example, have a distinctive profile that differs significantly from the Soviet pattern, even though these were considerably less significant for their trade balances throughout the 1960s and most of the 1970s than in the late 1950s. Their best-selling products have been their indigenous items, with the important exception of the T-54/55 tank. But East European designs must compete in the Third World against the best that other suppliers, Western and Third World, have to offer. With their military technology still rooted in the 1950s, the East European countries are at a growing disadvantage; most of their sales are appurtenances to larger Soviet deals. Since large Soviet fighter sales are usually accompanied by the sale of Czechoslovak jet trainers, Czechoslovakia has profited handsomely from this. In one exceptional case, Poland sold fifty of its indigenous TS-11 Iskara jet trainers to India in 1974. The Indians, expecting to use these inferior aircraft only as a temporary stopgap, paid a bargain price (Chopra 1978; Green, Swanborough, and Chopra 1982, 60-61). Eastern Europe can still serve as a Soviet surrogate in delicate diplomatic situations: when estranged temporarily from Moscow, Iraq turned to the East European countries, which were quite willing to supply some $1.3 billion in tanks, artillery, and sundry items (Snitch 1984, 118). Now that relations between Moscow and Baghdad have improved, however, Soviet armaments have largely replaced those of its WTO allies (SIPRI 1986b, 381-84).

In aircraft the East European countries' manufacturing capabilities are being overtaken by Third World producers. Like many Third World arms producers—such as Argentina, Brazil, Egypt, Indonesia, and South Africa—Eastern Europe's most sophisticated products are subsonic jet trainers and twin-engine transports. Other newly industrializing countries—including India, Israel, South Korea, and Taiwan—are co-producing or developing supersonic fighters more advanced than any East Europe product. (Among the best recent publications on Third World arms industries are Katz 1984; Miller 1980; and Ross 1981). East European aircraft, as well as their other military systems, are consequently losing not just their competitiveness but their very place in the international market. Eastern Europe, unable to sell its products on the basis of their quality, must depend upon political arrangements with Moscow for sales to Soviet clients in the Third World.

The strongest challenge to established East European arms suppliers may come from North Korea and India, which also co-produce Soviet equipment, and from China. North Korea cannot yet supply significant quantities of major weapon systems, but it has provided about 40 percent of Iran's ordinance and ammunition in Iraq war (Halloran 1982). India produces several Soviet systems, including MiG-27 fighters and T-72 tanks. Although India has rarely made major foreign arms transfers, recent indications are that it will market its military equipment more actively henceforth. Some Indian officials would even like to convert their country's military industries to provide spare parts to the Soviet Union (Cherian 1982, 52–61). China has sold considerable quantities of its versions of Soviet designs and provided Pakistan with facilities to overhaul these items. It has also sold Egypt spare parts for its MiG-21s that the latter can no longer obtain from the Soviet bloc, offered MiG-21s to the United States (Biddle 1984), and indeed become Iran's chief source of major weaponry in its war with the WTO-supported Iraq (SIPRI 1986b, 381–84). Czechoslovakia and Poland, lacking competitive military technology, are losing old clients and cannot find new ones. More than 70 percent of their arms transfers go to the Soviet Union or other Warsaw Pact countries (U.S. Arms Control and Disarmament Agency 1984). Their arms transfers have also suffered from the global recession and the Third World debt crisis that together cut total Third World arms purchases, from all sources, from $38.2 billion in 1982 to $30.5 billion in 1984 (Grimmett 1985).

Czechoslovakia and Poland are further challenged by the German Democratic Republic (GDR) and Romania. The GDR began rearming in 1956, but economic problems retarded this process until the late 1960s. Struggling to build its own armed forces, the GDR was in no position to assist others. The country was diplomatically isolated throughout the 1960s, and its assistance to Third World countries helped to establish its legitimacy in the global arena (Sodaro 1981). It first rushed support to the Middle East after the June 1967 debacle. But of equal importance was the invasion of Czechoslovakia in August 1968. The invasion "crippled the [Czechoslovak] economy, inflicted heavy damage on the productive forces, and isolated the country in international relations" (Pechota 1981, 91). Czechoslovakia has since that time kept a low diplomatic profile, abandoning its role as the East European leader in relations with the Third World. The GDR has stepped into this void.

But the East Germans cannot assume Czechoslovakia's role as an arms supplier. Their only military industries manufacture small arms, ammunition, spare parts, and small naval vessels. The GDR has considerable industrial potential but cannot yet execute a policy of assistance to the Third World based on the transfer of major weapon systems. Instead, it has concentrated on providing military advisors. By 1980, estimates of East German military advisors in Africa were on the order of 3,500 to 5,000 (Croan 1980; Kanet 1981, 308, 328). In global terms these numbers are far behind those of the superpowers, France, and even Cuba and Pakistan. The GDR's military representation abroad is about the same as Israel's, North Korea's, or Taiwan's.

Still, the rise of the GDR did transform the nature of East European relations with the Third World. Transfers of major weaponry are no longer their leading diplomatic instrument. That role is now assumed by military training, advice, and technical assistance. The significance of training and advice on combat effectiveness is suggested by William McNeill's (1982, 133) conclusion that the rediscovery of close-order drill was "certainly one of the major achievements of the seventeenth century, as remarkable in its way as the birth of modern science or any of the other breakthroughs of that age." The effectiveness of East German military training was demonstrated in the May 1978 rebellion in Zaire's Shaba province, where rebels trained in Angola by the GDR and armed by the WTO members were far more coordinated and resolute than they were in a similar rebellion fourteen months earlier (Valenta and Butler 1981, 153–55).

Romania seldom acts in concert with its Warsaw Pact allies. Still it has acquired the ability to supplement, challenge, and even counter their Third World arms sales. This was proven as Romania's arms transfers rose from about $80 million in 1979 to $1.1 billion by 1982. Sales to war-torn Iraq amounted to $825 million over these years, during which Romania also supplied the Soviet Union with some $625 million in military equipment. Thus, Romania can make some significant transfers, exacerbating the problems of its East European rivals. But it faces the same constraints as Czechoslovakia and Poland: most of its military technology is late-1950s' vintage, including the Orao. But Romania, unlike the others, has access to some Western military technology as well as greater incentives to utilize what advanced technology it can acquire.

4.2.2 Technical Assistance

As recent East German experience shows, military assistance need not be limited to transfers of major weapon systems. Training and technical assistance are established components in the WTO countries' repertoire of foreign policy instruments. According to the CIA (1978, 1980, 1986) and the U.S. Department of State (1983), the number of Soviet and East European military technicians increased from 3,635 to 10,125 between 1965 and 1970, a factor of 2.8. Following Sadat's expulsion of Soviet military advisors from Egypt in 1972, this figure dropped 18 percent, reaching 8,220 in 1975, but after 1975 the number of these technicians grew very sharply, at a rate of 25 percent from 1975 to 1977, 56 percent from 1977 to 1979, and 15 percent from 1979 to 1981, reaching in 1981 (as shown in Table 4–5) the record level of 18,205 persons. Since 1981, this figure has stagnated, reaching 18,375 military technicians in 1985. The Middle East and North Africa regions predominate; sub-Saharan Africa's contingents are concentrated mainly in Angola and Ethiopia, and, to a lesser degree, Mozambique.

Finally, if we compare military technicians with civilian technicians (called "economic" by U.S. sources, but who include teachers, medical personnel, etc.) we see that the military component represents about 16 percent of all technicians sent by the USSR and Eastern Europe in both 1979 and 1981. This percentage varies according to region and country. Thus in the Middle East, a generally average region for these figures, the percentages vary from 0 percent for Iran and Egypt (hardly surprising) to 9 percent and 4 percent for Iraq in 1979 and 1981, and up to higher percentages (29 to 80 percent) for North Yemen, South Yemen, and Syria. The percentage for Iraq may be explained by the relatively low number of military technicians for its arms purchases (550 in 1981), and an exceptionally large number of economic advisors (around 13,000). Only Algeria compares with Iraq in the latter regard with 11,150 economic technicians (26 percent), explicable by the large contingents in Angola, Ethiopia, and Mozambique, and also in Mali. India confirms its status as a special case, with a very low proportion (8 percent in 1981).

The Middle East and North Africa regions predominate, respectively with 33 percent and 25 percent of military technicians in 1981. Sub-Saharan Africa receives 29 percent of the personnel, a much greater proportion than that fraction total arms transfers which it receives. (These technicians would be concentrated in Angola and Ethiopia, and, to a lesser degree, Mozambique.) The large number of military technicians stationed in Afghanistan, over the above the combat forces themselves, contrasts with the low level of arms transfers to this country; the Soviets give the Afghan army much training but few arms, as if it were diffident of that army's combativity. According to the U.S. Arms Control and Disarmament Agency, the USSR delivered to Afghanistan military matériel worth $650 million (in current dollars) between 1978 and 1982, which is less than Angola and slightly more than Peru. Likewise, SIPRI records $408 million of deliveries (in 1975 dollars), but concentrated almost exclusively in 1978–1979. Since 1980, the Afghan army has received only $11 million in major weapon systems (in 1975 dollars), amounting to two AN-24 transports and fifteen SU-7B Fitters free of charge.

The specific role of the small European CMEA countries is difficult to evaluate, because the data are usually presented in aggregate form under the rubric "USSR and Eastern Europe." East European military technicians did represent, however, 11 percent of the total Soviet and East European military contingent in 1981, roughly corresponding with their 9.5 percent share of total arms sales. This share was proportionately greater in Latin America (26 percent, but which represents only 60 technicians), a bit higher in North Africa and sub-Saharan Africa (13 and 14 percent respectively), and slightly lower in the Middle East (8 percent). The particular role played by the East Germans helps to explain this (Valenta and Butler 1981). Indeed, the GDR has signed military cooperation agreements with several Third World movements and regimes: with the People's Movement for the Liberation of Angola (MPLA) in 1973, with Ethiopia, and recently with Nicaragua (Bolanos 1983). Moreover, the GDR and Cuba have signed a 25-year friendship treaty that provides for their continued support for Third World "struggles." All throughout the Angolan civil war, the East Germans took care of training as well as of medical aid for soldiers evacuated from Angola to the Congo (Brazzaville). There seem to have been up to 700 East German military advisors, but direct military assistance ceased after the victory of the MPLA. The GDR has supported Ethiopia since 1977, when Moscow's alliance with Somalia ended. According to the GDR defense minister himself, Ethiopia has received up to 1,500 military experts who engaged in combat during the offensive in Eritrea, and South Yemenites trained by the GDR fought in Ogaden (cited by Valenta and Butler 1981, 155). The GDR furnishes medical aid to Nicaragua and Afghanistan, and seriously wounded Nicaraguan and Afghan soldiers are treated in East Berlin.

As Table 4-5 shows, military technicians represent about 16 percent of all technicians sent by the USSR and Eastern Europe in both 1979 and 1981; however, by 1985 this figure fell to 13 percent, due to the leveling off in the number of military technicians mentioned above, as well as to a substantial increase in the number of civilian and economic advisors. This percentage varies a great deal according to region, country, and period of time. The low percentage for Iraq is explained by a very large number of economic advisors (about 15,600), with which, aside from Libya (with 44,000) only Algeria compares, although there are also large contingents in Angola, Mozambique, and Mali (while East-bloc economic technicians, strangely, appear to have disappeared from Ethiopia). India's very low proportion until the early 1980s confirms its status as a special case. Although it appears that in numerous cases, the number of military technicians and advisors is much higher than necessary (higher at least than the number of technicians and advisors sent by Western countries in similar cases), this nevertheless represents only a minority of the various Soviet and East European contingents (Pierre 1982, 75–76).

A total of 46,985 LDC military personnel were trained in the WTO countries over the whole period 1956–77; this figure rose to 51,930 for the period 1955–79; 57,795 for the period 1955–81; and 82,415 for the period 1955–85. If we assume that the number trained in 1955 alone is negligible, then these figures reflect a mean increase of 5.4 percent each year from 1977 to 1981, since which time the rate

Table 4-5. Military and nonmilitary technicians from USSR and East Europe in LDCs.

	1979a		1979a	1981b	1981b	1981b	1985c	1985c	1985c
	Milit. techni- cians	Econ. techni- cians^d	Milit. percent of total	Milit. techni- cians	Econ. techni- cians^d	Milit. percent of total	Milit. techni- cians	Econ. techni- cians^d	Milit. percent of total
TOTAL	15,865	80,830	16.4	18,205	95,685	16	18,375	122,745	13
North Africa	2,835	37,845	7	4,600	45,870	9.1	3,915	64,150	6
Algeria	1,015	11,500	8	2,000	11,150	15	615	17,150	3
Libya	1,820	23,500	7	2,600e	31,700	8e	3,300	44,000	7
Mauritania	0	6	0		50		0	50	0
Others	0	2,790	0		2,670		0	2,950f	0
Sub-Saharan Africa	3,990	10,440	27.7	5,300	14,730	26	5,365	14,680	27
Angola	1,400	2,760	34	1,600	3,900	29	1,050	2,475	30
Ethiopia	1,250	1,500	33	1,900	1,800	53	2,600	0	100
Guinea	85	645	12	50	660	7	70	620	10
Guin.-Bissau	60	50	55	50	275	15	85	210	29
Mali	180	485	27	205	425	32	50	505	9
Mozambique	525	800	40	550	1,800	23	950	1,400	40
Others	490	4,200	10	945	5,870	14	560	9,470	0
Lat. America	110	595	15.6	225	930	19.5	260	1,465	15

POLITICAL ECONOMY OF EAST–SOUTH MILITARY TRANSFERS 141

	1979[a]	1979[a]	1979[a]	1981[b]	1981[b]	1981[b]	1985[c]	1985[c]	1985[c]
	Milit. technicians	Econ. technicians[d]	Milit. percent of total	Milit. technicians	Econ. technicians[d]	Milit. percent of total	Milit. technicians	Econ. technicians[d]	Milit. percent of total
Middle East	4,780	25,905	15.6	5,925	27,150	17.9	0	0	0
Egypt	0	750	0	0	0	0	6,260	34,200	15
Iran	0	2,200	0	0	2,450	0	1,200	1,500[e]	44
Iraq	1,065	11,275	9	550	13,000	4	1,300	15,625	8
N. Yemen	130	160	45	700	175	80	310	650	32
S. Yemen	1,100	1,280	46	1,100	2,700	29	1,150	3,250	25
Syria	2,480	6,000	29	3,300	4,100	45	2,300	5,500	29
Others	0	4,240	0	275	4,725	5.5	50	7,675	1
South Asia	4,150	5,945	41	2,155	6,795	24	1,575	7,985	24
Afghanistan	4,000	3,700	52	2,000	3,750	35	2,025	5,525	30
Bangladesh	0	115	0	0	125	0	50	35	34
India	150	1,285	10	150	1,625	8	500	1,600	24
Nepal	0	10	0	0	15	0	0	10	0
Pakistan	0	750	0	5	1,150	0.4	0	955	0
Sri Lanka	0	85	0	0	125	0	0	90	0
East Asia	0	90	0	0	60	0	0	255	0
Europe	0	10[h]	0	0	150	0	0	10	0

[a] Source: CIA (1980, 15, 21).
[b] Source: U.S. Department of State (1983, 14, 20).
[c] Source: CIA (1986, 122–23).
[d] Includes nonmilitary personnel (teachers, doctors etc.).
[e] Probably all attributable to Libya.
[f] Morocco, 2,325; Tunisia, 625.
[g] Most departed before the end of the year.
[h] Malta.

of growth has doubled (CIA 1978, 1980, 1986; U.S. Department of State 1983). Angola, Ethiopia, and Mozambique had no personnel trained in the Eastern bloc before 1977, but between 1977 and 1981 this number rose sharply, to 180, 2,095, and 530 respectively, fluctuating thereafter until reaching in 1985 the levels of 1,500, 680, and 1,000. Although these countries receive comparable numbers of military advisors from WTO countries, they apparently follow very different training policies. Nicaragua had 260 military personnel trained between 1979 and 1981 but sent 1,200 for training in 1985; Afghanistan, which had no military trainees in the WTO countries in 1979, sent about 800 in both 1980 and 1981, this number rising to 1,300 per year from 1982 to 1985. The military personnel sent for training from the Middle East grew at an annual rate of about 5 percent between 1977 and 1981, and at a rate of 8 percent since then. North Yemen, however, shows a much more significant increase, sending 185 trainees from 1977 to 1979, 700 over the next two years, and 2,250 from 1982 to 1985.

Eastern Europe provides training for a growing proportion of Third World trainees in the WTO countries. This proportion, as low as 11 percent for the period 1956–79 and 12 percent for 1955–79, rose to 21 percent during 1982–85, reaching 30 percent in 1985 alone (2,835 as against 6,465 for the Soviet Union). This is still lower than the proportion of civilian students they train from the Third World (12,400 as against 14,690 for the USSR at the end of 1979, the most recent year for which this figure is available). The military contingent from the Third World in the East European countries, as a proportion of all students, was slightly greater than 4 percent in 1979, dropping thereafter to slightly less than that (CIA 1980, 16, 22–23). This corresponds with the generally decreasing significance of the East European countries as a source for transfers of major weapon systems to the Third World: their exports of major weapon systems to LDCs represent about 1 percent of Soviet exports for the period 1981–86 (SIPRI 1986a). The East European countries taken together, however, account for close to one-fifth of the level of total WTO transfers, including munitions and services (CIA 1986, 74). It follows that East European specialization in transfers other than major weapon systems has intensified, leaving the latter field to the

Soviets. There is every indication that future East European patterns of military transfers will continue to diverge from those of their regional hegemon.

4.2.3 Past and Future of East European Participation in the Global Arms Bazaar

Eastern Europe has lost its niche in the international arms market. The military equipment it offers is consistently less competitive not only in the European theater but also in the Third World. Many small and middle powers have also been compelled by economic and technological forces to contract their arms industries, but some have retained or even strengthened their place in the international arms market by specializing. Belgian small arms, Norwegian antiship missiles, and Swiss ordnance are just a few examples. However, with the important exception of Czechoslovak jet trainers, Eastern Europe has not been able to adjust in this manner. With research and development costs rising much faster than their military budgets, and with most avenues to foreign military technology cut off, the East European countries are hard pressed to keep up.

This is not to say that East European armaments are inconsequential. In specific cases, such as the resupply of Iraq in 1980–81, Eastern Europe can still transfer huge quantities. But this depends on the fortuitous combination of Soviet diplomatic requirements, client needs, and East European capabilities. The great majority of East European arms transfers to the Third World are marginal diplomatic oddities. Nevertheless, even small arms transfers can have an importance out of proportion to their size. Small sales to small states, insurgents, or terrorists can fortify unpopular rulers, aggravate civil wars, or panic whole polities. Unintended side effects can also result: regional powers have often used small-scale arms transfers to their adversaries as justification for large-scale military interventions.

Given this perspective, Eastern Europe's gradual transition from security assistance through arms transfers to a policy stressing human skills is a necessity clothed as a virtue. It is not that human skills are a preferable form of security assistance, but rather that this is the only marketable military commodity that Eastern Europe has left. By supplying military training, tactics, efficient organization, and logistic technology, Eastern Europe can play a crucial role in the survival of governments and in the success of putative autocrats. Moreover, the skills of military organization, discipline, and logistics can be instrumental in the civilian economic development of some least-developed countries. But this transformation is evidence of another decline in East European influence: transfers of major weapon systems in the past gave Eastern Europe access to some of the largest and most influential Third World countries, but the human military technology they now have to offer is most useful to the smallest and least developed.

Unless the East European countries make much greater efforts to modernize and expand their military industries, their position as arms suppliers will continue to erode. While the rest of the world continues to modernize, Eastern Europe still relies on technological investments made 15 to 30 years ago. Many Third World arms manufacturers have already passed them by. Other manufacturers of vintage Soviet designs — especially China and North Korea — sell uninhibited by Moscow's heavy hand.

If Eastern Europe is to update its military industries, the GDR and Romania are the likely candidates for rapid expansion. Their industries are the healthiest and most dynamic, they are diplomatically prominent, and they both have some access to foreign military technology. Czechoslovakia and Poland should not be dismissed; quiescent for years, burdened by economic problems arid Soviet suspicions, they still retain substantial potential. But unless the East European countries reorient their domestic priorities, their military industries will continue the USSR remains unsympathetic to their situation.

4.3 Soviet-East European Coordination of Military Production

The policy that guided Soviet promotion of East European military industries during the 1950s was equally applied to the newly established People's Republic of China. Starting in 1954, the Soviets

POLITICAL ECONOMY OF EAST–SOUTH MILITARY TRANSFERS   145

established factories to build a complete range of conventional armaments in China. These included MiG-15/17 and MiG-19 fighters, Il-28 tactical bombers, Mi-4 helicopters, and T-54 tanks, among others (Heymann 1975). When the Chinese expelled all Soviet technicians in August 1960, the USSR found itself confronted with a hostile power that it had itself armed. The Sino-Soviet split may also have helped to convince Moscow to cease issuing production licenses to its remaining allies. Events in East Berlin in 1953 and in Hungary and Poland in 1956 had already cast doubt on the trustworthiness of the East European allies, and after 1963 Romania increased its foreign policy independence. The Soviet Union would not then have found it hard to conclude that East European arms production no longer served its own best interests.

The most important indigenous program was undoubtedly the Czechoslovak L-29 Delfinjet trainer (Gunston 1983, 397-98), which remains the only foreign-designed military system on which the Soviet Union is totally dependent. The L-29 resulted from a bloc-sponsored competition for a trainer to replace the aging MiG-15UTI. A prototype fly-off was held in Moscow in August 1961, and for the first time a non-Soviet design triumphed. The L-29 was a significant achievement for a nation whose prior indigenous designs were piston-engine light planes. Its Czechoslovak designers had benefited from years of experience in co-producing Soviet jet fighters as well as from direct Soviet technical assistance. Czechoslovakia had hoped to sell its indigenous jet trainer worldwide, but the L-29 was hard pressed to compete in a market flooded with equally good or better machines from the West, and it focused its attention on the Warsaw Pact. The prestigious Soviet contract made selling to other allies less challenging, but this still required salesmanship. Poland's TS-11 Iskara lost the fly-off in Moscow at which the L-29 was selected, but Poland decided to produce the aircraft anyway and tried to sell it on the international market. But the success of the indigenous programs camouflaged the fact that East European military-industrial technology was not advancing. The Soviet co-production licenses of the 1950s—the source of much of the technology in Eastern Europe's indigenous programs—were not being renewed. After 1961, no East European country received new production licenses for any major Soviet weapon systems, with the exception of tanks. These countries faced a choice between keeping obsolescent items in production and ending production altogether.

4.3.1 The Decline of East European Military Industries from 1961 to 1978

Just as Eastern Europe's role in East–South arms transfers was declining in the early 1960s, its military industries were achieving their greatest strength and diversity. Old production lines continued to turn out Soviet-designed weaponry, while new facilities were being created to produce locally designed equipment. The East European countries were transferring imported Soviet technology to their own projects and, for the first time since the 1930s, were introducing indigenously developed weaponry. They lacked the research and development budgets, however, and in some cases the skills, to develop state-of-the-art combat systems. Indigenous East European programs were thus locked into a Catch-22: military industries could build diversity only by incorporating less-sophisticated military technologies dating from the late 1950s, which undermined the products' competitiveness because, dating from the late 1950s, they were increasingly outmoded.

Moscow might have justified in several ways its reluctance to share its military technology. It was abandoning its reliance on intermediaries in Third World arms agreements and could have wished to preclude competition. At the same time, the Soviets were becoming accustomed to earning foreign currency through arms transfers. Many of the earliest WTO arms transfers to the Third World were heavily subsidized by grants, soft loans, or payment in local currency or in goods and raw materials. Gradually the Soviet Union, like other major arms suppliers, began to make such financial assistance available only in exceptional cases and regularly insisted on prompt payment in hard currency (Pajak 1981; Laird 1984). As arms transfers emerged as a major component in Soviet exports, economically competitive allies became still less desirable. Moreover, the Soviet Union no longer needed East European factories to arm the Warsaw Pact. Khrushchev's shift to nuclear deterrence justified the reduction of conventional forces, permitting resources to be shifted to the civilian economy.

Technological and economic forces complicate arms production: new generations of weapon systems brought exponential increases in cost. In Western experience, the cost of each new generation of a weapon system is typically three to ten times that of its predecessor; military modernization has also had the perverse effect of pushing production rates down (White 1974). The Soviet economy operates in a different manner and its rate of technological progress is slower, but these forces are certainly present even if they are not as severe (Biery 1983). As technological modernization increases production costs, the Soviets may have felt compelled by economic necessity to reduce production rates. For example, in the ten years from 1949 to 1958, at least 14,000 MiG-15/17 fighters were produced. In the subsequent decade these were superseded by only 10,000 MiG-21s, which in turn were replaced with just 1,500 MiG-23/27s in the decade following that. Feeling the burdens of its own overcapacity, the Soviet Union had strong incentives to monopolize production of major weaponry within the Warsaw Pact.

4.3.2 The Controlled Renaissance of East European Military Industries since 1978

In the late 1970s East European arms industries began to show signs of modest revival. Military production moved laterally through the Warsaw Pact permitting Bulgaria, the GDR, and Romania to assume greater leadership in Third World arms transfers and security assistance. In 1978 the Soviets started modernizing East European arsenals with weaponry from the 1960s. Soviet transfers included MiG-23 fighters, Mi-24 helicopters, and SA-9 surface-to-air missiles, all of which had been shipped to Soviet clients in the Third World several years earlier. In the 1950s, such items would have been co-produced in Eastern Europe, but now the Soviet Union supplied Eastern Europe with "off-the-shelf" equipment just as it supplied its allies in the Third World. The Soviet Union moved production of its An-28 turboprop transport to Poland, which continues also to manufacture military helicopters, patrol vessels, and small arms.

Czechoslovakia continued producing its L-39 Albatross jet trainer (a modernized version of its L-29), armored personnel carriers, and artillery; and it has introduced a new indigenous self-propelled Howitzer, the 152-mm Dana.

The East European countries have tried to compensate for the lack of Soviet supply of military technology by trading such technology among themselves. Czechoslovakia, Hungary, and Poland all trade their respective indigenous armored vehicles, desiring to deal among themselves rather than to buy similar Soviet systems. Poland co-produces the Czechoslovak OT-64 armored personnel carrier, as does Hungary. Czechoslovakia and Poland both use Hungary's FUG scout car. This pattern creates minor problems for Warsaw Pact military standardization, but it enables the East European countries to subsidize one another's independent ventures. Such trading can only balance out their capabilities, however, and cannot substitute for new infusions of Soviet military technology.

The only major new military production license has been one enabling Czechoslovakia and Poland to begin manufacturing the Soviet T–72 tank. Moscow had already supplied large quantities to the Third World, so it was probable (perhaps explicitly guaranteed) that Eastern Europe would share in follow-on orders. In practice, the switch to producing the new tank has not been smooth, apparently because of the obsolescence of Eastern Europe's military-industrial base. There was a four-year lag in bringing it to series production after receiving the license in 1978, and the production rates since then have been quite low (100 units for Czechoslovakia and Poland together in 1982), while the old T-55s still continue to be produced (500 units in 1982). The defeat of Syrian T-72s by older Israeli machines in the 1982 war in Lebanon has further complicated matters by darkening future sales prospects (U.S. Department of Defense 1983: 80).

New licenses for fighter aircraft have not been reported. Because fighter technology has changed radically since the 1950s, when the last fighters built in Czechoslovakia or Poland were introduced, resumption of fighter production without considerable Soviet support would be extremely difficult and even with that support, perhaps impossible. The latest generation of Soviet fighters, the MiG-29 Fulcrum and Su-27 Flanker, have severely strained Soviet capabilities. Introduced a full decade after equivalent Western aircraft, they are still not in full-scale production. If Soviet factories are hard pressed to adapt to the new technologies involved (Strode 1984; Sweetman 1984), then East European licensees, who face a 25-year technological gap to cross, have bleak prospects.

The GDR is unable to arm its clients heavily but Romania can now do so. In the last twenty years, Romania has developed a military-industrial base technically equal to that of Czechoslovakia or Poland, though somewhat smaller. Because Romania lies outside the superpowers' main region of confrontation in central Europe, the country has never received as much attention from the Soviet Union as have its northern neighbors. In 1958 Romania successfully exploited its geographical position, convincing the Soviet Union to evacuate its troops from the country. In 1963 Romania began to steer its more independent foreign policy. This deviation became still more marked when Romania then began to develop its own military industries with non-Soviet technology. In 1969 it signed a contract with Britain to co-produce BN-2A transport aircraft. This agreement was superseded in 1979 by a license to produce British BAe-11 jet transports. In 1971 licenses were also secured for French Aerospatiale helicopters and Chinese fast patrol boats. Also in 1971, a collaborative venture was started with Yugoslavia that led to the trans-sonic Orao ground support fighter. The Orao, which relies on British, French, and Swedish subsystems, first flew in 1974.

Romania's capabilities are nevertheless severely limited. Aside from the Orao, its only major indigenous programs are production of an armored personnel carrier introduced in 1972 and modernization of imported T-54/55 tanks (Alexiev 1981, 7–18; Foss 1983, 51, 332–33; Munson 1983, 225–30). Romania has developed its military-industrial base more slowly than its northern neighbors theirs, but Romania's has continued to develop whereas the latter's, deprived of new Soviet military technology, have virtually stopped. Always ready to enhance its maverick profile, Romania has considered buying United States military equipment and has added to its stock of Soviet weaponry by purchasing equipment captured by Israel (U.S. Arms Control and Disarmament Agency 1984, 96–97).

4.4 "International Political Economy" or the "World-System"?: A False Opposition

It was suggested at the outset of this study that the hierarchical and bargaining models of Soviet-East European relations fail to capture important economic elements of the global political order that help to explain military transfers to the Third World, and that the international political economy and the world-system approaches illuminate significant aspects of those relations that would remain otherwise unclarified. Both these approaches indeed make clear the need for studies of global commerce in military commodities to give more attention to the autonomous role of international technological modernization in particular. Luke, for example, correctly takes account of this phenomenon in a general way when he asserts (1985, 347) that the Soviet Union's position in the world economy is semi peripheral, dependent on Western technologies while exporting core-like products to the Third World and Eastern Europe and peripheral products to core areas in the industrialized West. But Luke neglects significant phenomena that fail to conform with that pattern, including such important constants as Soviet imports of finished goods, particularly machinery, from other CMEA states – notably East Germany and Czechoslovakia. Yet this shortcoming is shared by much work done in the international political economy approach; its prodigious literature is dominated by concern with the commerce and commercial policies of the advanced industrial democracies of the West, although that emphasis is understandable since these countries among themselves account for the vast majority of world trade (Nye and Keohane 1977; Keohane 1984). The world-system approach, applied by Luke, has recently (compare Wallerstein 1976, 1982; Chase-Dunn 1980, 1981; Ost 1982; Tylecote and Lonsdale-Brown 1982) suggested that the CMEA countries are being integrated into the world capitalist system. Väyrynen (1983), however, does not take this into account; in his attempt at a general characterization of the semiperiphery in the global military-industrial order, he hardly mentions the Soviet Union or any East European country. Moreover, no subcategory of the semi-periphery that Väyrynen develops is defined by empirical criteria that any of the CMEA countries would meet. The root of this difficulty would seem to lie in the nature of the world-system approach itself, which seeks to abstract from the particular characteristics that the CMEA member-states have in common. However, although this analytical approach tends to fail to differentiate between the Soviet Union and the East European countries or among the latter individually, it does shed light on important features of their collective relations with other actors in global politics.

As is known, the member-states of the CMEA differ even among themselves concerning the basic role of foreign trade in centrally planned economies. Some planners in the East European countries feel that exports should function not to optimize capacity or resource allocation but instead to secure revenue for covering import requirements; others contend that the CMEA countries must merge into the international division of labor in order to improve their own economic efficiency and viability; and still others attempt to resolve this dispute by speaking of a "socialist international division of labor" that is distinct from the international division of labor more generally conceived. (Compare, for example, Paszyński 1981, 38–40, with Dobozi and Inotai 1981, 48–50; see also Lavigne 1981, 85–86.) Thus, the CMEA countries can today be treated as a homogeneous unit in the world economy only with difficulty.

From the fact that the East European states, motivated by Soviet intrabloc trading behavior, have responded to international economic developments by diversifying their general trade patterns and developing technical assistance capabilities, it follows that the international regime that is particular to the Soviet–East European region and governs military production and transfers to the Third World, has changed. In particular, it is the norms and rules if not the procedures as well, that regulate the intrabloc division of labor that have shifted, leading to general and differentiated changes in East European strategies for industrialization and economic growth (Clark and Bahry 1983). The present study reveals that international technological modernization and its repercussions within the WTO bloc are the principal developments motivating the observed shift in the international regime within that bloc that govern military transfers to the Third World. The international regime therefore emerges as an intervening variable that mediates the effect of the world economy on East European state behavior. This has occurred in other economic sectors as the Soviet Union and its East European allies have entered the world economy, of which their behavior therefore can be only less and less autonomous. They have become subject to global market forces affecting general commerce not only in military but also in nonmilitary products. As the role of the USSR as regional economic hegemon declines, it is increasingly evident that changes in the intrabloc economic regime may have autonomous effects on the international economic order (see Krasner 1982a, 503–9; 1982b, 186–94).

The general strengths and weaknesses of the international political economy and world-system approaches emerge from this summary of the light they shed on the particular topic at hand. Specifically, those strengths and weaknesses derive from the contrast between the levels of analysis to which each approach is addressed. International political economy is principally concerned with the relationship between the state and international-regime levels of analysis, whereas the world-system is mainly concerned with the regime and international-system levels of analysis. (It is possible to synthesize the clear and unequivocal advantages offered by the international political economy and world-system approaches — advantages that they hold over the two traditional models of Soviet–East-European relations, the hierarchical and bargaining models, neither of which compasses economic sources of the international behavior of states.) Recent work (Comisso 1986; Tyson 1986) suggests not just that the two approaches are not mutually exclusive, but, moreover, that a judicious combination of them can accommodate analytically based "within-group" differentiations among state actors whose common distinct attributes also provide a basis for treating them separately as a collective unit for the purpose of holistic interpretation.

The recent rebirth of interest in "international regimes" (Haas 1980; Krasner 1983; Young 1980), leading to a reemphasis on the significance of international norms (Cohen 1981; Kratochwil 1984), has rectified, but only in part, the tendency of the international political economy approach to slight normative perspectives on trade and development issues. To provide the continuity if not the enforcement of norms is a principal function of international institutions, which — whatever else they are or do — lose themselves all normative value if they do not remain the reified collective memory of the lessons of the life of nations. It would be fruitful to study — though we cannot do so here — how Marxism-Leninism as a system of organized knowledge has influenced the norms underlying the world trade system; this would provide still another perspective of East–South relations. (As Soviet and East European bargaining positions at UNCTAD have become less "ideological," for instance, those countries have increasingly introduced ideologically based operational initiatives into such forums as the International Law Committee and the United Nations Commission on International Trade Law.)

The so-called "world-system" approach, perhaps even more widely adopted among sociologists than among political scientists, affords another possible *optique* on East–South relations. However, like the international political economy approach, its principal focus is usually on West–West and West–South relations. Some practitioners assert that the Soviet Union and Eastern Europe actually stand in a neocolonial economic relationship to the West, importing mainly semi-manufactured and manufactured goods, and exporting mainly raw materials and natural resources (Chase-Dunn 1980, 1981; Tylecote and Lonsdale-Brown 1982; Wallerstein 1976, 1982). However, in all the "world-system" literature there are consistent shortcomings as regards treatment of Eastern Europe and the Soviet Union, and so also as regards East–South relations. Notably, because they do not have the requisite area specialization, they tend to abstract the particular characteristics of these countries, neglecting for example to differentiate between the Soviet Union and the small East European countries — and among the latter individually — with respect to their places in the international political economy (Ost 1982).

4.5 Conclusion: Soviet-East European Military Relations and Global Military-Industrial Development

The Soviet Union has tried three times since the late 1940s to standardize Warsaw Pact military procurement. The first initiative involved *Sovietization* of the East European military industries. This was accomplished by 1952, but reversed thereafter as the East European countries acquired the ability to develop their own modern weaponry. The second initiative involved the promotion of *specialization*, among the USSR's allies, in the production of particular types of weaponry. This move toward specialization ran afoul of the national imperative to achieve and maintain across-the-board capabilities. Differences in countries' degree of commitment to joint efforts led some projects to collapse while others prospered. The last Soviet initiative has sought to establish a *hierarchy* of military manufacturers, wherein the Soviet Union builds all major combat equipment and minor armaments such as small arms. This strategy appeals to East European self-interest and, being less coercive, has been more persuasive.

Since the early 1960s, Moscow has replaced the Third World as the largest buyer of East European military equipment. At about the same time, the USSR's preemption of Eastern Europe's role as a Third World arms supplier reopened the question of how it might utilize its allies' excess military-industrial capacity. The Soviets have responded by purchasing large quantities of East European hardware for their own use.

The coordination of military cooperation between the European socialist countries and the USSR seems to take three principal forms. First, certain East European countries occasionally act on behalf of the USSR when the latter does not wish to be directly involved. Thus, the first arms sales agreement signed between a socialist country and an LDC was the one between Czechoslovakia and Egypt in September 1955. It was followed later in the same decade by agreements with Syria, Iraq, Indonesia, and Guinea (Pechota 1981). Likewise, when the USSR decreed an embargo on arms sales to Iraq after the latter's attack on Iran, the GDR and Poland—and especially Romania—continued to deliver T-54 and T-55 tanks as resupply for the losses in the Gulf War (and the deliveries were even transited through Saudi Arabia). According to Valenta and Butler (1981, 150), Article Eight of the Treaty of Friendship, Cooperation, and Mutual Assistance signed between the GDR and the USSR in 1975, specifies that mutual military assistance would no longer be limited to Europe, as was previously the case. East German military advisors in Angola, Ethiopia, and Mozambique serve Soviet interests and are apparently supervised by Soviet personnel, as is surely the case for Cuban troops.

The second form of coordination of Soviet-East-European military cooperation involves the division of labor. Czechoslovakia appears to specialize in training tank teams and artillery support, the GDR in utilizing reconnaissance equipment and air traffic, Poland in training pilots and parachutists, and Hungary in the general training of infantry. Moreover, there exist instances where the coordination of arms sales and training services is arranged. For example, Hungary signed an agreement with Mozambique in November 1978, according to which it undertook to furnish the latter with tanks and planes (certainly produced by the USSR or another East European country since Hungary herself produces none), accompanied by Hungarian instructors and advisors to train the Mozambican troops to use these arms (cited by Kanet 1984, 180).

Finally, the CMEA countries have maintained since the early 1960s a common fund to assist "anti-imperialist" states and political movements. Each country contributes to the fund either transferable rubles or a quota of goods. According to Checinski (1977, 193), a former researcher at the Institute of War Economics Warsaw's Central School for Planning and Statistics, the USSR supplies arms and military equipment, while other CMEA members principally supply consumer goods.

The findings presented here reveal the need for substantial revision of standard interpretations of Soviet-East European relations and WTO armaments policy. In particular, more attention needs to be given to the autonomous role of international technological modernization. (See Sprout and Sprout, 1962. Compare Abonyi and Sylvain 1977; Clark and Bahry 1983.) The success of East European arms transfers depends not only on Soviet policy or local priorities, but also on the pace of global military modernization. East European arms transfers as a proportion of global totals peaked twice: first, in the 1950s when Soviet licenses gave East European military industries near state-of-the-art technology; and later in the 1960s when indigenous East European programs were at their height. In both instances, the sophistication and range of Eastern Europe's arms production made them internationally competitive.

The hierarchical and bargaining models are revealed as useful ideal types, but neither can be applied across the board to all facets of the military relationship. East European arms transfers generally fit hierarchical expectations. Soviet allies transfer arms to the Third World only where this suits Soviet purposes. In only one instance has a WTO member transferred arms in contradiction to Soviet policy: this occurred in 1975, when Romania briefly supported Holden Roberto's forces in the Angolan Civil War, while the Warsaw Pact backed the victorious MPLA. The only known refusal to transfer arms in support of Soviet objectives came in 1967–68, when Alexander Dubček's government in Czechoslovakia refused to help the WTO arm the federal government during the Nigerian Civil War (Gavshon, 1981: 242; Porter, 1984: 103). Even when East European countries transfer arms to countries in the gray areas of Soviet diplomacy, it is safe to assume that they act with the Kremlin's approval. But East European arms transfers are not as orderly as the hierarchical model assumes, and the roles played by individual countries correspond to no hierarchically determined political plan or principle.

WTO arms production corresponds superficially with hierarchic assumptions: major weapon systems are developed exclusively in the Soviet Union while East European military industries tend to concentrate on less sophisticated nonlethal support equipment. But Moscow's plans to establish a WTO-wide articulated division of labor in arms production have failed. Soviet efforts to orchestrate East European arms production have not met with success because the East European countries cannot be forced to manufacture what they do not wish to. Furthermore, Moscow cannot end East European projects simply because they are obsolete, redundant, or worrisome; its allies seek to maximize the competence and versatility of their own military industries and thus consistently prefer their own to Soviet designs. Moscow has not been able to direct East European military industries through mere fiat. The most effective tools of influence have been selective expansion of East European capabilities, offers of new production technology, and purchases of East European products. The crude hierarchy in WTO arms production that the Soviet Union has achieved comes from its success in convincing its allies that this is in their best economic and industrial interests. What hierarchy there is results principally from bargaining processes.

In the future, East European arms industries and arms transfers will be less relevant to the needs of the Warsaw Pact and of Third World clients, partly because of Eastern Europe's inability to match the pace of the superpowers' military modernization: a problem besetting the smaller NATO members as well. In Eastern Europe's case, however, the problem is exacerbated by the lack of Soviet support for their advanced hardware programs. It also reflects their inability to find a diplomatic role for their armaments. As is demonstrated by the evolution of Eastern Europe's military-industrial relations with the USSR, it is necessary, from the standpoint of political economy and development strategies, to distinguish between the effects of arms transfers on recipient countries and those of the transfer of arms-production technologies. Simple arms transfers tend to have less sophisticated effects, and these are usually limited to the macrolevel. All that is usually involved in the reallocation of a part of the recipient country's national product for the arms purchases, away from other potential uses of those economic resources. If personnel training is included as part of an arms-transfer agreement, then a possible microlevel effect would be the acquisition of some technical skills. Aside from this, simple arms transfers have no significant microlevel effects.

The East European countries' capabilities in manufacturing aircraft illustrate the problems this can create for their international marketability. Like many Third World arms producers — such as Argentina, Brazil, Egypt, and Indonesia — Eastern Europe's most sophisticated products are subsonic jet trainers and twin-engine transports. Other newly industrializing countries — including India, Israel, South Korea, and Taiwan — are co-producing or developing supersonic fighters and munitions more advanced than any East European product. But Eastern Europe's aircraft, like its other military systems, are losing not their competitiveness but their very place in the international market. Unable to sell its products on the basis of their quality, Eastern Europe must depend on political arrangements with Moscow for sales to Soviet clients in the Third World. (For recent analyses of the new Third World arms industries, see Miller 1980; Ross 1981; Neuman 1984a, 1984b.)

The marketability of East European arms depends not only on Soviet policy or local priorities but also on the pace of global military modernization. East European arms transfers as a proportion of global totals have peaked twice: once in the 1950s, when Soviet licenses gave East European military industries near state-of-the-art technology; and then in the 1960s, when indigenous East European programs were at their height. In both instances, what made them internationally competitive was the sophistication and range of the East European countries' own arms production.

These problems are not restricted to major weapon systems. North Korea, for example, has been aggressively marketing its artillery, small arms, and ammunition, all based on Soviet designs; China has received no Soviet military technology since 1962, but it has repeatedly demonstrated its willingness to share what it has. If these and other LDC-produced arms incorporate technology more "appropriate" for use in other LDCs, and if sales of these therefore rise, then the global arms market could gradually become segmented into two world markets for military goods: one for smaller, less sophisticated arms, for which production technology is more often transferred and in which greater competition might therefore be anticipated, perhaps thus resulting in higher demand as well; and another market for more sophisticated arms, for which production technology is less often transferred and in which we would consequently expect lower competition. If such an evolution of the world market were to occur, then the smaller, technologically advanced arms exporters (such as France and Sweden) could, like the East European countries, find themselves squeezed out by decreased demand in the high-technology market and increased competition in the low-technology market.

Evaluating the effects of the transfer of arms-production technology on the recipient country is more complicated, for it invokes all the considerations usually brought to "project evaluation" in developing countries. As in the case of technology generally, the transfer of advanced arms-production technology may contribute to splitting the recipient LDC economically in two. The outcome would be a set of economic sectors in which advanced techniques are principally employed, and another set in which traditional economic processes continue at work. This is neither a macrolevel nor a microlevel effect of technology transfer; we may well consider it a "mesolevel" effect. Almost the only empirical work on either the mesolevel or the microlevel is by Neuman (1978, 1981), who addresses U.S. arms-technology transfer to Iran before the fall of the Shah. In such work the level of technology transferred is very important (Spencer 1970: 115–29). It is customary to distinguish between "high" technology and "appropriate" technology. Whereas the traditional understanding of the appropriateness of technology is "appropriate to the level of economic development," this may be slightly ambiguous when military commodities are at issue. Any future research agenda should include the decision-making processes through which LDC leaders and their militaries resolve questions of arms acquisitions (Katz 1984).

References

ABONYI, Arpad, and Ivan J. SYLVAIN. 1977. "CMEA Integration and Policy Options for Eastern Europe: A Development Strategy of Dependent States." *Journal of Common Market Studies* 16, no. 2 (December): 132–154.

ALEXANDER, Arthur J. (1978) *Decision-Making in Soviet Weapons Procurement*. Adelphi Papers Nos. 147-148. London: International Institute for Strategic Studies.

ALEXIEV, Alex. 1981. "Romania and the Warsaw Pact: The Defense Policy of a Reluctant Ally." *Journal of Strategic Studies* 4, no. 1 (March): 7-18.

BIDDLE, W. 1984. "U.S. Navy May Get MiG's [sic] from China." *New York Times* (3 July): A/6.

BIERY, Frederick P. 1983. "Converging Lines: How Soviet and U.S. Tactical Aircraft Cost and Design Trends Compare." *Defense and Foreign Affairs* 11, no. 5 (May), 11-15, 49.

BOLANOS, M. (1983) "Interview." *Backgrounder* (30 September): 8-9.

BOND, D. L. 1983. "Macroeconomic Projections of the Burden of Defense on the Soviet Economy." In U.S. Congress 1983, 180-191.

BRZOSKA, M., and T. OHLSON, eds. 1986. *Arms Production in the Third World*. London: Taylor & Francis.

CAMPBELL, John. C. 1984. "Soviet Policy in Eastern Europe: An Overview." In *Soviet Policy in Eastern Europe*, edited by Sarah Meiklejohn Terry, 1-31. New Haven, Conn.: Yale University Press.

CHARI, P. R. 1979. "Indo-Soviet Military Cooperation: A Review." *Asian Survey* 19, no. 3 (March): 230-44.

CHASE-DUNN, Christopher. 1980. "Socialist States in the Capitalist World Economy." *Social Problems* 27, no. 5 (June): 505-25.

—. 1981. "Interstate System and Capitalist World Economy: One Logic or Two?" *International Studies Quarterly* 25, no. 1 (March): 12-42.

CHECINSKI, Michael. 1975. "The Cost of Armament Production and the Profitability of Armament Exports in Comecon Countries." *Osteuropa-Wirtschaft* 20, no. 2 (June): 117-42.

—. 1978. "Structural Causes of Soviet Arms Exports." *Osteuropa-Wirtschaft* 23, no. 3 (September): 169-81.

—. 1982. "The Military-Industrial Complex: Planned and Non-Planned Consequences of CMEA Defense Spending." In *The CMEA Five-Year Plan (1981-1985)*, ed. NATO Economics and Information Directorates, 237-255. [Brussels]: NATO.

CHERIAN, D. 1983. "HAL Cleared for Take-off?" *Business India*, 13-26 September, 52-61.

CHOPRA, Pushpindar Singh. 1978. "India's Air Academians [sic]: The Story of Flying Training in the Indian Air Force." *Air International* 14, no. 5 (July): 15-20, 39-40.

CIA. 1978. Central Intelligence Agency, National Foreign Assessment Center. *Communist Aid to Less Developed Countries of the Free World*. Washington, D.C.: Central Intelligence Agency.

—. 1980. Central Intelligence Agency, National Foreign Assessment Center. *Communist Aid Activities in Non-Communist Less Developed Countries, 1979 and 1954–1979*. Washington, D.C.: Central Intelligence Agency.

—. 1986. Central Intelligence Agency, Directorate of Intelligence. *Handbook of Economic Statistics, 1986*. CPAS 86-10002. Washington, DC: Central Intelligence Agency, September.

CLARK, Cal, and Donna BAHRY. 1983. "Dependent Development: A Socialist Variant." *International Studies Quarterly* 27, no. 3 (September): 271–93.

COHEN, Raymond. 1981. *International Politics: The Rules of the Game*. London: Longman.

COHN, Stanley H. 1983. "Economic Burden of Soviet Defense Production: Qualitative and Quantitative Aspects." In U.S. Congress (1983), 192–207.

COMISSO, Ellen. 1986. "Introduction: State Structures, Political Processes, and Collective Choice in CMEA States." *International Organization* 40, no. 2 (Spring): 195–238.

CROAN, Melvin. 1980. "A New Africa Korps?" *Washington Quarterly* 3, no. 1 (Winter): 21–37.

CUTLER, Robert M. 1983. "East–South Relations at UNCTAD: Global Political Economy and the CMEA." *International Organization* 37, no. 1 (Winter): 121–142. [Reprinted in this volume.]

—. (1984). "Economic Issues in East–South Relations." *Problems of Communism* 33, no. 4 (July–August): 73–80. [Reprinted in this volume.]

DESPINEY, Barbara. 1980. "Pays socialistes et nouvel ordre économique international." In *Stratégies des pays socialistes dans l'échange international*, coordinated by Marie Lavigne, 94–110. Paris: Economica.

—. 1984. "Le nouvel ordre économique international et les pays socialistes." In *L'URSS et l'Europe de l'Est en 1983–84*, edited by Thomas Schrieber, 9–26. Notes et études documentaires 4767. Paris: Documentation française.

DESPRÉS, Laure. 1985. *Les ventes d'armes et la coopération militaire entre l'URSS, les pays socialistes européens et les pays en voie de développement non membres du CAEM*. Paris: Université de Paris-I, Centre d'économie internationale des pays socialistes (March).

DOBOZI, István, and András INOTAI. 1981. "Prospects of Economic Cooperation between CMEA Countries and Developing Countries." In Saunders 1981, 48–65.

DUSSAUGE, Pierre. 1985. *L'industrie française de l'armement*. Paris: Economica.

EFRAT, Moshe. 1983. "The Economics of Soviet Arms Transfers to the Third World: A Case Study, Egypt." *Soviet Studies* 35, no. 4 (October): 437–456.

ERICKSON, John. 1982. "Military Management and Modernization within the Warsaw Pact." *The Warsaw Pact: Political Purpose and Military Means*, edited by Robert W. Clawson and Lawrence S. Kaplan, 213–255. Wilmington, Del.: Scholarly Resources Press.

ERICSON, Paul G., and Ronald S. MILLER. 1979. "Soviet Foreign Economic Behavior: A Balance of Payments Perspective." In U.S. Congress, Joint Economic Committee, *Soviet Economy in a Time of Change*, Part 2: 208–243. Washington, D.C.: U.S. Government Printing Office.

FOSS, Christopher F. 1983. *Jane's Armour and Artillery, 1983–84*. London: Jane's Publishing Company.

FRIEDMAN, Edward, ed. 1982. *Ascent and Decline in the World-System*. Beverly Hills, Calif.: Sage Publications.

GAVSHON, Arthur. 1981. *Crisis in Africa: Battleground of East and West*. New York: Penguin.

GREEN, William, Gordon SWANBOROUGH, and P. S. CHOPRA, eds. 1982. *The Indian Air Force and Its Aircraft*. London: Ducimus Books.

GRIMMETT, Richard F. 1982. *Trends in Conventional Arms Transfers to the Third World by Major Supplier, 1974–1983*. Washington, D.C.: Congressional Research Service.

—. 1984. *Trends in Conventional Arms Transfers to the Third World by Major Supplier, 1976–1983*. Washington, D.C.: Congressional Research Service.

—. 1985. *Trends in Conventional Arms Transfers to the Third World by Major Supplier, 1977–1984*. Washington, D.C.: Congressional Research Service, April.

GUNSTON, Bill. 1983. *The Aircraft of the Soviet Union*. London: Osprey.

HAAS, Ernst B. 1980. Why Collaborate? Issue-Linkage and International Regimes. *World Politics* 32, no. 3 (April): 357–405.

HEYMANN, Hans, Jr. 1975. *China's Approach to Technology Acquisition*. Rand Report R-1573. Santa Monica, Calif.: Rand Corporation, February.

HUTCHINGS, Raymond L. 1978. "Regular Trends in Soviet Arms Exports to the Third World." *Osteuropa-Wirtschaft* 23, no. 3 (September): 182–202.

—. 1983. *Soviet–East European Relations: Consolidation and Conflict, 1968–1980*. Madison, Wisc.: University of Wisconsin Press.

KAMOFF-NICOLSKY, G. 1980. *Soviet and East European Arms Deliveries to Less Developed Countries, 1955–1980: An Interpretation of Trends*. Ottawa: Department of National Defence, Research and Analysis Establishment (September).

KANET, Roger E. 1981. "Patterns of East European Economic Involvement in the Third World." In Radu 1981, 303-32.

—. 1984. "Soviet and East European Arms Transfers to the Third World: Strategic, Political and Economic Factors." In *External Economic Relations of CMEA Countries: Their Significance and Impact in a Global Perspective*, ed. NATO Economics and Information Directorates, 171-194. Brussels: NATO.

KATZ, James Everett, ed. 1984. *Arms Production in Developing Countries: An Analysis of Decision-Making*. Lexington, Mass.: D.C. Heath, Lexington Books.

KEOHANE, Robert O. 1984. *After Hegemony: Cooperation and Discord in the World Political Economy*. Princeton, N.J.: Princeton University Press.

KRASNER, Stephen D. 1982a. Regimes and the Limits of Realism: Regimes as Autonomous Variables. *International Organization* 36, no. 2 (Spring): 497-510.

—. 1982b. "Structural Causes and Regime Consequences: Regimes as Intervening Variables.' *International Organization* 36, no. 2 (Spring): 185-205.

—, ed. (1983). *International Regimes*. Ithaca, N.Y: Cornell University Press.

KRATOCHWIL, Friedrich. 1984, The Force of Prescriptions. *International Organization* 38, no. 4 (Autumn): 685-708.

LAIRD, Robbin F. 1983. *Soviet Arms Trade with the Non-Communist Third World in the 1970s and the 1980s*. Washington, D.C.: Wharton Econometric Forecasting Associates.

—. 1984 "Soviet Arms Trade with the Noncommunist Third World." In *The Soviet Union in the 1980s*, edited by Eric P. Hoffmann, 196-213. New York: Academy of Political Science.

LAVIGNE, Marie (1981). [Comment]. In Saunders 1981, 85-86. London: Macmillan.

LEWIS, William H. 1985. "Emerging Choices for the Soviets in Third World Arms Transfers Policy." In U.S. Arms Control and Disarmament Agency, *World Military Expenditures and Arms Transfers, 1985,* 30-34. Washington, D.C.: U.S. Government Printing Office (August).

LUKE, Timothy W. 1985. "Technology and Soviet Foreign Trade: On the Political Economy of an Underdeveloped Superpower." *International Studies Quarterly* 29, no. 3 (September): 327-353.

MAKIYAMA, Hideko, comp. 1980. *The New International Economic Order: Selected Documents, 1976*. New York: UNITAR.

MALLMANN, Wolfgang. 1979. "Arms Transfers to the Third World: Trends and Changing Patterns in the 1970s." *Bulletin of Peace Proposals* 10, no. 3: 301-307.

McNEILL, William H. 1982. *The Pursuit of Power: Technology, Armed Force, and Society since A.D. 1000.* Chicago, Ill.: University of Chicago Press.

MELMAN, Seymour. 1982. "The Conversion of the Military Economy: The USSR." In *The Political Economy of Arms Reduction: Reversing Economic Delay,* edited by L.J. Dumas, 69-90. Boulder, Colo.: Westview.

MILLER, Steven E. 1980. *Arms and the Third World: Indigenous Weapons Production.* PSIS Occasional Paper 3/1980. Geneva: Graduate Institute of International Studies, Program for Strategic and International Security Studies (December).

MOSLEY, Hugh G. 1984. *The Arms Race: Economic and Social Consequences.* Lexington, Mass.: Lexington Books.

MUNSON, Kenneth. 1983. "Renaissance of Romania's Aircraft Industry." *Jane's Defence Review* 4, no. 3: 225-230.

NEUMAN, Stephanie G. 1978. "Security, Military Expenditures and Socioeconomic Development: Reflections on Iran." *Orbis* 22, no. 3 (Fall): 569-594.

—. 1981. "Arms Transfers, Indigenous Defense Production and Dependency: The Case of Iran." In *The Security of the Persian Gulf,* edited by Hossein Amirsadeghi, 131-150. London: Croom Helm

—. 1984a. Third World Arms Production and the Global Arms Transfer System. In Katz 1984, 15-37.

—. 1984b. "Third World Military Industries." *International Organization* 38, no. 1 (Winter): 167-198.

NYE, Joseph S., and Robert O. KEOHANE. 1977. *Power and Interdependence: World Politics in Transition.* Boston, Mass.: Little, Brown.

OFER, Gur. 1976. "Soviet Military Aid to the Middle East: An Economic Balance Sheet." In United States Congress, Joint Economic Committee, *Soviet Economy in a New Perspective,* 216-239. Washington, D.C.: U.S. Government Printing Office.

OST, David. 1982. "Socialist World Market as Strategy for Ascent?" In Friedman 1982, 229-54.

PAJAK, Roger F. 1981. "Soviet Arms Transfers as an Instrument of Influence." *Survival* 23, no. 4 (July-August): 165-173.

PAPP, Daniel S. 1983. "Communist Military Assistance: An Overview." In *Communist Nations' Military Assistance,* edited by John F. Copper and Daniel S. Papp. Boulder, Colo.: Westview Press.

PASZYŃSKI, Marian. 1981. "The Economic Interest of the CMEA Countries in Relations with Developing Countries." In Saunders 1981, 33-47.

PECHOTA, Vratislav. 1981. "Czechoslovakia and the Third World." In Radu 1981, 77-105.

PIERRE, Andrew J. 1982. *The Global Politics of Arms Sales.* Princeton, N.J.: Princeton University Press.

PORTER, Bruce D. 1984. *The USSR in Third World Conflicts: Soviet Arms and Diplomacy in Local Wars, 1945–1980.* New York: Cambridge University Press.

RADU, Michael, ed. 1981. *Eastern Europe and the Third World.* New York: Praeger Publishers.

REMINGTON, Robin Alison. 1971. *The Warsaw Pact: Case Studies in Communist Conflict Resolution.* Cambridge, Mass.: MIT Press.

ROBERTS, Cynthia A. 1983. Soviet Arms-Transfer Policy and the Decision to Upgrade Syrian Air Defenses. *Survival* 25, no. 4 (July–August): 154–164.

ROSS, Andrew L. 1981. "Arms Production in Developing Countries: The Continuing Proliferation of Conventional Weapons." Note N-1615. Santa Monica, Calif.: Rand Corporation (October).

ROTHSTEIN, Robert L. 1984a. "Consensual Knowledge and International Coordination." *International Organization* 38, no. 4 (Autumn): 733–762.

—. 1984b. "Regime-Creation by a Coalition of the Weak: Lessons from the NIEO and the Integrated Program for Commodities." *International Studies Quarterly* 28, no. 3 (September): 307–328.

SAUNDERS, Christopher T., ed. 1981. *East–West–South: Economic Interactions between Three Worlds.* London: Macmillan.

SCHRODT, Philip A. 1983. "The Effect of Arms Transfers on Supplier-Recipient Behavior: A Statistical Test for the Middle East and North Africa." Paper presented to the Annual Convention, International Studies Association, Mexico City (April).

SIPRI. 1984a. Stockholm International Peace Research Institute. Computerized Data Files and Archives, June.

—. (1984b) Stockholm International Peace Research Institute. *World Armaments and Disarmament: SIPRI Yearbook, 1984.* London: Taylor and Francis.

—. (1985) Stockholm International Peace Research Institute. Computerized Data Files and Archives, August.

—. (1986a) Stockholm International Peace Research Institute. Computerized Data Files and Archives, December.

—. (1986b) Stockholm International Peace Research Institute. *World Armaments and Disarmament: SIPRI Yearbook, 1986.* New York: Oxford University Press.

SNITCH, Thomas H. 1984. "East European Involvement in the World's Arms Market." In U.S. Arms Control and Disarmament Agency, *World Military Expenditures and Arms Transfers, 1972–1982*, 117–121. ACDA Publication 117. Washington, D.C.: U.S. Government Printing Office (April).

SODARO, Michael. 1981. "The GDR and the Third World: Supplicant and Surrogate." In Radu 1981, 106–141.

SPENCER, Daniel Lloyd. 1970. *Technology Gap in Perspective: Strategy of International Technology Transfer*. New York: Spartan Books.

SPROUT, Harold, and Margaret SPROUT. 1962. *Foundations of International Politics*. Princeton, N.J: Van Nostrand.

STRODE, Rebecca V. 1984. "Soviet Design Policy and Its Implications for U.S. Combat Aircraft Procurement." *Air University Review* 35, no. 2 (January–February): 46–61.

SWEETMAN, Bill. 1984. "New Soviet Combat Aircraft: Quality with Quantity?" *International Defense Review* 17, no. 1 (January): 35–38.

TsSU. 1974. Tsentral'noe statisticheskoe upravlenie pri Sovete ministrov SSSR. *Narodnoe khoziaistvo SSSR v 1973 g.* [The National Economy of the USSR in 1973]. Moscow: Statistika.

—. 1975. Tsentral'noe statisticheskoe upravlenie pri Sovete ministrov SSSR. *Narodnoe khoziaistvo SSSR v 1974 g.* [The National Economy of the USSR in 1974]. Moscow: Statistika.

—. 1980. Tsentral'noe statisticheskoe upravlenie pri Sovete ministrov SSSR. *Narodnoe khoziaistvo SSSR v 1979 g.* [The National Economy of the USSR in 1979]. Moscow: Statistika.

—. 1983. Tsentral'noe statisticheskoe upravlenie pri Sovete ministrov SSSR. *Narodnoe khoziaistvo SSSR v 1982 g.* [The National Economy of the USSR in 1982]. Moscow: Statistika.

—. 1984. Tsentral'noe statisticheskoe upravlenie pri Sovete ministrov SSSR. *Narodnoe khoziaistvo SSSR v 1983 g.* [The National Economy of the USSR in 1983]. Moscow: Statistika.

—. 1985. Tsentral'noe statisticheskoe upravlenie pri Sovete ministrov SSSR. *Narodnoe khoziaistvo SSSR v 1984 g.* [The National Economy of the USSR in 1984]. Moscow: Statistika.

—. 1986. Tsentral'noe statisticheskoe upravlenie pri Sovete ministrov SSSR. *Narodnoe khoziaistvo SSSR v 1985 g.* [The National Economy of the USSR in 1985]. Moscow: Statistika.

TYLECOTE, Andrew B., and Marian L. LONSDALE-BROWN. 1982. "State Socialism and Development: Why Russian and Chinese Ascent Halted." In Friedman 1982, 255–88.

TYSON, Laura D'Andrea. 1986. "The Debt Crisis and Adjustment Responses in Eastern Europe: A Comparative Perspective." *International Organization* 40, no. 2 (Spring): 239–85.

U.S. ARMS CONTROL AND DISARMAMENT AGENCY. (1984) *World Military Expenditures and Arms Transfers, 1972–1982*. Washington, D.C.: U.S. Government Printing Office.

U.S. CONGRESS (1983). United States Congress, Joint Economic Committee. *Soviet Military Economic Relations*. Washington, D.C.: U.S. Government Printing Office.

U.S. DEPARTMENT OF DEFENSE. 1983. United States Government, Department of Defense. *Soviet Military Power, 1983*. Washington, D.C.: U.S. Government Printing Office.

U.S. DEPARTMENT OF STATE. (1982) United States Government, Department of State. *Conventional Arms Transfers in the Third World, 1982–1981*, Special Report 102. Washington, D.C.: U.S. Government Printing Office.

—. 1983. United States Government, Department of State. *Soviet and East European Aid to the Third World, 1981*. Washington, D.C.: U.S. Government Printing Office.

VALENTA, Jiri, and Shannon BUTLER. 1981. "East German Security Policies in Africa." In Radu 1981, 142–68.

VANOUS, Jan. 1981. "Soviet and Eastern European Foreign Trade in the 1970s: A Quantitative Assessment." In United States Congress, Joint Economic Committee, *East European Economic Assessment*, Part 2: 685–715. Washington, D.C.: U.S. Government Printing Office.

VÄYRYNEN, Raimo. 1983. "Semiperipheral Countries in the Global Economic and Military Order." In *Militarization and Arms Production*, edited by H. Tuomi and R. Väyrynen, 163–92. New York: St. Martin's Press.

WALLERSTEIN, I. 1976. "Semi-Peripheral Countries and the Contemporary World Crisis." *Theory and Society* 3, no. 4 (Winter): 461–483.

—. 1982. "Socialist States: Mercantilist Strategies and Revolutionary Objectives." In Friedman 1982, 289–300.

WEFA. 1982. Wharton Econometric Forecasting Associates. "Soviet Exports of Arms to Developing Countries." *Centrally Planned Economies: Current Analysis* (22 January).

—. 1984. Wharton Econometric Forecasting Associates. "Soviet Exports of Arms to Developing Countries." *Centrally Planned Economies: Current Analysis* (9 April).

—. 1986a. Wharton Econometric Forecasting Associates. "Soviet Exports of Arms to Developing Countries." *Centrally Planned Economies: Current Analysis* (24 April).

—. 1986b. Wharton Econometric Forecasting Associates. "Soviet Exports of Arms to Developing Countries." *Centrally Planned Economies: Current Analysis* (16 August).

WHITE, William D. 1974. *U.S. Tactical Air Power: Missions, Forces, and Costs*. Washington, D.C.: Brookings Institution.

WOLFE, Thomas. W. 1965. *The Evolving Nature of the Warsaw Pact*, Rand Research Memorandum RM-4835. Santa Monica, Calif.: Rand Corporation (December).

YOUNG, Oran R. 1980. "International Regimes: Problems of Concept Formation." *World Politics* 32, no. 3 (April): 331-356.

ZOETER, Joan Parpart. 1982. "U.S.S.R.: Hard Currency Trade and Payments." In United States Congress, Joint Economic Committee, *Soviet Economy in the 1980s: Problems and Prospects*, Part 2: 479-506. Washington, D.C.: U.S. Government Printing Office.

5 East–South Relations in Global Perspective

This chapter analyzes the development of East–South studies across the fields of economic, ideological, legal-financial, and military domains of international behavior. It briefly treats the three decades up until 1947 when the USSR was the only member of the "East" and then concentrates attention on periodizing the development of East–South relations since then up until Gorbachev's coming to power in 1985. It then situates the four preceding chapters of this book in that framework, systematizing a view of their coverage of the subject, before concluding by suggesting some topics for further research.

Keywords: Soviet, bloc, developing, South, global, political, economy

5.1 Introductory Remarks

In recent years the study of East-bloc relations with the developing countries has acquired both a new impetus and a broader scope from the standpoint of international security affair. Throughout the 1960s and much of the 1970s, scholars concentrated principally on bilateral Soviet relations with individual Third World countries, frequently focusing on military assistance. (For early studies of Soviet "foreign aid" in general, see such ground-breaking but forgotten studies as: Berliner 1958; Carter 1969; Goldman 1967; Müller 1967.) International events in the last dozen years have forced a reorientation of that focus. The non-Soviet European members of the Soviet bloc have come of age in international relations. The current changes within the socialist states of Eastern Europe as well as in their relations with the world at large have given East–South studies a real dynamism. The very situation also multiplies the information available for analysis. However, the topic means different things to different people. It is useful to review the international sociology of East–South studies, which displays remarkable, if not wholly surprising, national profiles.

The development of East–South studies in a given country seems conditioned simultaneously by historical trends in the development of international studies in the given country and (not always unrelated) the national preoccupations of that country's international policy. For example, North Americans (but Canadians to a lesser degree) tend still to focus—though by no means so exclusively as in the past—on Soviet political behavior in the Third World and its military and strategic aspects in particular. Of course, for quite some time after the end of the Second World War, East–South relations *did* consist principally of Soviet moral and material support to local communist parties plus East-bloc arms transfers to anticolonial revolutionary movements and the independent governments formed by those movements whose revolts were successful. During this time, while much of the "developed" world was merely trying to assure its *own* economic reconstruction in the aftermath of the War, the United States had intact, not only the vastest economic resources but also the vastest academic infrastructure. Upon this infrastructure, those resources built formidable collections of the materials necessary for studying the subject, reinforcing U.S. dominance in defining the perspective for studying Soviet influence in the developing world (as East–South relations were then called). The dominant Soviet perspective at the time did not controvert but only inverted that perspective, without challenging its premises.

The situation in Europe has been a bit different. Today both East and West Europeans (though the British to a lesser degree) focus as much on economic as on political aspects of East–South relations (as Chapter 3 suggests). Partly for this reason, they give East European countries a higher profile in their treatments of the subject. The French tend to be particularly innovative in their approach, and the Hungarians (and to a lesser degree the Poles) particularly inventive in their analyses. In both these countries, for different reasons, the sociology of the social sciences had made economics (but not econometrics for its own sake) the discipline of choice for students of contemporary international affairs.

It used to be the case that cross-fertilization in East–South studies was greater internationally within disciplines than nationally across disciplines. Especially in larger countries, well-institutionalized disciplinary professional associations still tend today to narrow rather than to broaden incentive structures for research in

EAST–SOUTH RELATIONS IN GLOBAL PERSPECTIVE   171

academia. However, cross-fertilization today is gaining internationally, if not also nationally, across disciplines. This phenomenon emerged as a response to the need for the production of knowledge concerning the unintended international consequences of the 1973-74 oil embargo. The postwar rebuilding of the European scholarly infrastructure (where incentive structures do not discourage such cooperation as much as in North America) and training of a new generation also contributed that development in the sociology of knowledge.

5.2 Dimensions for an Analytical Synthesis

It is possible to grasp the evolution of East–South studies, and the differences in orientations toward them, possible by characterizing them in three dimensions. These are a chronological periodization of the overall subject, the geographical regionalization of the global phenomenon, and the varying thematic emphases of particular approaches and studies. I summarize all of these in the present section, then extend the discussion of chronological periodization in the next one.

5.2.1 The Longitudinal Dimension of East–South Relations

A chronological periodization of relations between the Soviet bloc (which by definition consisted of one country for four decades) and the developing world would be tripartite: 1917–47, 1948–73, and 1974–present.

The period from 1917 to 1947 has two subperiods. The first subperiod, 1917–33, begins with the Bolshevik Revolution ends with Hitler's coming to power, because this event altered the Soviet orientation toward the world at large. The second subperiod, 1933-47, signifies the remainder of this time during which the USSR continued to be the only member of the "East." It ends with the creation of Marxist-Leninist states in East Central Europe.

The second major period runs from 1948 until 1973. Relations between the Soviet Union and the East Central European communist states began to undergo fundamental shifts in the mid-1950s, following Khrushchev's de-Stalinization speech and the uprisings in Hungary and Poland. Although communist rule in East Central Europe appeared on the scene in the mid- and late 1940s, it is not really proper to speak of any significant relative autonomy of those states from the Soviet Union, in their international relations, until the mid-1950s. Also, decolonization began in the Third World only in the mid-1950s; the Bandung Conference was held at this time. These events transformed Soviet policy toward the developing world. Partly in response to them, Khrushchev introduced important doctrinal changes into the Soviet philosophy of international relations. These changes reflected and motivated an evolution in East-West relations as well. Stalin's death in 1953 and the Polish and Hungarian events in 1956 motivated changes in the functioning of the Council of Mutual Economic Assistance (CMEA). From that time forward, therefore, it is therefore proper to consider the Soviet Union and smaller East European communist countries as two distinct actors within an Eastern "bloc" vis-à-vis the South.

The third period starts as the biennium 1973-1974 marks a divide. Politically, these years were a high-water mark for U.S.-Soviet détente, but economically they mark the OPEC embargo and the rise in world oil prices. This development held implications for the smaller CMEA countries' economic relations with the global economy as well as with the Soviet Union. These years also mark the United Nations General Assembly's adoption of the Charter of the Economic Rights and Duties of States, which effectively launched the Third World's diplomatic and economic offensive on behalf of a New International Economic Order (NIEO).

It is probably the case that that East-South relations beginning in 1985 will, in retrospect, appear as another major period distinct from the 1974-85. However, the exact contours of such a new period are not yet clear. (But see Campbell and MacFarlane 1989; Valenta and Cibulka 1990.) To the degree that the years 1985-89 are considered here, therefore, they are treated as a part of the 1974-85 tranche. Moreover, research and scholarship on East-South relations typically requires several years (and sometimes longer) to "catch up" to the newest developments.

5.2.2 The Geographical Dimension of East-South Relations

The changes in the world economy unleashed by the OPEC states in 1973-1974 had significant implications for relations within the East bloc as well as for West-South and East-West relations. In particular, they motivated significant changes in CMEA pricing for raw materials including oil. These changes constituted a turning-point not only in Soviet-East-European relations but also in the international relations of the East European states within the international system at large. That is because the Soviet Union turned increasingly to the world market for the sale of its natural resources. Deprived of Soviet resources, or unable to pay world market prices for them, the small CMEA states also turned to the world market both for raw materials and for the foreign exchange necessary to participate in the world market. Their economic dependence on the USSR decreased and their economic dependence on the world market increased.

This dimension of the analysis is threefold. One may enumerate its three aspects as being relations between (1) the Soviet Union and the Third World, (2) Eastern Europe and the Third World, and (3) the Soviet Union and Eastern Europe. The patterns of economic conduct of the East European countries in world politics became increasingly distinct from those of the Soviet Union. A finer-grained analysis would also introduce, since about 1973, a distinction between West European and North American sectors of the "West." This could be done not on an *a priori* but on an *ad hoc* basis as required by the phenomena under discussion. For example, the North America/Western Europe distinction would be important for the analysis of Eastern Europe's economic relations with the Soviet Union but not for the analysis of Soviet ideological relations with the Third World.

Particularly as we approach the present day, it is important to distinguish between Soviet relations with the West and South on the one hand, and East European relations with the West and South on the other. The increased relative autonomy of the Eastern European communist states' international relations, from the Soviet template, is very evident in during the early 1980s, when the two halves of Europe maintained a less than frozen aspect while Soviet–West European relations entered the deep-freeze.

5.2.3 The Thematic Dimension of East–South Relations

5.2.3.1 Partial Globalistic Approaches
To put East–South relations into global perspective, it is thus necessary not only to extend the geographic field of analysis to the planetary level, but also to compass the multifaceted nature of those relations. Political scientists have elaborated two perspectives that might be able to capture the multifarious nature of East–South relations. These are "international political economy" and the "world-system" (as discussed in Chapter 4). Each of these approaches is, for different reasons, of relatively limited assistance insofar as the study of East–South relations is concerned.

"International political economy," as practiced by political scientists, largely concerns the commerce and the commercial policies of the advanced industrial democracies of the West, which of course account among themselves for the vast majority of world trade. To the degree that this approach is concerned with North–South issues, these are really West–South issues. Only when that approach overlaps with the study of what may be called "international public policy" does it address East–South issues, and then under the umbrella rubric of "trade and development." The analysis of economic relations is more directly connected with an international political economy approach, which focuses on the interplay between the state and the international-regime levels of analysis and sometimes reduces itself to a discussion of bilateral trade patterns.

The world-system approach focuses principally on West–West and West–South relations. Practitioners of this approach sometimes disagree among themselves as to which there exists a "socialist world-system" (the East) independent of and counterposed against a "capitalist world-system" (comprising the West and South together).

5.2.3.2 Five Major Themes

The obvious interrelationship of economic and military issues emerges. Yet there are two additional aspects of East–South relations that are too often overlooked or not integrated with these other aspects. These are the legal-financial and ideological aspects. Such a quadripartite distinction in international studies goes far back, even to the opening paragraphs of Thucydides's (2008, 11) *Peloponnesian War*: "But as the power of Hellas grew, and the acquisition of wealth became more an objective [economics], the revenues of the states increasing [finance], tyrannies were by their means established almost everywhere [ideology] ... and Hellas began to fit out fleets and apply herself more closely to the sea [military]."

It is worthwhile to distinguish briefly between the economic and the legal-financial, and to clarify what is meant by the ideological. "Economic" relations concern the relatively mundane patterns of world commerce, and the habitual modes of actions by individuals within countries and trading organizations which produce and reproduce those patterns. "Legal-financial" relations cover aspects such as commercial and payments regimes, and international agreements and institutions that mediate them. As such, legal-financial relations are distinct from, although related to, economic relations proper.

Concerning the "ideological" aspect of relations, Marxism-Leninism as a system of organized knowledge has had the potential to influence the norms underlying the organization of the world trade system. The recent rebirth of interest in "international regimes," leading to a re-emphasis on the significance of international norms, has helped to rectify the tendency of the international political economy approach to downplay normative perspectives on trade and development issues. But the Marxist-Leninist approach has never suffered from this analytical deficiency. Indeed, until very recently, as the CMEA countries' bargaining positions at the United Nations Conference on Trade and Development have become less "ideological" at the same time as they introduced ideologically based operational initiatives into such forums as the

International Law Committee and the United Nations Commission on International Trade Law. (See Chapter 2.)

5.3 The First Chronological Tranche, 1917–47

This tentative overview analysis attempts to discern whether there is any relationship between the quality or quantity of East–West relations and the quality or quantity of East–South relations.

5.3.1 From the Revolution until Hitler's Rise to Power, 1917–33

During the first decade and a half of Bolshevik rule, economic ties with the West were extended as more and more Western countries recognized the Soviet regime. Indeed, the Bolsheviks sought economic assistance as much as they sought diplomatic recognition for its own sake. However, with the exceptions of German reparations and protectionist policies within the capitalist world, economic matters were less explicitly on the agenda of world politics of the era. The Soviet Union did seek to extend economic ties with those countries of what we now call the South, but these were unaffected by the extension or non-extension of such ties to the Soviet Union by the West. Because of the quite low volume of overall Soviet foreign trade, the issue of legal-financial relations does not greatly enter at this stage. The same is true of military relations in the sense of commerce in military goods or the sending of Soviet advisors to Third World colonies.

China, however, is something of an exception to this last statement, if one considers "ideological" rather than military advisors. Indeed, Soviet relations with a good deal of the colonial world were greatly ideological, mediated though CPSU attempts to influence, through the Communist International, the activities of the communist parties in the European colonies. In this respect here India joins China as focus of "ideological" attention.

Against the background of the 1925 Treaty of Locarno, which confirmed the status quo of Germany's western borders while opening to Germany the possibility of playing off the Western powers against the Soviets, Soviet policy sought two ways to escape its isolation. First, it attempted further rapprochement with other states dissatisfied by the status quo: and not only Germany and Italy but also Japan, which sought to revise the territorial boundaries established on the Chinese mainland in particular. Second, the Soviet Union worked outside the League of Nations, which it was not invited to join until the mid-1930s, so as to establish its own security system. The latter effort was only partly successful; nevertheless, the Soviets had by the mid-1920s signed "conciliation treaties," which included neutrality and non-aggression, with Lithuania and the "Third World" (in quotation marks because of the anachronism) countries of Turkey, Afghanistan, and Persia. By the early 1930s, the combination of Japanese aggression on the Asian mainland and the emergence of the Nazis as the dominant party in Germany led the Soviet Union to conclude further bilateral pacts of neutrality and nonaggression with Finland, Estonia, Latvia, Poland, France, and Italy.

All those diplomatic initiatives aimed to create a stable and predictable international environment, as non-threatening as possible, that would protect the status quo in Eastern Europe against the potential fallout from Locarno. The Soviet leaders pursued this course of action because they felt threatened by the Western powers. The Allied intervention in the Russian Civil War and upon the Soviet ostracism from the community of nations resulting from their signing the 1922 Rapallo Treaty with Germany created this sense of threat.

5.3.2 From Hitler's Rise to the Birth of the Soviet Bloc, 1933–47

During the period from 1933 to 1947, Soviet policy was mainly Eurocentric. The exception to this Eurocentrism was Stalin's concern with China (i.e. with keeping it fragmented). The Soviets gave some attention to the various independence movements in the European colonies (Algeria, India, Indochina) but these interests were marginal. Also, they were set against the overwhelming Soviet concerns with assuring the integrity of its European borders and, later, its security by imposing communist-party rule in the states of East Central Europe. The only significant modality of Soviet influence on the "South" during this period would be the ideological.

Military, economic, legal-financial, and political ties were overwhelmed by Stalin's obsession with European security.

During the mid- and late 1940s the Soviet Union ceased to be the only communist-party state in the world. The one-party states created in East Central Europe, however, had (with the exception of Yugoslavia), no effective autonomy at all of Stalin. Concerned as they were with reconstruction following the Second World War, the Soviets did not engage in significant relations with the "South," but some of the preexisting patterns of economic ties were restored. Regarding the East Central European states, Stalin extracted economic resources, not least including the seizure and transport to within Soviet borders of physical industrial plant, in the name of war reparations.

With the exception of Great Britain, the United States, and Germany (and perhaps France), it is fair to say that Soviet foreign relations during this period gave at least as much attention to interparty relations in the Comintern framework as to traditional interstate relations. Certainly, Soviet relations with the Third World during this period were more conditioned by interparty than by interstate relations, despite Stalin's inclinations to *Realpolitik*. Yet even in Western Europe, Soviet relations with other communist parties were largely conditioned other forces and had little autonomous dynamic of their own. The nature of Soviet relations with communist parties in the developing world were in turn affected by Soviet relations with European communist parties, specifically the doctrinal changes promulgated by the Third International during the 1930s (Hammond, 1965). Those changes involved a broadening of the social base to which the communist parties sought to appeal, and a less hostile attitude toward cooperation with other political parties. These changes were a coordinated attempt to stem the tide of European fascism under theory and practice of the "popular front."

5.4 The Second Chronological Tranche, 1948–73

Notwithstanding the significance of the year 1956 in the evolution of international relations within the Soviet bloc, this period may be divided into subperiods by the transitional triennia of 1961-63 and 1967-69. This subperiodization has more to do with East-West relations than with East: the years 1961-63 marked the end of a nascent thaw in U.S.-Soviet relations that had proceeded haltingly in the late 1950s and (not without interruptions) the very early 1960s; the years 1967-69 marked the Warsaw Pact's invasion of Czechoslovakia but also the beginning of the period that saw the conclusion of major arms limitation accords between East and West. At the same time, however, these two dates are important in the history of the development of the South.

For example, 1962 marks the Cairo Declaration, which gave birth to UNCTAD; and the years 1961-63 include the Bay of Pigs debacle, the Cuban Missile Crisis, and the independence of dozens of states in Africa, as well as the expansion of Soviet-Indian trade. The years 1967-69, on the other hand, include the Six-Day War in the Middle East and the associated Soviet assertion in this region. This experience taught the Soviets that they did not need Eastern Europe as an intermediary in arms transfers and that they could themselves profit from direct sales to the Third World, which would bring them significant hard currency revenue.

The Soviets were ideologically driven in their attempt to curry favor among the newly independent nations (Lowenthal 1977), but the latter did not respond uniformly (Laïdi 1984). There were brief East-West détentes, one in the early 1960s and the other in the early and mid-1970s; in both instances, various aspects of East-South relations (respectively, Vietnam and Angola/Afghanistan) appear to have undermined whatever success there may have been in the East-West détentes (Golan 1988). However, their breakdown may have been due as much to Western misperceptions of ongoing East-South relations as to anything else (Donaldson 1981; Korbonski and Fukuyama 1987; Melchers 1980).

In the late 1960s and early 1970s, the Soviets developed the preference, in fact just like between the two World Wars and immediately after the Second, and indeed just like Russian Empire throughout the nineteenth century, for inclusion in a general security system. Absent that, the Soviet Union fell and now falls back on a combination of *status quo* and revisionist components into a single, differentially applied, line. Such a strategy enables the USSR to seek to have its interests taken into account while at the same time articulating the view that the existing system is really not satisfactory as it stands.

> The "natural allies" doctrine is of a piece with the socialist offensive in international law, finding expression through it, in multilateral negotiations over global economic issues. The Soviets chose the Non-Aligned Movement as the forum for propagating this doctrine, because its membership is more restrictive than the "Group of 77" at UNCTAD, particularly in excluding many Latin American countries. The farther-reaching interpretation of the "natural allies" doctrine articulated by Cuba and other Soviet clients in the Non-Aligned Movement in fact fell by the wayside when the presidency of the Movement rotated from Cuba to India in 1982. The reason was that the full and unadulterated "natural allies" doctrine robbed the Non-Aligned Movement of the foreign-policy autonomy from both East and West that was its original purpose. (Cutler 1987, 89)

Thus the USSR plays the Third World against the West whenever possible. If interests agree with those of the latter, then it will allow the West to refute the Third World's objections: the disinclination to establish an authoritative international institution to regulate transnational technology transfer is an example. In other cases, the Soviet Union will seek to mobilize the Third World against the West. The situation is quite analogous to the mid-1930s, when the Soviets played the revisionist powers of Germany, Italy, and Japan off against the *status quo* powers if England, France, and the United States (Cutler, 1987: 95–96).

5.5 The Third Chronological Tranche, 1974–85

As the chapters in this volume address more the economic and legal-financial than the political-strategies aspects of East–South relations, so this section does as well. (See Table 5-1; for the latter aspects, particularly dealing with changes under Gorbachev, see Kolodziej and Kanet 1989; Duncan and Ekedahl 1990.)

The OPEC oil embargo led the Soviets to alter their policy of supplying Eastern Europe, with virtually as much oil and gas as they could consume, at prices lower than those of the world market. The Soviets forced through a change in the pricing of raw materials inside CMEA. In addition, they limited the quantities they would sell to their allies in order to gain increasing amounts of hard currency. The small East European countries were not left to fend for themselves entirely. Nevertheless, they were obliged to pay hard currency for energy supplies purchased on the world market. This put them in increasingly dire straits. As a result, they began to look more intently at commerce with not only the West, but also the Third World, as a hard-currency source. (For a selection of views from the Soviet Union, Eastern Europe, Western Europe, and the United States, see Jackman 1985; also Kanet 1987.)

Expanding arms transfers was an obvious market for hard-currency gains. (See Chapter 4.) However, the Soviets, who had earlier relied on their East European allies as proxies in arms transfers to the Third World, ceased transferring state-of-the-art production technology to them. Moscow began selling on the world market itself, all the while enforcing stricter terms of sale for both their non-military and military products. (Here is a particular example of the need, now generally recognized, to integrate East–South economic affairs systematically into the study of national and international security.)

Table 5-1. Thematic and temporal distribution of chapters in this book.

	USSR as the only member of the "East" (bloc)	E. Eur. considered as subordinate to the USSR	E. Eur. considered as showing relative autonomy of the USSR
	1917–1947	1948–1973	1974–1985
Chapter 1		Economic & Military	
Chapter 2		Economic & Legal-financial	
Chapter 3			Economic, Legal-financial & Ideological
Chapter 4		Military & Economic	

Source: Constructed by the author.

Since 1974 all five fields of activity of both East–West and East–South relations become relevant: military, economic, legal-financial, ideological, and political. At the same time, the activity of the smaller East European states in global economics world politics develops more and more autonomously of the Soviet Union (Audeoud et al. 1985; Bożyk 1988; Lavigne 1986). This is also the most complex period. Having failed in the attempt to encourage specialization in military production among their smaller East European allies, the Soviets have sought to establish a hierarchy of military manufacturers. In this hierarchy, the Soviet Union builds all major combat equipment plus minor armaments such as small arms. Yet another form of coordination of military cooperation that has emerged involves the division of labor. This appeals to East European self-interest and, being less coercive, is more persuasive. For example, Czechoslovakia appears to specialize in training tank teams and artillery support, the GDR in utilizing reconnaissance equipment and air traffic, Poland in training pilots and parachutists, and Hungary in the general training of infantry. Moreover, the provision of arms sales and training services is sometimes coordinated in such a manner.

With the United Nations General Assembly's declaration in 1974 of the Charter of the Economic Rights and Duties of States, trumpeting the charge on behalf of a New International Economic Order, it becomes analytically necessary to separate the economic sphere of East–South activity into commercial relations on the one hand, and regime-creation on the other. In the second of these, the legal-financial, ideological, and political aspects of East–South and East–West relations become almost inseparably intermingled; and East–South economic relations become only one leg of the East–West–South commercial triangle. A comprehensive assessment of those relations consequently would entails consideration of such diverse phenomena as the increased politicization of East–West trade, the acute debt of the East European countries, growing East European imports of Third World natural resources and manufactures, and the increasingly scarce and expensive labor force in the member countries of the Council of Mutual Economic Assistance (CMEA). This list of phenomena makes clear the need to take into account analyses emerging not only from the discipline of international politics, but also from those of international economics and international law. (See Chapter 3.)

These developments have unfolded just as the Third World has come to articulate its demands for the restructuring of international economic relations and to press ever more strongly. From the standpoint of U.S.-Soviet competition for influence in the Third World (Hough 1986; Shulman 1986), the East European countries' desire, now shared by the Soviet Union under Gorbachev, to deepen economic relations with the Third World acquires a specifically political character. The analysis of commercial flows, and so the international political economy of these exchanges, follows as always from sectoral analysis of trade statistics. At the same time, one should not lose sight of the strategic implications of the political economy of East-South military transfers; however, it is also necessary also to focus on the Soviet and East European policy responses to the New International Economic Order (NIEO) advocated by the developing countries.

Two specific questions may provide particular points of focus in this respect. The first question is: Which of the Third World's NIEO-related demands for changes in existing international regimes governing trade and development are supported by the CMEA countries? The second is: What are divergences of interest and policy among the latter themselves, with respect to political and economic relations with the Third World.

To begin to form an answer, one may take as point of departure the international forums in which specifically economic negotiations are conducted. The United Nations Conference on Trade and Development (UNCTAD) is where the NIEO has been most continuously elaborated and most consistently developed by the Third World. It is an especially appropriate forum for understanding the joint Soviet-East European attempt to address the NIEO, because the CMEA countries participate at UNCTAD — and only at UNCTAD — as the collective caucus called "Group D." (See Chapter 2.) Moreover, UNCTAD's comprehensiveness permits the analysis to operationalize the concept of "international regime" in concrete terms, thus delimiting the various issue areas that deserve study.

The UNCTAD negotiations over the Generalized System of Preferences (GSP) exemplify the overlap among East–South economic relations on the one hand and, on the other hand, the legal-financial and ideological components of those relations. When the Soviet and East European countries agreed to lower their tariff barriers against exports by developing countries, the latter quite rightly objected to the meaninglessness of the move: East-bloc imports of these commodities depend not upon putatively higher consumer demand, resulting from lower tariff barriers, but rather upon the provisions for imports that are built into the respective CMEA member-countries' annual economic plans. To this objection, the Soviets and East Europeans replied by volunteering to organize seminars bringing together personnel from their own economic planning and foreign trade ministries with their counterparts from the developing countries, so as to facilitate the incorporation of the latter's exports into the former's plans.

The response from the developing countries has been favorable. Any agreed export contracts fall into frameworks of overarching long-term intergovernmental agreements for bilateral economic ties, a device that the Soviets have long preferred in organizing their foreign trade planning. Such bilateral intergovernmental agreements also govern transfer of technology from the CMEA countries to the developing countries. Therefore, the East bloc does not feel affected by developing countries' demands for international controls upon technology between from a parent transnational corporation and its subsidiary based in a developing country. Here, indeed, interests of CMEA and developing countries coincide: the former may benefit from international regulation because they too import Western technologies.

UNCTAD provides another example of this in the negotiations over an Integrated Program for Commodities that would establish international buffer stocks to regulate commodity prices, along with an international agency that would control available supply. In the late 1960s the Soviets felt that they could support the idea of such buffer stocks only as a temporary measure. When the developing countries then threatened to take their complaints to GATT, of which the Soviet Union is not a member, the USSR acceded to the use of UNCTAD as a forum. Finally, in 1976, the Soviets and their bloc came out in favor of creating these buffer stocks in order to stabilize commodity prices, but only in the framework of a particular form of in agreement, the terms of which, it was further asserted, would not apply to intra-CMEA trade. A stable world market price would be necessary to allow producing countries to proceed with economic development in an orderly fashion, that would not be subject to uncertainty over foreign-trade earnings from their principal commodity exports.

Multilateral global economic negotiations have become the principal forum where the USSR pushes the socialist offensive in international law in general and, in particular, the doctrine that the East are "natural allies" of the South. (See Chapter 2.) The USSR uses not just UNCTAD but also other forums, such as the United Nations Conference on the Law of the Sea and UNESCO's work on a New World Information and Communications Order, to erect international regimes that take into account their state interests. They use such institutions as the International Law Commission (ILC) to shape the overarching framework of international law that regulates the rights and duties of states and of nonstate actors. The East bloc as a whole works through the United Nations Commission on International Trade Law (UNCITRAL) to transform the existing system of international commerce. Treaty law among socialist states also influences the elaboration of international norms in this area.

Participation in regime-formation is a way for a state such as the Soviet Union to get its foot in the door in policy arenas where it has no traditional place. In international economic negotiations, for instance, the extremely low level of Soviet foreign trade and the nonconvertibility of the ruble make the USSR a peripheral actor, the West and the Third World are the principals. Precisely in such nontraditional (i.e. nonterritorial) issues of the postcolonial era, the socialist offensive in international law acquires its significance as a structural analogue of the Soviet strategy of interwar collective security, when two broad groups of states could be distinguished in world politics: the status quo powers (England, France, and the

United States; today, "the West") and the revisionist powers (Germany, Italy, and Japan; today, the Third World).

> In particular: the United States is the analogue of Germany; the Third World is the analogue of the western members of the League of Nations; the general system of international law is the analogue of the League's collective-security mechanism; and the doctrine that the socialist countries are the "natural allies" of the developing countries against international imperialism is the analogue of the USSR's entente with England and France, a counterweight against Germany organized under the aegis of collective security. During the interwar period the Soviets attempted both to deal bilaterally with their principal enemy (Germany) and simultaneously to restrain Germany through multilateral arrangements, collective security in particular. Today the Soviets attempt to deal bilaterally with their new principal enemy (the United States), and simultaneously to restrain the United States through multilateral arrangements in international law that also include the developing countries. (Cutler 1987, 96)

The early 1970s were a major turning point in the Soviet theory of international law, motivated principally by the need to justify the political détente necessary to end the Soviet Union's economic isolation from the West. As Grzybowski (1987, 185–86) put it, "the Soviet Union has accepted traditional forms of international agreements and has sought to participate in various scientific research programs" in order to promote trade and economic cooperation, but the "law of diplomacy" remains "an area that Soviet practices have effectively made a channel for systematic espionage."

It is worth noting that the recent socialist offensive in international law, combined with the substitution of the United States for Germany in the role of the Soviet Union's principal enemy, explains contemporary Soviet strategy in international politics as a present-day structural analogue of Soviet collective-security strategy between the two world wars (Cutler 1987). In particular: the United States is the analogue of Germany; the Third World is the analogue of the western members of the League of Nations; the general system of international law is the analogue of the League's collective security mechanism; and the doctrine that the socialist countries are the "natural allies" of the developing countries against international imperialism is the analogue of the USSR's entente with England and France as a counterweight against Germany organized under the aegis of collective security. During the interwar period the Soviets attempted both to deal bilaterally with their principal enemy (Germany) and simultaneously to restrain Germany through multilateral arrangements, collective security in particular. Today the Soviets attempt to deal bilaterally with their new principal enemy (the United States), and simultaneously to restrain the United States through multilateral arrangements in international law that also include the developing countries.

Looking at the more specifically ideological aspects of East–South relations since 1974, it seems clear that the doctrine that the socialist countries are the "natural allies" of the third world is a piece with the socialist offensive in international law. It finds expression, through legal argumentation, in multilateral negotiations over global economic issues. (See Chapter 3.) The Soviets chose the Non-Aligned Movement as the forum for propagating this doctrine, because its membership is more restrictive than the Group of Seventy-seven at UNCTAD, which actually includes over 120 developing countries. (For example, many Latin American countries are members of the Group of Seventy-seven but not of the Non-Aligned Movement.) In fact, the farther-reaching interpretation of the "natural allies" doctrine articulated by Cuba and other Soviet clients in the Non-Aligned Movement fell by the wayside when the presidency of the Movement rotated from Cuba to India in 1982. The reason was that the full and unadulterated natural-allies doctrine robbed the Non-Aligned Movement of the foreign-policy autonomy from both East and West that was its original purpose. (For a general political treatment, see Allison 1988.)

5.6 Concluding Remarks

A rough list of general issue areas within the evolving international economic order provides an approach to the problem of operationalizing the issues falling within the scope of this short paper. That list would necessarily include development financing, international trade, industrialization and technology transfer, food and natural resources, institutional and organizational policies, and social issues It would be possible to use these rubrics as conceptual foci for elaborating analyses of competing international regimes within a given issue area. (The implications of those regimes for various approaches to economic development—such as "self-reliance," "basic needs," and "rural development"—could also then be specified.)

A useful topic to address in this context would be: What specific joint East-South action has been taken on behalf of common interests, how effective has that action been toward which goals, and what other joint action is conceivable? Application of the "international regime" concept in analyzing the foregoing question, which permits incorporation the notion of issue areas in debates over the economic redistribution of the world product, itself leads to a broadening of the analysis beyond the international organizations themselves.

The "socialist development strategies" in the 1960s and 1970s become interesting in this context. Assessing the political significance of such strategies include analysis of the influence of Marxist-Leninist ideology (as a system of knowledge) on the development of international regimes. That is because the use of knowledge affects how issue areas are defined and how issue-specific debates are couched. An example is the influence of the "Group D" countries on the Charter of the Economic Rights and Duties of States, approved by the United Nations General Assembly.

It is unlikely that any unified or consensus approach to the study of East-South relations will emerge. There is, after all, no unified or consensus approach even to the study of East-West relations. Yet a common general awareness has grown over the years among researchers on East-West relations. Due in part to significantly increased contact among East-West specialists internationally, and not just since Gorbachev, mutual understanding has increased within this specialist community.

The last comment to be made is that, in general, the status of East-South relations has been more or less independent of the status of East-West relations. This is significant, because it was a staple of American political discourse in the early 1970s, that U.S.-Soviet détente would promote Soviet good behavior in the Third World. Senior American officials tried to explain to the public how this was not necessarily so, but journalists were generally not interested in the complications.

It may appear that the political nature of East–South relations was result of East–West relations from the Bolshevik Revolution through the early 1930s, but in fact ideological Leninist strictures were the common cause pushing the Soviets to incite violent revolution both in Europe and in their colonies (the South) as well. From 1933 to 1947, on the other hand, East–South relations did not seem generally to depend terribly much on East–West relations, mainly because international affairs in Europe constrained the Soviets to seek more regular relations with the West European states. After Stalin's death, Khrushchev broached the idea of a "zone of peace" in the Third World, but this was discarded after his ouster.

Following that, Brezhnev's 1971 "Peace Plan" foreign-policy program was essentially a compromise between the need for good relations with the West for technological imports on the one hand and, on the other hand, the apparat-driven ideological, but also economic, imperative to make geopolitical gains in the Third World (Volten 1982). It follows that in that theater, none of the general Western strategies of deterrence, inducement, or convergence (Simes 1985) succeeded in its goal; and that the same result is likely to be the general case for other political systems of a similar type.

References

ALLISON, Roy. 1988. *The Soviet Union and the Strategy of Non-alignment in the Third World*. Cambridge: Cambridge University Press.

AUDEOUD, Oliver, Marc GJIDARA, Joëlle NGUYEN DUY TAN, and Patrick RAMBAUD. 1985. *La coopération économique à long terme avec les pays socialistes*. Paris: Presses universitaires de France.

BERLINER, Joseph S. 1958 *Soviet Economic Aid: The New Aid and Trade Policy in Underdeveloped Countries*. New York: Frederick A. Praeger.

BOŻYK, Paweł, ed. 1988. *Global Challenges and East European Responses*. Warsaw: Polish Scientific Publishers.

CAMPBELL, Kurt M., and S. Neil MacFARLANE, eds. 1989. *Gorbachev's Third World Dilemmas*. London: Routledge.

CARTER, James Richard. 1969. *The Net Cost of Soviet Foreign Aid*. New York: Praeger Publishers.

CUTLER, Robert M. 1987. "The Soviet Union and World Order." In *Global Peace and Security: Trends and Challenges*, edited by Wolfram F. Hanrieder, 76–100. Boulder, Colo.: Westview Press.

DONALDSON, Robert H., ed. 1981. *The Soviet Union in the Third World: Successes and Failures*. Boulder, Colo.: Westview Press.

DUNCAN, W. Raymond, and Carolyn McGiffert EKEDAHL. 1990. *Moscow and the Third World under Gorbachev*. Boulder, Colo.: Westview Press.

FEUCHTWANGER, E.J., and Peter NAILOR, eds. 1981. *The Soviet Union and the Third World*. London: Macmillan Press.

GOLAN, Galia. 1988. *The Soviet Union and National Liberation Movements in the Third World*. Boston, Mass.: Unwin Hyman.

GOLDMAN, Marshall I. 1967. *Soviet Foreign Aid*. New York: Frederick A. Praeger.

GRZYBOWSKI, Kazimierz. 1987. *Soviet International Law and World Economic Order*. Durham, N.C.: Duke University Press.

HAMMOND, Thomas T., comp. and ed. 1965. *Soviet Foreign Relations and World Communism: A Selected, Annotated Bibliography of 7,000 Books in 30 Languages*. Princeton, N.J.: Princeton University Press.

HOUGH, Jerry F. 1986. *The Struggle for the Third World: Soviet Debates and American Options*. Washington, D.C.: Brookings Institution.

KANET, Roger E., ed. 1987. *The Soviet Union, Eastern Europe and the Third World*. Cambridge: Cambridge University Press.

KOLODZIEJ, Edward A., and Roger E. KANET, eds. 1989. *The Limits of Soviet Power in the Developing World: Thermidor in the Revolutionary Struggle*. London: Macmillan Press.

KORBONSKI, Andrzej, and Francis FUKUYAMA, eds. 1987. *The Soviet Union and the Third World: The Last Three Decades*. Ithaca, N.Y.: Cornell University Press.

LAVIGNE, Marie, ed. 1986. *Les relations Est–Sud dans l'économie mondiale*. Paris: Economica.

LAÏDI, Zaki, dir. 1984. *L'URSS vue du Tiers Monde*. Paris: Éditions Karthala.

LOWENTHAL, Richard. 1977. *Model or Ally? The Communist Powers and the Developing Countries*. New York: Oxford University Press.

MELCHERS, Konrad. 1980 *Die sowjetische Afrikapolitik von Chruschtschow bis Breschnew*. Berlin: Oberbaum.

MÜLLER, Kurt 1967. *The Foreign Aid Programs of the Soviet Bloc and China*, translated [from the German 1964 edition] by Richard H. Weber and Michael Roloff. New York: Walker & Company.

SHULMAN, Marshall D., ed. 1986. *East–West Tensions in the Third World*. New York: W.W. Norton.

SIMES, Dimitri K. 1985. "Can the West Affect Soviet Thinking?" In *Soviet Politics in the 1980s*, edited by Helmut Sonnenfeldt, 161-169. Boulder, Colo.: Westview Press.

THUCYDIDES. 2008. *The Landmark Thucydides: A Comprehensive Guide to the Peloponnesian War*, edited by Robert B. Strassler. New York: Simon & Schuster.

VALENTA, Jiri, and Frank CIBULKA, eds. 1990. *Gorbachev's New Thinking and Third World Conflicts*. New Brunswick. N.J.: Transaction Publishers.

VOLTEN, Peter M.E. 1982. *Brezhnev's Peace Program: A Study of Soviet Domestic Political Process and Power*. Boulder, Colo.: Westview Press.

om # Index

The letter *t* following a page number denotes a table.

A

Abonyi, Arpad, 159
ACDA. *See* Arms Control and Disarmament Agency (U.S. Government entity)
Adomeit, Hannes, 58
Afghanistan: coups in, 21, 51; GDR military assistance to, 139; Soviet economic assistance to, 41, 42t, 44, 51–52, 132; Soviet foreign trade with, 51; Soviet ideological views of, 51, 132; Soviet intervention in, 19, 21, 23; Soviet military assistance to, 132, 138–39, 141t, 142; Soviet security policy and, 177, 179; Soviet withdrawal from, 22
Africa. *See individual countries and regions*
Africa, East. *See* East Africa
Africa, North. *See* North Africa
Africa, sub-Saharan. *See* sub-Saharan Africa
Aganbegian, Abel, 20, 23
Albania, 97; CMEA activity of, 32
Albright, David E., 12, 58
Alexander, Arthur J., 160
Alexiev, Alex, 160
Algeria, 48, 177; Soviet economic assistance to, 42t, 44; Soviet foreign trade with, 29t; WTO military assistance to, 121, 132, 137, 139, 140t

Allison, Roy, 189
America, Latin. *See* Latin America
Amur River, 38
An, Tai Sung, 58
Angola, 18, 179; civil war in, 136, 138–139, 156; Soviet military assistance to, 22, 54; WTO military assistance to, 132, 136–39, 140t, 142, 155
Argentina, 134, 158; Soviet economic assistance to, 42t; Soviet foreign trade with, 45, 55
Arms Control and Disarmament Agency (ACDA, U.S. Government entity), 167
Asia, 21. *See also individual countries and regions*
Asia, East. *See* East Asia
Asia, South. *See* South Asia
Aswan High Dam, 43, 47
Audeoud, Oliver, 189
Ausch, Sándor, 99, 110
Averkin, A.G., 88

B

Bahry, Donna, 161
Bandung Conference, 172
Bangladesh, 51–53; Soviet economic assistance to, 42t, 53; Soviet foreign trade with, 53; WTO military assistance to, 141t
Baumer, Max, 88
Berliner, Joseph S., 189
Berrios, Ruben, 111

Biberaj, Elez, 111
Biddle, W., 160
Bién, Andrzej, 100, 111
Biery, Frederick P., 160
Bogomolov, Oleg, 103-4, 111
Bolanos, M., 160
Bolivia, 55; Soviet economic assistance to, 42t
Bond, Daniel L., 160
Borisov, Oleg B., 58
Botos, Katalin, 88
Bovin, Aleksandr, 23
Bożyk, Paweł, 189
Brainard, Lawrence J., 89
Bratstvo (gas pipeline), 35
Brazil, 131, 134, 158; Soviet economic assistance to, 42t; Soviet foreign trade with, 29t, 45, 55
Brezhnev, Leonid I., 20, 21, 22, 44, 57, 189
Brzoska, Michael, 12, 160
Bulgaria, 36, 62, 147; CMEA activity of, 28, 32; politics of, 31; Soviet foreign trade with, 29t, 32
Burma, Soviet economic assistance to, 42t
Butler, Shannon, 167
Butler, William E., 111
Buvailik, G.E., 89
Bykov, Anatolii A., 89

C

Cambodia, Soviet economic assistance to, 42t
Cameroon, 54; Soviet economic assistance to, 42t
Campbell, John C., 160
Campbell, Kurt M., 189
Canada, 28t

Carter, Jimmy, 121, 189
Central African Republic, Soviet economic assistance to, 42t
Central Intelligence Agency (CIA), 124-25, 126t, 126-27, 127t, 128, 137 161
Chad, Soviet economic assistance to, 42t
Charter of the Economic Rights and Duties of States. *See* New International Economic Order
Chase-Dunn, Christopher, 160
Checinski, Michael, 156, 160
Chekhutov, Andrei I., 91
Chemokomplex (Hungarian firm), 104
Cherian, D., 160
Chile, Soviet economic assistance to, 42t
China, People's Republic of: military assistance of, 137-38, 144-45; Soviet economic assistance to, 38; Soviet foreign policy and, 20, 44, 51, 54, 57, 178; Soviet foreign trade with, 29t, 38; Soviet ideological views of, 33-34, 39, 57, 177-178; Soviet security policy and, 18-19, 52, 158
China, Republic of, 134, 136, 158
Chopra, Pushpindar S., 159, 161
Churchill, Winston, 15
CIA. *See* Central Intelligence Agency
Cibulka, Frank, 191
Clark, Cal M., 161
Cline, Ray S., 58
CMEA. *See* Council for Mutual Economic Assistance
Cohen, Raymond, 161
Cohn, Stanley H., 161

Colombia, 55; Soviet economic assistance to, 42t
Comecon. *See* Council for Mutual Economic Assistance
Comisso, Ellen, 161
Common Fund. *See* United Nations Conference on Trade and Development, Common Fund for Commodities
Conference on Security and Cooperation in Europe (CSCE), 17
Congo: GDR military assistance to, 138–39; Soviet economic assistance to, 42t
Copper, John D., 111
Costa Rica, 55
Côte d'Ivoire, 53, 54
Council for Mutual Economic Assistance (CMEA): as an integration organization, 35–37; at UNCTAD as Group D, 61–64, 69–72, 74, 76–83, 85–88; compared with EEC, 61, 80–83; Comprehensive Program of Socialist Economic Integration of, 34; economic relations with LDCs of, 95–100, 103–11, 175; enlargement beyond Eastern Europe of, 39–40; foundation and institutional development of, 31–35; General Conditions of Delivery of Goods, 85; juridical personality, 80, 82; structure of trade in, 18, 33–37, 173. *See also individual members*; Eastern Europe, military assistance of; United Nations Conference on Trade and Development, Group D (socialist states) at

Croan, Melvin, 161
CSCE. *See* Conference on Security and Cooperation in Europe
Csepel (Hungarian firm), 104
Cuba, 47; CMEA activity of, 28, 34, 39; cooperation with GDR, 138; in G77, 62; in Non-Aligned Movement, 187; Missile Crisis (1962), 54, 179; Soviet economic assistance to, 21, 31, 39; Soviet foreign policy and, 18, 38; Soviet foreign trade with, 29t, 39, 40; Soviet military assistance to, 40, 58, 136, 155
Cutler, Robert M., 15–17, 23, 111, 161, 191
Czechoslovakia: CMEA activity of, 28, 32, 33, 62, 109; East European foreign trade with, 109; economic relations with LDCs of, 64, 70, 98; invasion of, 34, 181; military assistance of, 46, 135–36, 144, 145, 146, 149–50, 156, 157, 184; politics of, 31–32, 109; Soviet foreign trade with, 29t, 36
Czerwinski, Edward J., 58

D

Dallin, Alexander, 89
Danilov, Evgenii A., 95, 107–8, 111
De Fiumel, Henryk, 89, 111
Decaye, Jocelyne, 105, 111
decolonization, 15, 17, 119, 172
Denmark, Soviet foreign trade with, 55
Department of Defense (U.S. Government entity), 167

Desolère, Michel, 92
Després, Laure, 12, 160
Despiney, Barbara, 79, 89, 105, 111, 161
Dessemontet, François, 89
developing countries. *See* less-developed countries
Diambou, Jean, 99, 112
Dibb, Paul, 58
Dobozi, István, 105, 111, 112, 161
Donaldson, Robert H., 58, 190
Druzhba (oil pipeline), 35
Dubček, Alexander, 156
Duncan, W. Raymond, 190
Dussauge, Pierre, 162

E

East Africa, 54. *See also individual countries*
East Asia: Soviet economic assistance to, 42t; Soviet foreign policy and, 58; WTO military assistance to, 141t. *See also individual countries*
East Germany. *See* German Democratic Republic
East Turkestan, 38
Eastern Europe
foreign trade of: commodities in, 67, 173; energy in, 37, 50, 173; intra-CMEA, 34; LDCs in, 37, 78-80, 96-99, 106, 109-110, 115, 172-73, 180-85; industrialized West in, 70, 174; Soviet Union in, 31-38; tripartite industrial cooperation in, 80, 104, 106, 109; world markets in, 16, 38, 62, 66, 96.
military assistance to LDCs from, 116-19, 131-39, 142-59, 169
relations with Soviet Union of: coordination of military production in, 144-50; foreign trade in, 32-37, 40, 100; global military-industrial development and, 154-59; hierarchical vs. bargaining models of military production in, 115-17, 149, 151, 155-56
See also individual countries; Council for Mutual Economic Assistance; Warsaw Treaty Organization
ECOSOC. *See* United Nations Economic and Social Council
Ecuador, 55
EEC. *See* European Economic Community
Efrat, Moshe, 162
Egypt: Soviet economic assistance to, 42t, 43-45, 47; Soviet foreign trade with, 29t, 44, 47; Soviet military assistance to, 46-48, 119, 134-35, 137, 155, 158; WTO military assistance to, 141t. *See also* Aswan High Dam; Suez Canal; Nasser, Gamal Abdel
Ekedahl, Carolyn McG., 190
El Salvador, 55
Equatorial Guinea, Soviet economic assistance to, 42t
Erickson, John, 162
Erickson, Richard J., 90
Ericson, Paul G., 124, 162
Ethiopia: CMEA economic assistance to, 140; GDR military

INDEX 197

assistance to, 138–40, 143, 156; Soviet economic assistance to, 42t, 54; Soviet foreign policy and, 18, 22–23, 54; Soviet military assistance to, 54; WTO military assistance to, 140t, 143
Europe, Eastern. See Eastern Europe
Europe, Western. See Western Europe
European Economic Community (EEC): compared with CMEA, 62, 80–83; juridical personality of, 82, 108; relations with CMEA, 69; Soviet perspectives on, 72, 80. See also Treaty of Rome (1957)

F

Feldebrugge, F.J.M., 112
Feuchtwanger, Edgar J., 190
Filimonova, T.V., 90
Fink, Karl Hermann, 90
Finland, 108, 177; Soviet foreign trade with, 29t, 55
Fomin, B.S., 90
Fomin, V.V., 90
Foreign Trade Research Institute (Warsaw), 106
Foss, Christopher F., 162
France: foreign trade of, 28t; military assistance of, 120, 137; military industry of, 122, 149, 160; participation in TIC by, 106; Soviet foreign policy and, 179, 180, 182, 187–88; Soviet foreign trade with, 29t
Freedman, Robert O., 59
Friedman, Edward, 162
Freymond, Jacques, 24

Fukuyama, Francis, 190

G

G77. See Group of Seventy-seven
Gallatin, Albert, 11
Gardner, Richard N., 90
Gati, Toby T., 102
GATT. See General Agreement on Tariffs and Trade
Gavshon, Arthur, 162
GDR. See German Democratic Republic
General Agreement on Tariffs and Trade (GATT), 64, 67, 72, 83, 86, 184
Generalized System of Preferences. See United Nations Conference on Trade and Development, Generalized System of Preferences
German Democratic Republic (GDR): CMEA activity of, 28, 32–33; foreign relations with LDCs of, 97–98; military assistance to LDCs of, 136–39, 148, 150, 156, 184; military industry of, 136, 145, 148; politics of, 145; Soviet economic assistance to, 33; Soviet foreign trade with, 29t, 30, 36, 55
Germany, Federal Republic of, 74; foreign trade of, 28t; Soviet foreign trade with, 29t, 30, 36, 40, 55
Ghana, 53, 54; Soviet economic assistance to, 42t
Gheorghiu-Dej, Gheorghe, 34
Gibraltar, Straits of, 56
Gjidara, Marc, 189
Gitelman, Zvi, 59

Glassman, Jon D., 59
Golan, Galia, 190
Goldman, Marshall I., 190
Gorbachev, Mikhail S.: coming to power of, 19–20; consolidation of power of, 22–23; new political thinking of, 20, 22
Gosovic, Branislav, 90
Greece, Soviet economic assistance to, 42t
Green, William, 162
Grimmett, Richard F., 162
Group of 77. *See* Group of Seventy-seven
Group of Seventy-seven (G77), 62, 75–76; relations with CMEA countries at UNCTAD of, 70, 71–72, 73 75–77, 86, 89, 105; Soviet perspectives on, 102
Grzybowski, Kazimierz, 190
GSP. *See* United Nations Conference on Trade and Development, Generalized System of Preferences
Gu Guan-fu, 112
Guinea: Soviet economic assistance to, 42t; Soviet foreign policy and, 53–54; WTO military assistance to, 132, 140t, 155
Guinea-Bissau: Soviet economic assistance to, 42t; WTO military assistance to, 140t
Gulf of Aden, 53
Gunston, Bill, 162
Gutman, Patrick, 105–6, 112
Guyana, 55

H

Haas, Ernst B., 162

Hall, William, 90
Hammond, Thomas T., 190
hard currency
  Soviet foreign trade and:
    Eastern Europe in, 181;
    Hungary in, 99; Iraq in, 50;
    North Korea in, 39
  Soviet sources of: arms sales, 124–31, 126t, 127t, 146; gold sales, 125; merchant marine, 55–56; natural resources, 34, 36, 48, 130
Havana Charter. *See* International Trade Organization, Havana Charter
Helsinki Conference. *See* Conference on Security and Cooperation in Europe
Heymann, Hans, Jr., 162
Holzman, Franklyn D., 59
Hough, Jerry F., 23, 190
Hungary: at UNCTAD, 62; CMEA activity of, 28, 32, 79, 100, 109; economy of, system reform of, 70; LDCs in foreign economic relations of, 64, 99, 103–4; LDCs in foreign military assistance of, 148, 155, 183; politics of, 31, 145, 172–73; Soviet economic assistance to, 33; Soviet foreign trade with, 28, 29t, 36
Hutchings, Raymond L, 129, 162

I

IBEC. *See* International Bank for Economic Cooperation
IIB. *See* International Investment Bank

INDEX 199

ILC. *See* United Nations General Assembly, International Law Commission
IMEMO. *See* Institute of World Economy and International Relations (Moscow)
IMF. *See* International Monetary Fund
India: military industry of, 134–35, 150; Soviet economic assistance to, 40–41, 42t, 43–45, 44t, 52; Soviet foreign policy and, 40, 51–52, 57, 177–78, 181, 187; Soviet foreign trade with, 29t, 44, 47, 51–52, 180; Soviet military assistance to, 52, 119, 122–23; war with Pakistan of, 51; WTO military assistance to, 132, 137, 140, 141t, 142
Indian Ocean, 45, 53; Soviet security policy and, 50
Indonesia, Soviet economic assistance to, 42t
industrialized West, 43, 74, 80, 87, 119, 139, 150, 176. *See also individual countries*; Soviet Union, foreign trade of, industrialized West in; United Nations Conference on Trade and Development, Group B (advanced capitalist states) at
Inotai, András, 105, 161
Inozemtsev, Nikolai N., 24
Institute of Economics of the World Socialist System (Moscow), 103, 107
Institute of War Economics (Warsaw), 156
Institute of World Economics (Budapest), 106

Institute of World Economy and International Relations (IMEMO, Moscow), 66
Integrated Program for Commodities. *See* United Nations Conference on Trade and Development, Common Fund for Commodities
International Bank for Economic Cooperation (IBEC), 33, 34
International Investment Bank (IIB), 34
international law
  East European perspectives on: international trade law in, 98; intra-CMEA relations seen from, 107–10
  socialist offensive in, 71–72, 76, 81, 84, 153, 180, 183, 185–87
  Soviet perspectives on: ideological struggle in, 84; international organizations in, 68–69, 81, 84–85; multilateral diplomacy in, 86; norm-creation in, 73–74, 84–85, 87; status of UNCTAD Common Fund for Commodities in, 69
International Monetary Fund (IMF), 64, 86
international relations
  East European perspectives on world markets in, 100–2, 105
  East–South relations in: academic studies of, 97–100, 109–10, 169–71, 174–76, 180–83, 187–89; Soviet perspectives on, 100–3

international organizations in, 64–65. *See also individual international organizations*
Soviet perspectives on:
changes under Gorbachev in, 22; LDCs in, 100, 189; world markets in, 100–2
Western theories about: international political economy approach in, 96, 110, 116, 118–19, 150, 152–53, 174–75; regime theory in, 85, 88, 116, 175; world-system approach in, 118, 150–52, 174
International Trade Organization (ITO), 83; Havana Charter (1948), 61; Soviet perspectives on, 63–65
Iran
military assistance to: from China, 137; from North Korea, 138; from WTO members, 131, 141t, 155
Soviet nonmilitary relations with: economic assistance in, 42t, 43–44, 50; foreign trade in, 29t, 44, 50; security policy in, 50
Iraq
military assistance to: from China, 135; from East European WTO members, 134, 136, 137, 139, 141t, 143; from the Soviet Union, 46, 122, 132, 155
Soviet nonmilitary relations with: economic assistance in, 42t, 43, 44; foreign policy and, 50; foreign trade with, 29t, 44, 47, 50, 52
Isfahan, 50

Israel: Egyptian relations with, 46, 48; military industry of, 134, 158; Soviet foreign policy and, 49
Italy, Soviet foreign trade with, 28t, 29t
ITO. *See* International Trade Organization
Ivanov, A., 90
Ivanov, Ivan D., 94

J

Jackson–Vanik amendment. *See* United States, Trade Act of 1974
Jacobsen, Hanns-Dieter, 88
Jacobson, Harold K., 90
Jain, J.R., 59
Jamaica, 55
Japan, 56, 177, 180, 186; foreign trade of, 28t; Soviet foreign policy and, 20; Soviet foreign trade with, 29t, 36, 55
Joint Economic Committee (U.S. Congressional entity), 167
Jordan, 48, 119, 120
Juda, Lawrence, 90
Judet, Pierre, 90

K

Kahn, Philippe, 90
Kamoff-Nicolsky, 162
Kanet, Roger E., 11, 24, 25, 59, 98–99, 112, 163, 190
Kapur, Harish, 11
Karp, Aaron, 12
Katner, Garth T., 24
Katz, James E., 163
Kenya, Soviet economic assistance to, 42t
Keohane, Robert O., 163, 164

Khrushchev, Nikita S.: CMEA reform under, 33; de-Stalinization speech of, 36, 171; ouster of, 34; Soviet foreign policy under 17, 36, 40, 43–44, 172, 189
Khvoinik, Pavel I., 90
Kiss, A.C., 90
Kiembai (USSR), 37
Klerr, Jerzy, 91, 107, 112
Kolodziej, Edward A., 190
Koloskov, Boris T., 58
Korbonski, Andrzej, 91, 190
Korea, North: military assistance of, 134, 136, 144, 158; Soviet economic assistance to, 31, 39; Soviet foreign trade with, 38–39;
Kostecki, Michel [Maciej] M., 91, 112
Korea, South, 39, 134, 158
Krasner, Stephen D., 85, 88, 91, 163
Krasnov, Gennadii A., 91
Kratochwil, Friedrich, 163
Kulig, Jan, 113
Kulski, Wladyslaw W., 59
Kursk (USSR), 37
Kurtzman, Joel, 91, 95, 97, 112

L

Laïdi, Zaki, 190
Laird, Robbin F., 126, 163
Lall, Sanjaya, 77, 91
Laos, Soviet economic assistance to, 42t
Laszlo, Ervin, 91, 95, 97, 112
Latin America: Soviet economic assistance to, 42t, 44, 55; Soviet foreign policy and, 20–21, 55; Soviet foreign trade with, 55; WTO military assistance to, 138. *See also individual countries*
Lavigne, Marie, 95, 112, 163, 190
LDCs. *See* less-developed countries
Lederer, Ivo J., 59
less-developed countries (LDCs): CMEA foreign trade with, 67, 70–72, 75–80, 95, 99–101; economic determinants of demand for Soviet arms by, 119–23; economic competition with CMEA of, 105–7; Soviet economic assistance to, 31, 40–46 42t, 44t, 108–9; Soviet foreign policy and, 16–17, 20, 21–22, 45, 64–65, 86–87; Soviet foreign trade with, 29t, 40–46; Soviet military assistance to, 41, 119–10, 120t, 123, 130t, 131–33; Soviet perspectives on, 100–3, 102t. *See also individual countries*; Group of Seventy-seven; tripartite industrial cooperation; United Nations Conference on Trade and Development
Lewis, William H., 163
Libya, 48, 121, 129, 132, 139; WTO military assistance to, 140t
Lindell, John O., 91
Liner Conferences. *See* United Nations Conference on Trade and Development, Codes of Conduct, Liner Conferences
Lonsdale-Brown, Marian L., 166
Löwenthal, Richard, 59, 190
Luke, Timothy W., 150, 163
Luterbacher, Urs, 11

Lydolph, Paul E., 11

M

MacFarlane, S. Neil, 189
Machowski, Heinrich, 24
Maggs, Peter B., 112
Maire, Jean-Paul, 91
Makiyama, Hideko, 1980
Malacca, Straits of, 56
Malaysia, 56
Mali: Soviet economic assistance to, 42t, 54; Soviet foreign policy and, 54; WTO military assistance to, 132, 137, 139, 140t
Mallmann, Wolfgang, 163
Marer, Paul, 59
Matejka, Harriet, 70, 79, 91, 99, 112
Mauritania, Soviet economic assistance to, 42t; WTO military assistance to, 140t
MccGwire, Michael, 59
McDonnell, John, 59
McLane, Charles, 59
McMillan, Carl H., 66, 91, 113
McNeill, William, 136, 164
Melchers, Konrad, 190
Melman, Seymour, 1982
Mexico, 55
MFN. *See* most-favored-nation clause
Middle East: GDR military assistance to, 135; Soviet economic assistance to, 31, 42t; Soviet foreign policy and, 17, 46, 48–49, 50, 57–58, 179; Soviet military assistance to, 46; WTO military assistance to, 120t, 137–38, 141t, 142. *See also individual countries*

military assistance and cooperation. *See individual countries*
Milenkovitch, Michael M., 113
Miller, Ronald S., 124, 162
Miller, Steven E., 164
Minakov, Aleksandr I., 91
Mir (high-voltage electricity-transmission line), 35
Mitchell, Donald W., 59
Mongolia: CMEA activity of, 28, 32, 62; Soviet foreign trade with, 29t
Morocco: Soviet economic assistance to, 42t, 131; Soviet foreign trade with, 48
Morozov, Grigorii I., 81–82, 84–85, 91, 108
Mosley, Hugh G., 164
most-favored-nation clause (MFN), 72
Moulioukova, Dina, 25
Mozambique: GDR military assistance to, 142; Soviet foreign policy and, 53, 132, 137–38, 139, WTO military assistance to, 137–38, 139, 140t, 142, 155
MPLA. *See* Angola, civil war in
Müller, Kurt, 190
multilateralization: of East-South trade, 78, 99; of intra-CMEA trade, 33, 34, 66; of transferable ruble, 66, 78–79, 99–100, 107, 109

N

Naik, J.A., 59
Nailor, Peter, 190
NAM. *See* Non-Aligned Movement
Namikas, Lisa, 24
Nasser, Gamal Abdel, 43, 46, 47

NATO. *See* North Atlantic Treaty Organization
Natufe, Omajuwa I., 60
Nepal: Soviet economic assistance to, 42t; WTO military assistance to, 141t
Netherlands, 49, 80; foreign trade of, 28t; Soviet foreign trade with, 55
Neuman, Stephanie G., 159, 164
New International Economic Order (NIEO): Charter of the Economic Rights and Duties of States as founding document of, 68–69, 172, 182, 188; CMEA response to, 62, 65–66, 88, 103, 182–83
newly industrializing countries (NICs), 103–4, 131, 134, 158
Nguyen Duy Tan, Joëlle, 189
Nicaragua, 139, 142
NICs. *See* newly industrializing countries
NIEO. *See* New International Economic Order
Niger, Soviet economic assistance to, 42t
Nigeria, 54, 121, 132; Soviet economic assistance to, 42t
Non-Aligned Movement (NAM), 16, 102, 180, 187; foundation of, 172. *See also* international law, socialist offensive in
North Africa: Soviet economic assistance to, 31; Soviet foreign policy and, 58; WTO military assistance to, 121, 137–38, 140t. *See also individual countries*

North Atlantic Treaty Organization (NATO), 19, 33, 117, 157
North Korea, Soviet foreign trade with, 29t, 39–40
North-South dialogue. *See* New International Economic Order
Nosiadek, Grzegorz, 100, 111
Nötzold, Jürgen, 113
Nye, Joseph S., 164

O

Obminskii, Ernest E., 95, 101–2, 113
Ofer, Gur, 123, 164
Ohlson, Thomas, 12, 160
oil embargo (1973), effect on intra-CMEA relations of, 36–37, 48–49, 121–22, 125, 171–72, 180
OPEC. *See* Organization of the Petroleum Exporting Countries
Organization of the Petroleum Exporting Countries (OPEC). *See individual countries*
Orenburg (USSR), 35
Osakwe, Chris, 92
Ost, David, 164

P

Pajak, Roger F., 113
Pajestka, Josef, 113
Pakistan: Soviet economic assistance to, 42t, 44, 52, 53; Soviet foreign policy and, 51–53; Soviet foreign trade with, 52–53; WTO military assistance to, 135, 136, 141t
Panama Canal, 56
Papp, Daniel S., 24, 111, 124, 164
Parvin, Manouchar, 60

Paszyński, Marian, 105, 113, 164
Pechota, Vratislav, 98, 113, 164
Persian Gulf, Soviet foreign policy and, 45, 50
Peru: Soviet economic assistance to, 42t; Soviet military assistance to, 120
Piekalkewicz, Jaroslaw, 58
Pierre, Andrew J., 165
Pinegin, Boris M., 92
Poland
  CMEA activity of, 28, 32, 62
  economy of: Soviet assistance to, 33; system reform of, 70, 109
  foreign trade of: Eastern Europe in, 79, 100, 107, 109; LDCs in, 64; Soviet Union in, 29t, 32, 36, 55
  military assistance of, 134–36, 144, 145, 147–49, 155, 182
  politics of: intra-elite, 21, 31; social protest and, 145, 172
  Soviet foreign policy and, 177
Polezhaev, V., 90
Popov, Valerii D., 95, 108, 109, 113
Porter, Bruce D., 165
Prebisch, Raúl, 65

R

Radu, Michael, 95, 97, 98, 113, 165
Radvanyi, Janos, 98–99, 114
Rajski, Jerzy, 92
Rambaud, Patrick, 189
Remington, Robin A., 165
restrictive business practices. *See* United Nations Conference on Trade and

Development, Codes of Conduct, Restrictive Business Practices
Robert, Annette, 114
Roberts, Cynthia A., 123, 165
Roffe, Pedro, 92
Romania: arms-production industry of, 135, 136, 144, 147, 149; CMEA activity of, 28, 32, 33–34, 35, 62; foreign policy of, 145, 149; LDCs in foreign trade of, 96; military assistance of, 136, 147, 155, 156; oil industry of, 36; politics of, 31; Soviet foreign trade with, 29t
Romer, J.-Christophe, 92
Ross, Andrew L, 165
Rothstein, Robert L., 165
Rubinstein, Alvin Z., 60, 92
Russian Empire, 179
Rwanda, Soviet economic assistance to, 42t

S

Sadat, Anwar, 46–47, 137
Sakhalin Island, 56
Sárközy, Tamas, 92
Saudi Arabia, 48, 155
Saunders, Christopher T., 95, 97, 114, 165
Savin, V.A., 60
Schaefer, Henry W., 60
Schiering, Wulf-Peter, 92
Schrodt, Philip A., 165
Schultz, Siegfried, 24
Schwartz, Charles A., 92
Schwartz, Morton, 60
Sen Gupta, Bhabani, 60
Senegal, Soviet economic assistance to, 42t
Shattan, Joseph J., 60

Shulman, Marshall D., 190
Sierra Leone, Soviet economic assistance to, 42t
Simai, Mihaly, 104, 114
Simes, Dimitri K., 191
Singapore, 56
SIPRI. *See* Stockholm International Peace Research Institute
Smith, Glen A., 60
Snitch, Thomas H., 166
Sodaro, Michael, 97, 98, 114, 166
Somalia: Soviet economic assistance to, 42t, 53–54; Soviet foreign policy and, 139
South Africa, Republic of, 134
South Asia: Soviet economic assistance to, 42t; WTO military assistance to, 141t. *See also individual countries*
Soviet Union (USSR)
  Academy of Sciences. *See names of individual institutes*
  economy of, system reform of, 18
  foreign policy of: CMEA and East European integration in, 21, 31, 34, 37; foreign trade in, 57; LDCs in, 41; marine fleet in, 55–56. *See also individual countries and regions*
  foreign trade of: change over time in, 27–31, 35; Eastern Europe in, 31–38; economic assistance in, 40–41, 42t 43; economic determinants of arms sales to LDCs by, 122–33; economic planning and, 30, 101; energy in, 27, 36; exports in, 27, 30, 35, 39, 52, 142, 146; imports in, 27, 30–31; industrialized West in, 28t, 185; LDCs in, 16, 38–58, 185; technology in, 19, 27–28, 30–31, 67, 101, 102–3, 188. *See also individual countries and regions*; hard currency, Soviet sources of; technology
Spandar'ian, Viktor B., 93
Spencer, Daniel L., 166
Sprout, Harold, 166
Sprout, Margaret, 166
Sri Lanka: Soviet economic assistance to, 42t; WTO military assistance to, 141t
Staar, Richard F., 60
Stalin, Iosif V., 15, 33, 84, 172, 177–78, 189
Steinert, Marlis, 11
Stevens, Christopher, 60
Stroke, Rebecca V., 166
Stockholm International Peace Research Institute (SIPRI), 165
Sub-Saharan Africa: Soviet economic assistance to, 31, 44, 53–55; Soviet foreign policy and, 53; Soviet foreign trade with, 53–55; WTO military assistance to, 137, 138, 140t. *See also individual countries*
Sudan, Soviet economic assistance to, 42t
Suez Canal, 43, 47, 56
Swanborough, Gordon, 162
Sweden, 159; Soviet foreign trade with, 55
Sweetman, Bill, 166
Sylvain, Ivan J., 159

Syria, 148; Soviet economic assistance to, 42t; Soviet foreign trade with, 29t, 48; Soviet military assistance to, 46, 48; WTO military assistance to, 121–22, 132, 137, 141t, 155
Szentes, Tamás, 103, 114
Szporluk, Roman, 60

T

Taiwan. *See* China, Republic of
Tanzania, Soviet economic assistance to, 42t
Tartarin, Robert, 12
technology: East–South transfer of, 78–79, 98, 104, 106–7, 115–16, 158–59, 180, 184; WTO military-industrial, 134–35, 136, 143–50, 156, 181. *See also* United Nations Conference on Trade and Development, Codes of Conduct, Transfer of Technology; Soviet Union, foreign trade of, technology in
Third World. *See* less-developed countries
Thucydides, 175, 191
TIC. *See* tripartite industrial cooperation
Tiraspolsky, Anita, 108, 114
Touscoz, Jean, 90, 93
transferable ruble: convertibility of, 78–79; multilateralization of, 66, 78–79, 99–100, 107, 109
Treaty of Locarno (1925), 176
Treaty of Rome (1957), 80
tripartite industrial cooperation (TIC), 80, 104, 106, 109
Tumanov, V.A., 93

Tunisia, Soviet economic assistance to, 42t
Tunkin, Grigorii I., 84, 93
Turkey, 131, 177; Soviet economic assistance to, 42t, 44, 45, 49, 52; Soviet foreign trade with, 49–50; Soviet security policy and, 49
turnkey plants, 104
Tylecote, Andrew B., 166
Tyson, Laura D'Andrea, 167

U

Uganda, Soviet economic assistance to, 42t
Ulam, Adam B., 60
UN General Assembly. *See* United Nations General Assembly
UNCITRAL. *See* United Nations Commission on International Trade Law
UNCTAD. *See* United Nations Conference on Trade and Development
UNGA. *See* United Nations General Assembly
UNIDO. *See* United Nations Industrial Development Organization
Union of Soviet Socialist Republics. *See* Soviet Union
United Kingdom: foreign trade of, 28t; Soviet foreign trade with, 29t, 55
United Nations Commission on International Trade Law (UNCITRAL), 68, 84, 185
United Nations Conference on Trade and Development

(UNCTAD), 11, 16, 61–94, 96, 153, 180, 187
Codes of Conduct: Liner Conferences, 66, 72, 74–75, 87; Restrictive Business Practices, 75, 81; Transfer of Technology, 66, 75–78, 81, 87
Common Fund for Commodities, 66–69, 80, 87
foundation and institutional development of, 61–65, 83, 85, 88, 179
Generalized System of Preferences (GSP), 66, 69, 72, 87, 184
Group B (advanced capitalist states) at, 62, 71, 73– 77, 81–82, 86
Group D (socialist states) at, 60–80, 83–88, 96, 183–85
Soviet perspectives on, 65–68, 73
United Nations Economic and Social Council (ECOSOC), 88
United Nations General Assembly (UNGA), 83, 84, 94; Charter of the Economic Rights and Duties of States, 68–69, 172, 182, 188; International Law Commission (ILC), 68–69, 71–72, 85, 185; Sixth Committee, 69, 85
United Nations Industrial Development Organization (UNIDO), 80
United States: foreign trade of, 28t; military assistance of, 122, 149; Soviet foreign policy and, 15, 18–19, 22, 49; Soviet foreign trade with, 29t, 31, 36; Soviet international strategy and, 51, 56, 178, 180, 183, 186; Trade Act of 1974, 49. *See also individual government entities*
Upper Volta, Soviet economic assistance to, 42t
Uruguay, 55; Soviet economic assistance to, 42t
USSR. *See* Soviet Union
Ussuri River, 38
Ust-Ilim (USSR), 37

V

Valenta, Jiri, 167, 191
Valkenier, Elizabeth K., 24, 95, 100–102, 105, 114
Vanous, Jan, 167
Väyrynen, Raimo, 151, 167
Vel'iaminov, Georgii M., 73–74, 93
Venezuela, 55
Vereinigte Edelstahlwerke (Austrian firm), 104
Vietnam, 23, 38, 39, 57, 62, 125, 179; Soviet economic assistance to, 21, 31; Soviet foreign trade with, 29t, 39–40; Soviet military assistance to, 46
Volten, Peter M.E., 191
Volvo (Swedish firm), 104
Vucinich, Wayne S., 59

W

Wallerstein, Immanuel, 167
Walters, Robert S., 60
Warsaw Pact. *See* Warsaw Treaty Organization
Warsaw Treaty Organization (WTO), 33, 116, 117, 129, 156, 179. *See also individual countries*

WEFA. *See* Wharton Econometric Forecasting Associates
Weinstein, Warren, 60
West Germany. *See* Federal Republic of Germany
Western Europe: economic relations with Eastern Europe of, 35; foreign trade of, 33; Soviet foreign policy and, 178; Soviet foreign trade with, 29t, 57; Soviet perspectives on, 174
Wharton Econometric Forecasting Associates (WEFA), 167, 168
White, William D., 168
Wolfe, Thomas W., 168
Wright, Arthur W., 60
WTO. *See* Warsaw Treaty Organization

Y

Yemen, North, 48; Soviet economic assistance to, 42t; WTO military assistance to, 137, 141t, 142
Yemen, South, 48, 56; GDR military assistance to, 139; Soviet economic assistance to, 42t; WTO military assistance to, 132, 137, 141t
Young, Oran R., 168
Yugoslavia, 32, 97, 113, 149, 178; politics of, 31, 32; Soviet foreign trade with, 29t

Z

Zacher, Lech, 91, 107, 112
Zaire, 136
Zambia, 119, 132; Soviet economic assistance to, 42t
Zevin, Leon, 106, 114
Zoeter, Joan Parpart, 124, 168
Zorin, Valerian A., 94
Zurawicki, Leon, 106, 114

SOVIET AND POST-SOVIET POLITICS AND SOCIETY
Edited by Dr. Andreas Umland | ISSN 1614-3515

1   Андреас Умланд (ред.) | Воплощение Европейской конвенции по правам человека в России. Философские, юридические и эмпирические исследования | ISBN 3-89821-387-0

2   Christian Wipperfürth | Russland – ein vertrauenswürdiger Partner? Grundlagen, Hintergründe und Praxis gegenwärtiger russischer Außenpolitik | Mit einem Vorwort von Heinz Timmermann | ISBN 3-89821-401-X

3   Manja Hussner | Die Übernahme internationalen Rechts in die russische und deutsche Rechtsordnung. Eine vergleichende Analyse zur Völkerrechtsfreundlichkeit der Verfassungen der Russländischen Föderation und der Bundesrepublik Deutschland | Mit einem Vorwort von Rainer Arnold | ISBN 3-89821-438-9

4   Matthew Tejada | Bulgaria's Democratic Consolidation and the Kozloduy Nuclear Power Plant (KNPP). The Unattainability of Closure | With a foreword by Richard J. Crampton | ISBN 3-89821-439-7

5   Марк Григорьевич Меерович | Квадратные метры, определяющие сознание. Государственная жилищная политика в СССР. 1921 – 1941 гг | ISBN 3-89821-474-5

6   Andrei P. Tsygankov, Pavel A. Tsygankov (Eds.) | New Directions in Russian International Studies | ISBN 3-89821-422-2

7   Марк Григорьевич Меерович | Как власть народ к труду приучала. Жилище в СССР – средство управления людьми. 1917 – 1941 гг. | С предисловием Елены Осокиной | ISBN 3-89821-495-8

8   David J. Galbreath | Nation-Building and Minority Politics in Post-Socialist States. Interests, Influence and Identities in Estonia and Latvia | With a foreword by David J. Smith | ISBN 3-89821-467-2

9   Алексей Юрьевич Безугольный | Народы Кавказа в Вооруженных силах СССР в годы Великой Отечественной войны 1941-1945 гг. | С предисловием Николая Бугая | ISBN 3-89821-475-3

10 Вячеслав Лихачев и Владимир Прибыловский (ред.) | Русское Национальное Единство, 1990-2000. В 2-х томах | ISBN 3-89821-523-7

11 Николай Бугай (ред.) | Народы стран Балтии в условиях сталинизма (1940-е – 1950-е годы). Документированная история | ISBN 3-89821-525-3

12 Ingmar Bredies (Hrsg.) | Zur Anatomie der Orange Revolution in der Ukraine. Wechsel des Elitenregimes oder Triumph des Parlamentarismus? | ISBN 3-89821-524-5

13 Anastasia V. Mitrofanova | The Politicization of Russian Orthodoxy. Actors and Ideas | With a foreword by William C. Gay | ISBN 3-89821-481-8

14 Nathan D. Larson | Alexander Solzhenitsyn and the Russo-Jewish Question | ISBN 3-89821-483-4

15 Guido Houben | Kulturpolitik und Ethnizität. Staatliche Kunstförderung im Russland der neunziger Jahre | Mit einem Vorwort von Gert Weisskirchen | ISBN 3-89821-542-3

16 Leonid Luks | Der russische „Sonderweg"? Aufsätze zur neuesten Geschichte Russlands im europäischen Kontext | ISBN 3-89821-496-6

17 Евгений Мороз | История «Мёртвой воды» – от страшной сказки к большой политике. Политическое неоязычество в постсоветской России | ISBN 3-89821-551-2

18 Александр Верховский и Галина Кожевникова (ред.) | Этническая и религиозная интолерантность в российских СМИ. Результаты мониторинга 2001-2004 гг. | ISBN 3-89821-569-5

19 Christian Ganzer | Sowjetisches Erbe und ukrainische Nation. Das Museum der Geschichte des Zaporoger Kosakentums auf der Insel Chortycja | Mit einem Vorwort von Frank Golczewski | ISBN 3-89821-504-0

20 Эльза-Баир Гучинова | Помнить нельзя забыть. Антропология депортационной травмы калмыков | С предисловием Кэролайн Хамфри | ISBN 3-89821-506-7

21 Юлия Лидерман | Мотивы «проверки» и «испытания» в постсоветской культуре. Советское прошлое в российском кинематографе 1990-х годов | С предисловием Евгения Марголита | ISBN 3-89821-511-3

22 Tanya Lokshina, Ray Thomas, Mary Mayer (Eds.) | The Imposition of a Fake Political Settlement in the Northern Caucasus. The 2003 Chechen Presidential Election | ISBN 3-89821-436-2

23 Timothy McCajor Hall, Rosie Read (Eds.) | Changes in the Heart of Europe. Recent Ethnographies of Czechs, Slovaks, Roma, and Sorbs | With an afterword by Zdeněk Salzmann | ISBN 3-89821-606-3

24 *Christian Autengruber* | Die politischen Parteien in Bulgarien und Rumänien. Eine vergleichende Analyse seit Beginn der 90er Jahre | Mit einem Vorwort von Dorothée de Nève | ISBN 3-89821-476-1

25 *Annette Freyberg-Inan with Radu Cristescu* | The Ghosts in Our Classrooms, or: John Dewey Meets Ceauşescu. The Promise and the Failures of Civic Education in Romania | ISBN 3-89821-416-8

26 *John B. Dunlop* | The 2002 Dubrovka and 2004 Beslan Hostage Crises. A Critique of Russian Counter-Terrorism | With a foreword by Donald N. Jensen | ISBN 3-89821-608-X

27 *Peter Koller* | Das touristische Potenzial von Kam"janec'–Podil's'kyj. Eine fremdenverkehrsgeographische Untersuchung der Zukunftsperspektiven und Maßnahmenplanung zur Destinationsentwicklung des „ukrainischen Rothenburg" | Mit einem Vorwort von Kristiane Klemm | ISBN 3-89821-640-3

28 *Françoise Daucé, Elisabeth Sieca-Kozlowski (Eds.)* | Dedovshchina in the Post-Soviet Military. Hazing of Russian Army Conscripts in a Comparative Perspective | With a foreword by Dale Herspring | ISBN 3-89821-616-0

29 *Florian Strasser* | Zivilgesellschaftliche Einflüsse auf die Orange Revolution. Die gewaltlose Massenbewegung und die ukrainische Wahlkrise 2004 | Mit einem Vorwort von Egbert Jahn | ISBN 3-89821-648-9

30 *Rebecca S. Katz* | The Georgian Regime Crisis of 2003-2004. A Case Study in Post-Soviet Media Representation of Politics, Crime and Corruption | ISBN 3-89821-413-3

31 *Vladimir Kantor* | Willkür oder Freiheit. Beiträge zur russischen Geschichtsphilosophie | Ediert von Dagmar Herrmann sowie mit einem Vorwort versehen von Leonid Luks | ISBN 3-89821-589-X

32 *Laura A. Victoir* | The Russian Land Estate Today. A Case Study of Cultural Politics in Post-Soviet Russia | With a foreword by Priscilla Roosevelt | ISBN 3-89821-426-5

33 *Ivan Katchanovski* | Cleft Countries. Regional Political Divisions and Cultures in Post-Soviet Ukraine and Moldova | With a foreword by Francis Fukuyama | ISBN 3-89821-558-X

34 *Florian Mühlfried* | Postsowjetische Feiern. Das Georgische Bankett im Wandel | Mit einem Vorwort von Kevin Tuite | ISBN 3-89821-601-2

35 *Roger Griffin, Werner Loh, Andreas Umland (Eds.)* | Fascism Past and Present, West and East. An International Debate on Concepts and Cases in the Comparative Study of the Extreme Right | With an afterword by Walter Laqueur | ISBN 3-89821-674-8

36 *Sebastian Schlegel* | Der „Weiße Archipel". Sowjetische Atomstädte 1945-1991 | Mit einem Geleitwort von Thomas Bohn | ISBN 3-89821-679-9

37 *Vyacheslav Likhachev* | Political Anti-Semitism in Post-Soviet Russia. Actors and Ideas in 1991-2003 | Edited and translated from Russian by Eugene Veklerov | ISBN 3-89821-529-5

38 *Josette Baer (Ed.)* | Preparing Liberty in Central Europe. Political Texts from the Spring of Nations 1848 to the Spring of Prague 1968 | With a foreword by Zdeněk V. David | ISBN 3-89821-546-5

39 *Михаил Лукьянов* | Российский консерватизм и реформа, 1907-1914 | С предисловием Марка Д. Стейнберга | ISBN 3-89821-503-2

40 *Nicola Melloni* | Market Without Economy. The 1998 Russian Financial Crisis | With a foreword by Eiji Furukawa | ISBN 3-89821-407-9

41 *Dmitrij Chmelnizki* | Die Architektur Stalins | Bd. 1: Studien zu Ideologie und Stil | Bd. 2: Bilddokumentation | Mit einem Vorwort von Bruno Flierl | ISBN 3-89821-515-6

42 *Katja Yafimava* | Post-Soviet Russian-Belarussian Relationships. The Role of Gas Transit Pipelines | With a foreword by Jonathan P. Stern | ISBN 3-89821-655-1

43 *Boris Chavkin* | Verflechtungen der deutschen und russischen Zeitgeschichte. Aufsätze und Archivfunde zu den Beziehungen Deutschlands und der Sowjetunion von 1917 bis 1991 | Ediert von Markus Edlinger sowie mit einem Vorwort versehen von Leonid Luks | ISBN 3-89821-756-6

44 *Anastasija Grynenko in Zusammenarbeit mit Claudia Dathe* | Die Terminologie des Gerichtswesens der Ukraine und Deutschlands im Vergleich. Eine übersetzungswissenschaftliche Analyse juristischer Fachbegriffe im Deutschen, Ukrainischen und Russischen | Mit einem Vorwort von Ulrich Hartmann | ISBN 3-89821-691-8

45 *Anton Burkov* | The Impact of the European Convention on Human Rights on Russian Law. Legislation and Application in 1996-2006 | With a foreword by Françoise Hampson | ISBN 978-3-89821-639-5

46 *Stina Torjesen, Indra Overland (Eds.)* | International Election Observers in Post-Soviet Azerbaijan. Geopolitical Pawns or Agents of Change? | ISBN 978-3-89821-743-9

47 *Taras Kuzio* | Ukraine – Crimea – Russia. Triangle of Conflict | ISBN 978-3-89821-761-3

48 *Claudia Šabić* | „Ich erinnere mich nicht, aber L'viv!" Zur Funktion kultureller Faktoren für die Institutionalisierung und Entwicklung einer ukrainischen Region | Mit einem Vorwort von Melanie Tatur | ISBN 978-3-89821-752-1

49 *Marlies Bilz* | Tatarstan in der Transformation. Nationaler Diskurs und Politische Praxis 1988-1994 | Mit einem Vorwort von Frank Golczewski | ISBN 978-3-89821-722-4

50 *Марлен Ларюэль (ред.)* | Современные интерпретации русского национализма | ISBN 978-3-89821-795-8

51 *Sonja Schüler* | Die ethnische Dimension der Armut. Roma im postsozialistischen Rumänien | Mit einem Vorwort von Anton Sterbling | ISBN 978-3-89821-776-7

52 *Галина Кожевникова* | Радикальный национализм в России и противодействие ему. Сборник докладов Центра «Сова» за 2004-2007 гг. | С предисловием Александра Верховского | ISBN 978-3-89821-721-7

53 *Галина Кожевникова и Владимир Прибыловский* | Российская власть в биографиях I. Высшие должностные лица РФ в 2004 г. | ISBN 978-3-89821-796-5

54 *Галина Кожевникова и Владимир Прибыловский* | Российская власть в биографиях II. Члены Правительства РФ в 2004 г. | ISBN 978-3-89821-797-2

55 *Галина Кожевникова и Владимир Прибыловский* | Российская власть в биографиях III. Руководители федеральных служб и агентств РФ в 2004 г.| ISBN 978-3-89821-798-9

56 *Ileana Petroniu* | Privatisierung in Transformationsökonomien. Determinanten der Restrukturierungsbereitschaft am Beispiel Polens, Rumäniens und der Ukraine | Mit einem Vorwort von Rainer W. Schäfer | ISBN 978-3-89821-790-3

57 *Christian Wipperfürth* | Russland und seine GUS-Nachbarn. Hintergründe, aktuelle Entwicklungen und Konflikte in einer ressourcenreichen Region| ISBN 978-3-89821-801-6

58 *Togzhan Kassenova* | From Antagonism to Partnership. The Uneasy Path of the U.S.-Russian Cooperative Threat Reduction | With a foreword by Christoph Bluth | ISBN 978-3-89821-707-1

59 *Alexander Höllwerth* | Das sakrale eurasische Imperium des Aleksandr Dugin. Eine Diskursanalyse zum postsowjetischen russischen Rechtsextremismus | Mit einem Vorwort von Dirk Uffelmann | ISBN 978-3-89821-813-9

60 *Олег Рябов* | «Россия-Матушка». Национализм, гендер и война в России XX века | С предисловием Елены Гощило | ISBN 978-3-89821-487-2

61 *Ivan Maistrenko* | Borot'bism. A Chapter in the History of the Ukrainian Revolution | With a new Introduction by Chris Ford | Translated by George S. N. Luckyj with the assistance of Ivan L. Rudnytsky | Second, Revised and Expanded Edition ISBN 978-3-8382-1107-7

62 *Maryna Romanets* | Anamorphosic Texts and Reconfigured Visions. Improvised Traditions in Contemporary Ukrainian and Irish Literature | ISBN 978-3-89821-576-3

63 *Paul D'Anieri and Taras Kuzio (Eds.)* | Aspects of the Orange Revolution I. Democratization and Elections in Post-Communist Ukraine | ISBN 978-3-89821-698-2

64 *Bohdan Harasymiw in collaboration with Oleh S. Ilnytzkyj (Eds.)* | Aspects of the Orange Revolution II. Information and Manipulation Strategies in the 2004 Ukrainian Presidential Elections | ISBN 978-3-89821-699-9

65 *Ingmar Bredies, Andreas Umland and Valentin Yakushik (Eds.)* | Aspects of the Orange Revolution III. The Context and Dynamics of the 2004 Ukrainian Presidential Elections | ISBN 978-3-89821-803-0

66 *Ingmar Bredies, Andreas Umland and Valentin Yakushik (Eds.)* | Aspects of the Orange Revolution IV. Foreign Assistance and Civic Action in the 2004 Ukrainian Presidential Elections | ISBN 978-3-89821-808-5

67 *Ingmar Bredies, Andreas Umland and Valentin Yakushik (Eds.)* | Aspects of the Orange Revolution V. Institutional Observation Reports on the 2004 Ukrainian Presidential Elections | ISBN 978-3-89821-809-2

68 *Taras Kuzio (Ed.)* | Aspects of the Orange Revolution VI. Post-Communist Democratic Revolutions in Comparative Perspective | ISBN 978-3-89821-820-7

69 *Tim Bohse* | Autoritarismus statt Selbstverwaltung. Die Transformation der kommunalen Politik in der Stadt Kaliningrad 1990-2005 | Mit einem Geleitwort von Stefan Troebst | ISBN 978-3-89821-782-8

70 *David Rupp* | Die Rußländische Föderation und die russischsprachige Minderheit in Lettland. Eine Fallstudie zur Anwaltspolitik Moskaus gegenüber den russophonen Minderheiten im „Nahen Ausland" von 1991 bis 2002 | Mit einem Vorwort von Helmut Wagner | ISBN 978-3-89821-778-1

71 *Taras Kuzio* | Theoretical and Comparative Perspectives on Nationalism. New Directions in Cross-Cultural and Post-Communist Studies | With a foreword by Paul Robert Magocsi | ISBN 978-3-89821-815-3

72 *Christine Teichmann* | Die Hochschultransformation im heutigen Osteuropa. Kontinuität und Wandel bei der Entwicklung des postkommunistischen Universitätswesens | Mit einem Vorwort von Oskar Anweiler | ISBN 978-3-89821-842-8

73 *Julia Kusznir* | Der politische Einfluss von Wirtschaftseliten in russischen Regionen. Eine Analyse am Beispiel der Erdöl- und Erdgasindustrie, 1992-2005 | Mit einem Vorwort von Wolfgang Eichwede | ISBN 978-3-89821-821-4

74 *Alena Vysotskaya* | Russland, Belarus und die EU-Osterweiterung. Zur Minderheitenfrage und zum Problem der Freizügigkeit des Personenverkehrs | Mit einem Vorwort von Katlijn Malfliet | ISBN 978-3-89821-822-1

75 *Heiko Pleines (Hrsg.)* | Corporate Governance in post-sozialistischen Volkswirtschaften | ISBN 978-3-89821-766-8

76 *Stefan Ihrig* | Wer sind die Moldawier? Rumänismus versus Moldowanismus in Historiographie und Schulbüchern der Republik Moldova, 1991-2006 | Mit einem Vorwort von Holm Sundhaussen | ISBN 978-3-89821-466-7

77 *Galina Kozhevnikova in collaboration with Alexander Verkhovsky and Eugene Veklerov* | Ultra-Nationalism and Hate Crimes in Contemporary Russia. The 2004-2006 Annual Reports of Moscow's SOVA Center | With a foreword by Stephen D. Shenfield | ISBN 978-3-89821-868-9

78 *Florian Küchler* | The Role of the European Union in Moldova's Transnistria Conflict | With a foreword by Christopher Hill | ISBN 978-3-89821-850-4

79 *Bernd Rechel* | The Long Way Back to Europe. Minority Protection in Bulgaria | With a foreword by Richard Crampton | ISBN 978-3-89821-863-4

80 *Peter W. Rodgers* | Nation, Region and History in Post-Communist Transitions. Identity Politics in Ukraine, 1991-2006 | With a foreword by Vera Tolz | ISBN 978-3-89821-903-7

81 *Stephanie Solywoda* | The Life and Work of Semen L. Frank. A Study of Russian Religious Philosophy | With a foreword by Philip Walters | ISBN 978-3-89821-457-5

82 *Vera Sokolova* | Cultural Politics of Ethnicity. Discourses on Roma in Communist Czechoslovakia | ISBN 978-3-89821-864-1

83 *Natalya Shevchik Ketenci* | Kazakhstani Enterprises in Transition. The Role of Historical Regional Development in Kazakhstan's Post-Soviet Economic Transformation | ISBN 978-3-89821-831-3

84 *Martin Malek, Anna Schor-Tschudnowskaja (Hgg.)* | Europa im Tschetschenienkrieg. Zwischen politischer Ohnmacht und Gleichgültigkeit | Mit einem Vorwort von Lipchan Basajewa | ISBN 978-3-89821-676-0

85 *Stefan Meister* | Das postsowjetische Universitätswesen zwischen nationalem und internationalem Wandel. Die Entwicklung der regionalen Hochschule in Russland als Gradmesser der Systemtransformation | Mit einem Vorwort von Joan DeBardeleben | ISBN 978-3-89821-891-7

86 *Konstantin Sheiko in collaboration with Stephen Brown* | Nationalist Imaginings of the Russian Past. Anatolii Fomenko and the Rise of Alternative History in Post-Communist Russia | With a foreword by Donald Ostrowski | ISBN 978-3-89821-915-0

87 *Sabine Jenni* | Wie stark ist das „Einige Russland"? Zur Parteibindung der Eliten und zum Wahlerfolg der Machtpartei im Dezember 2007 | Mit einem Vorwort von Klaus Armingeon | ISBN 978-3-89821-961-7

88 *Thomas Borén* | Meeting-Places of Transformation. Urban Identity, Spatial Representations and Local Politics in Post-Soviet St Petersburg | ISBN 978-3-89821-739-2

89 *Aygul Ashirova* | Stalinismus und Stalin-Kult in Zentralasien. Turkmenistan 1924-1953 | Mit einem Vorwort von Leonid Luks | ISBN 978-3-89821-987-7

90 *Leonid Luks* | Freiheit oder imperiale Größe? Essays zu einem russischen Dilemma | ISBN 978-3-8382-0011-8

91 *Christopher Gilley* | The 'Change of Signposts' in the Ukrainian Emigration. A Contribution to the History of Sovietophilism in the 1920s | With a foreword by Frank Golczewski | ISBN 978-3-89821-965-5

92 *Philipp Casula, Jeronim Perovic (Eds.)* | Identities and Politics During the Putin Presidency. The Discursive Foundations of Russia's Stability | With a foreword by Heiko Haumann | ISBN 978-3-8382-0015-6

93 *Marcel Viëtor* | Europa und die Frage nach seinen Grenzen im Osten. Zur Konstruktion ‚europäischer Identität' in Geschichte und Gegenwart | Mit einem Vorwort von Albrecht Lehmann | ISBN 978-3-8382-0045-3

94 *Ben Hellman, Andrei Rogachevskii* | Filming the Unfilmable. Casper Wrede's 'One Day in the Life of Ivan Denisovich' | Second, Revised and Expanded Edition | ISBN 978-3-8382-0044-6

95 *Eva Fuchslocher* | Vaterland, Sprache, Glaube. Orthodoxie und Nationenbildung am Beispiel Georgiens | Mit einem Vorwort von Christina von Braun | ISBN 978-3-89821-884-9

96 *Vladimir Kantor* | Das Westlertum und der Weg Russlands. Zur Entwicklung der russischen Literatur und Philosophie | Ediert von Dagmar Herrmann | Mit einem Beitrag von Nikolaus Lobkowicz | ISBN 978-3-8382-0102-3

97 *Kamran Musayev* | Die postsowjetische Transformation im Baltikum und Südkaukasus. Eine vergleichende Untersuchung der politischen Entwicklung Lettlands und Aserbaidschans 1985-2009 | Mit einem Vorwort von Leonid Luks | Ediert von Sandro Henschel | ISBN 978-3-8382-0103-0

98 Tatiana Zhurzhenko | Borderlands into Bordered Lands. Geopolitics of Identity in Post-Soviet Ukraine | With a foreword by Dieter Segert | ISBN 978-3-8382-0042-2

99 Кирилл Галушко, Лидия Смола (ред.) | Пределы падения – варианты украинского будущего. Аналитико-прогностические исследования | ISBN 978-3-8382-0148-1

100 Michael Minkenberg (Ed.) | Historical Legacies and the Radical Right in Post-Cold War Central and Eastern Europe | With an afterword by Sabrina P. Ramet | ISBN 978-3-8382-0124-5

101 David-Emil Wickström | Rocking St. Petersburg. Transcultural Flows and Identity Politics in the St. Petersburg Popular Music Scene | With a foreword by Yngvar B. Steinholt | Second, Revised and Expanded Edition | ISBN 978-3-8382-0100-9

102 Eva Zabka | Eine neue „Zeit der Wirren"? Der spät- und postsowjetische Systemwandel 1985-2000 im Spiegel russischer gesellschaftspolitischer Diskurse | Mit einem Vorwort von Margareta Mommsen | ISBN 978-3-8382-0161-0

103 Ulrike Ziemer | Ethnic Belonging, Gender and Cultural Practices. Youth Identitites in Contemporary Russia | With a foreword by Anoop Nayak | ISBN 978-3-8382-0152-8

104 Ksenia Chepikova | ‚Einiges Russland' - eine zweite KPdSU? Aspekte der Identitätskonstruktion einer postsowjetischen „Partei der Macht" | Mit einem Vorwort von Torsten Oppelland | ISBN 978-3-8382-0311-9

105 Леонид Люкс | Западничество или евразийство? Демократия или идеократия? Сборник статей об исторических дилеммах России | С предисловием Владимира Кантора | ISBN 978-3-8382-0211-2

106 Anna Dost | Das russische Verfassungsrecht auf dem Weg zum Föderalismus und zurück. Zum Konflikt von Rechtsnormen und -wirklichkeit in der Russländischen Föderation von 1991 bis 2009 | Mit einem Vorwort von Alexander Blankenagel | ISBN 978-3-8382-0292-1

107 Philipp Herzog | Sozialistische Völkerfreundschaft, nationaler Widerstand oder harmloser Zeitvertreib? Zur politischen Funktion der Volkskunst im sowjetischen Estland | Mit einem Vorwort von Andreas Kappeler | ISBN 978-3-8382-0216-7

108 Marlène Laruelle (Ed.) | Russian Nationalism, Foreign Policy, and Identity Debates in Putin's Russia. New Ideological Patterns after the Orange Revolution | ISBN 978-3-8382-0325-6

109 Michail Logvinov | Russlands Kampf gegen den internationalen Terrorismus. Eine kritische Bestandsaufnahme des Bekämpfungsansatzes | Mit einem Geleitwort von Hans-Henning Schröder und einem Vorwort von Eckhard Jesse | ISBN 978-3-8382-0329-4

110 John B. Dunlop | The Moscow Bombings of September 1999. Examinations of Russian Terrorist Attacks at the Onset of Vladimir Putin's Rule | Second, Revised and Expanded Edition | ISBN 978-3-8382-0388-1

111 Андрей А. Ковалёв | Свидетельство из-за кулис российской политики I. Можно ли делать добро из зла? (Воспоминания и размышления о последних советских и первых послесоветских годах) | With a foreword by Peter Reddaway | ISBN 978-3-8382-0302-7

112 Андрей А. Ковалёв | Свидетельство из-за кулис российской политики II. Угроза для себя и окружающих (Наблюдения и предостережения относительно происходящего после 2000 г.) | ISBN 978-3-8382-0303-4

113 Bernd Kappenberg | Zeichen setzen für Europa. Der Gebrauch europäischer lateinischer Sonderzeichen in der deutschen Öffentlichkeit | Mit einem Vorwort von Peter Schlobinski | ISBN 978-3-89821-749-1

114 Ivo Mijnssen | The Quest for an Ideal Youth in Putin's Russia I. Back to Our Future! History, Modernity, and Patriotism according to Nashi, 2005-2013 | With a foreword by Jeronim Perović | Second, Revised and Expanded Edition | ISBN 978-3-8382-0368-3

115 Jussi Lassila | The Quest for an Ideal Youth in Putin's Russia II. The Search for Distinctive Conformism in the Political Communication of Nashi, 2005-2009 | With a foreword by Kirill Postoutenko | Second, Revised and Expanded Edition | ISBN 978-3-8382-0415-4

116 Valerio Trabandt | Neue Nachbarn, gute Nachbarschaft? Die EU als internationaler Akteur am Beispiel ihrer Demokratieförderung in Belarus und der Ukraine 2004-2009 | Mit einem Vorwort von Jutta Joachim | ISBN 978-3-8382-0437-6

117 Fabian Pfeiffer | Estlands Außen- und Sicherheitspolitik I. Der estnische Atlantizismus nach der wiedererlangten Unabhängigkeit 1991-2004 | Mit einem Vorwort von Helmut Hubel | ISBN 978-3-8382-0127-6

118 Jana Podßuweit | Estlands Außen- und Sicherheitspolitik II. Handlungsoptionen eines Kleinstaates im Rahmen seiner EU-Mitgliedschaft (2004-2008) | Mit einem Vorwort von Helmut Hubel | ISBN 978-3-8382-0440-6

119 Karin Pointner | Estlands Außen- und Sicherheitspolitik III. Eine gedächtnispolitische Analyse estnischer Entwicklungskooperation 2006-2010 | Mit einem Vorwort von Karin Liebhart | ISBN 978-3-8382-0435-2

120 Ruslana Vovk | Die Offenheit der ukrainischen Verfassung für das Völkerrecht und die europäische Integration | Mit einem Vorwort von Alexander Blankenagel | ISBN 978-3-8382-0481-9

121 *Mykhaylo Banakh* | Die Relevanz der Zivilgesellschaft bei den postkommunistischen Transformationsprozessen in mittel- und osteuropäischen Ländern. Das Beispiel der spät- und postsowjetischen Ukraine 1986-2009 | Mit einem Vorwort von Gerhard Simon | ISBN 978-3-8382-0499-4

122 *Michael Moser* | Language Policy and the Discourse on Languages in Ukraine under President Viktor Yanukovych (25 February 2010–28 October 2012) | ISBN 978-3-8382-0497-0 (Paperback edition) | ISBN 978-3-8382-0507-6 (Hardcover edition)

123 *Nicole Krome* | Russischer Netzwerkkapitalismus Restrukturierungsprozesse in der Russischen Föderation am Beispiel des Luftfahrtunternehmens „Aviastar" | Mit einem Vorwort von Petra Stykow | ISBN 978-3-8382-0534-2

124 *David R. Marples* | 'Our Glorious Past'. Lukashenka's Belarus and the Great Patriotic War | ISBN 978-3-8382-0574-8 (Paperback edition) | ISBN 978-3-8382-0675-2 (Hardcover edition)

125 *Ulf Walther* | Russlands „neuer Adel". Die Macht des Geheimdienstes von Gorbatschow bis Putin | Mit einem Vorwort von Hans-Georg Wieck | ISBN 978-3-8382-0584-7

126 *Simon Geissbühler (Hrsg.)* | Kiew – Revolution 3.0. Der Euromaidan 2013/14 und die Zukunftsperspektiven der Ukraine | ISBN 978-3-8382-0581-6 (Paperback edition) | ISBN 978-3-8382-0681-3 (Hardcover edition)

127 *Andrey Makarychev* | Russia and the EU in a Multipolar World. Discourses, Identities, Norms | With a foreword by Klaus Segbers | ISBN 978-3-8382-0629-5

128 *Roland Scharff* | Kasachstan als postsowjetischer Wohlfahrtsstaat. Die Transformation des sozialen Schutzsystems | Mit einem Vorwort von Joachim Ahrens | ISBN 978-3-8382-0622-6

129 *Katja Grupp* | Bild Lücke Deutschland. Kaliningrader Studierende sprechen über Deutschland | Mit einem Vorwort von Martin Schulz | ISBN 978-3-8382-0552-6

130 *Konstantin Sheiko, Stephen Brown* | History as Therapy. Alternative History and Nationalist Imaginings in Russia, 1991-2014 | ISBN 978-3-8382-0665-3

131 *Elisa Kriza* | Alexander Solzhenitsyn: Cold War Icon, Gulag Author, Russian Nationalist? A Study of the Western Reception of his Literary Writings, Historical Interpretations, and Political Ideas | With a foreword by Andrei Rogatchevski | ISBN 978-3-8382-0589-2 (Paperback edition) | ISBN 978-3-8382-0690-5 (Hardcover edition)

132 *Serghei Golunov* | The Elephant in the Room. Corruption and Cheating in Russian Universities | ISBN 978-3-8382-0570-0

133 *Manja Hussner, Rainer Arnold (Hgg.)* | Verfassungsgerichtsbarkeit in Zentralasien I. Sammlung von Verfassungstexten | ISBN 978-3-8382-0595-3

134 *Nikolay Mitrokhin* | Die „Russische Partei". Die Bewegung der russischen Nationalisten in der UdSSR 1953-1985 | Aus dem Russischen übertragen von einem Übersetzerteam unter der Leitung von Larisa Schippel | ISBN 978-3-8382-0024-8

135 *Manja Hussner, Rainer Arnold (Hgg.)* | Verfassungsgerichtsbarkeit in Zentralasien II. Sammlung von Verfassungstexten | ISBN 978-3-8382-0597-7

136 *Manfred Zeller* | Das sowjetische Fieber. Fußballfans im poststalinistischen Vielvölkerreich | Mit einem Vorwort von Nikolaus Katzer | ISBN 978-3-8382-0757-5

137 *Kristin Schreiter* | Stellung und Entwicklungspotential zivilgesellschaftlicher Gruppen in Russland. Menschenrechtsorganisationen im Vergleich | ISBN 978-3-8382-0673-8

138 *David R. Marples, Frederick V. Mills (Eds.)* | Ukraine's Euromaidan. Analyses of a Civil Revolution | ISBN 978-3-8382-0660-8

139 *Bernd Kappenberg* | Setting Signs for Europe. Why Diacritics Matter for European Integration | With a foreword by Peter Schlobinski | ISBN 978-3-8382-0663-9

140 *René Lenz* | Internationalisierung, Kooperation und Transfer. Externe bildungspolitische Akteure in der Russischen Föderation | Mit einem Vorwort von Frank Ettrich | ISBN 978-3-8382-0751-3

141 *Juri Plusnin, Yana Zausaeva, Natalia Zhidkevich, Artemy Pozanenko* | Wandering Workers. Mores, Behavior, Way of Life, and Political Status of Domestic Russian Labor Migrants | Translated by Julia Kazantseva | ISBN 978-3-8382-0653-0

142 *David J. Smith (Eds.)* | Latvia – A Work in Progress? 100 Years of State- and Nation-Building | ISBN 978-3-8382-0648-6

143 *Инна Чувычкина (ред.)* | Экспортные нефте- и газопроводы на постсоветском пространстве. Анализ трубопроводной политики в свете теории международных отношений | ISBN 978-3-8382-0822-0

144 *Johann Zajaczkowski* | Russland – eine pragmatische Großmacht? Eine rollentheoretische Untersuchung russischer Außenpolitik am Beispiel der Zusammenarbeit mit den USA nach 9/11 und des Georgienkrieges von 2008 | Mit einem Vorwort von Siegfried Schieder | ISBN 978-3-8382-0837-4

145 *Boris Popivanov* | Changing Images of the Left in Bulgaria. The Challenge of Post-Communism in the Early 21st Century | ISBN 978-3-8382-0667-7

146 *Lenka Krátká* | A History of the Czechoslovak Ocean Shipping Company 1948-1989. How a Small, Landlocked Country Ran Maritime Business During the Cold War | ISBN 978-3-8382-0666-0

147 *Alexander Sergunin* | Explaining Russian Foreign Policy Behavior. Theory and Practice | ISBN 978-3-8382-0752-0

148 *Darya Malyutina* | Migrant Friendships in a Super-Diverse City. Russian-Speakers and their Social Relationships in London in the 21st Century | With a foreword by Claire Dwyer | ISBN 978-3-8382-0652-3

149 *Alexander Sergunin, Valery Konyshev* | Russia in the Arctic. Hard or Soft Power? | ISBN 978-3-8382-0753-7

150 *John J. Maresca* | Helsinki Revisited. A Key U.S. Negotiator's Memoirs on the Development of the CSCE into the OSCE | With a foreword by Hafiz Pashayev | ISBN 978-3-8382-0852-7

151 *Jardar Østbø* | The New Third Rome. Readings of a Russian Nationalist Myth | With a foreword by Pål Kolstø | ISBN 978-3-8382-0870-1

152 *Simon Kordonsky* | Socio-Economic Foundations of the Russian Post-Soviet Regime. The Resource-Based Economy and Estate-Based Social Structure of Contemporary Russia | With a foreword by Svetlana Barsukova | ISBN 978-3-8382-0775-9

153 *Duncan Leitch* | Assisting Reform in Post-Communist Ukraine 2000–2012. The Illusions of Donors and the Disillusion of Beneficiaries | With a foreword by Kataryna Wolczuk | ISBN 978-3-8382-0844-2

154 *Abel Polese* | Limits of a Post-Soviet State. How Informality Replaces, Renegotiates, and Reshapes Governance in Contemporary Ukraine | With a foreword by Colin Williams | ISBN 978-3-8382-0845-9

155 *Mikhail Suslov (Ed.)* | Digital Orthodoxy in the Post-Soviet World. The Russian Orthodox Church and Web 2.0 | With a foreword by Father Cyril Hovorun | ISBN 978-3-8382-0871-8

156 *Leonid Luks* | Zwei „Sonderwege"? Russisch-deutsche Parallelen und Kontraste (1917-2014). Vergleichende Essays | ISBN 978-3-8382-0823-7

157 *Vladimir V. Karacharovskiy, Ovsey I. Shkaratan, Gordey A. Yastrebov* | Towards a New Russian Work Culture. Can Western Companies and Expatriates Change Russian Society? | With a foreword by Elena N. Danilova | Translated by Julia Kazantseva | ISBN 978-3-8382-0902-9

158 *Edmund Griffiths* | Aleksandr Prokhanov and Post-Soviet Esotericism | ISBN 978-3-8382-0963-0

159 *Timm Beichelt, Susann Worschech (Eds.)* | Transnational Ukraine? Networks and Ties that Influence(d) Contemporary Ukraine | ISBN 978-3-8382-0944-9

160 *Mieste Hotopp-Riecke* | Die Tataren der Krim zwischen Assimilation und Selbstbehauptung. Der Aufbau des krimtatarischen Bildungswesens nach Deportation und Heimkehr (1990-2005) | Mit einem Vorwort von Swetlana Czerwonnaja | ISBN 978-3-89821-940-2

161 *Olga Bertelsen (Ed.)* | Revolution and War in Contemporary Ukraine. The Challenge of Change | ISBN 978-3-8382-1016-2

162 *Natalya Ryabinska* | Ukraine's Post-Communist Mass Media. Between Capture and Commercialization | With a foreword by Marta Dyczok | ISBN 978-3-8382-1011-7

163 *Alexandra Cotofana, James M. Nyce (Eds.)* | Religion and Magic in Socialist and Post-Socialist Contexts. Historic and Ethnographic Case Studies of Orthodoxy, Heterodoxy, and Alternative Spirituality | With a foreword by Patrick L. Michelson | ISBN 978-3-8382-0989-0

164 *Nozima Akhrarkhodjaeva* | The Instrumentalisation of Mass Media in Electoral Authoritarian Regimes. Evidence from Russia's Presidential Election Campaigns of 2000 and 2008 | ISBN 978-3-8382-1013-1

165 *Yulia Krasheninnikova* | Informal Healthcare in Contemporary Russia. Sociographic Essays on the Post-Soviet Infrastructure for Alternative Healing Practices | ISBN 978-3-8382-0970-8

166 *Peter Kaiser* | Das Schachbrett der Macht. Die Handlungsspielräume eines sowjetischen Funktionärs unter Stalin am Beispiel des Generalsekretärs des Komsomol Aleksandr Kosarev (1929-1938) | Mit einem Vorwort von Dietmar Neutatz | ISBN 978-3-8382-1052-0

167 *Oksana Kim* | The Effects and Implications of Kazakhstan's Adoption of International Financial Reporting Standards. A Resource Dependence Perspective | With a foreword by Svetlana Vlady | ISBN 978-3-8382-0987-6

168 *Anna Sanina* | Patriotic Education in Contemporary Russia. Sociological Studies in the Making of the Post-Soviet Citizen | With a foreword by Anna Oldfield | ISBN 978-3-8382-0993-7

169 *Rudolf Wolters* | Spezialist in Sibirien Faksimile der 1933 erschienenen ersten Ausgabe | Mit einem Vorwort von Dmitrij Chmelnizki | ISBN 978-3-8382-0515-1

170 *Michal Vit, Magdalena M. Baran (Eds.)* | Transregional versus National Perspectives on Contemporary Central European History. Studies on the Building of Nation-States and Their Cooperation in the 20th and 21st Century | With a foreword by Petr Vágner | ISBN 978-3-8382-1015-5

171 *Philip Gamaghelyan* | Conflict Resolution Beyond the International Relations Paradigm. Evolving Designs as a Transformative Practice in Nagorno-Karabakh and Syria | With a foreword by Susan Allen | ISBN 978-3-8382-1057-5

172 *Maria Shagina* | Joining a Prestigious Club. Cooperation with Europarties and Its Impact on Party Development in Georgia, Moldova, and Ukraine 2004–2015 | With a foreword by Kataryna Wolczuk | ISBN 978-3-8382-1084-1

173 *Alexandra Cotofana, James M. Nyce (Eds.)* | Religion and Magic in Socialist and Post-Socialist Contexts II. Baltic, Eastern European, and Post-USSR Case Studies | With a foreword by Anita Stasulane | ISBN 978-3-8382-0990-6

174 *Barbara Kunz* | Kind Words, Cruise Missiles, and Everything in Between. The Use of Power Resources in U.S. Policies towards Poland, Ukraine, and Belarus 1989–2008 | With a foreword by William Hill | ISBN 978-3-8382-1065-0

175 *Eduard Klein* | Bildungskorruption in Russland und der Ukraine. Eine komparative Analyse der Performanz staatlicher Antikorruptionsmaßnahmen im Hochschulsektor am Beispiel universitärer Aufnahmeprüfungen | Mit einem Vorwort von Heiko Pleines | ISBN 978-3-8382-0995-1

176 *Markus Soldner* | Politischer Kapitalismus im postsowjetischen Russland. Die politische, wirtschaftliche und mediale Transformation in den 1990er Jahren | Mit einem Vorwort von Wolfgang Ismayr | ISBN 978-3-8382-1222-7

177 *Anton Oleinik* | Building Ukraine from Within. A Sociological, Institutional, and Economic Analysis of a Nation-State in the Making | ISBN 978-3-8382-1150-3

178 *Peter Rollberg, Marlene Laruelle (Eds.)* | Mass Media in the Post-Soviet World. Market Forces, State Actors, and Political Manipulation in the Informational Environment after Communism | ISBN 978-3-8382-1116-9

179 *Mikhail Minakov* | Development and Dystopia. Studies in Post-Soviet Ukraine and Eastern Europe | With a foreword by Alexander Etkind | ISBN 978-3-8382-1112-1

180 *Aijan Sharshenova* | The European Union's Democracy Promotion in Central Asia. A Study of Political Interests, Influence, and Development in Kazakhstan and Kyrgyzstan in 2007–2013 | With a foreword by Gordon Crawford | ISBN 978-3-8382-1151-0

181 *Andrey Makarychev, Alexandra Yatsyk (Eds.)* | Boris Nemtsov and Russian Politics. Power and Resistance | With a foreword by Zhanna Nemtsova | ISBN 978-3-8382-1122-0

182 *Sophie Falsini* | The Euromaidan's Effect on Civil Society. Why and How Ukrainian Social Capital Increased after the Revolution of Dignity | With a foreword by Susann Worschech | ISBN 978-3-8382-1131-2

183 *Valentyna Romanova, Andreas Umland (Eds.)* | Ukraine's Decentralization. Challenges and Implications of the Local Governance Reform after the Euromaidan Revolution | ISBN 978-3-8382-1162-6

184 *Leonid Luks* | A Fateful Triangle. Essays on Contemporary Russian, German and Polish History | ISBN 978-3-8382-1143-5

185 *John B. Dunlop* | The February 2015 Assassination of Boris Nemtsov and the Flawed Trial of his Alleged Killers. An Exploration of Russia's "Crime of the 21st Century" | ISBN 978-3-8382-1188-6

186 *Vasile Rotaru* | Russia, the EU, and the Eastern Partnership. Building Bridges or Digging Trenches? | ISBN 978-3-8382-1134-3

187 *Marina Lebedeva* | Russian Studies of International Relations. From the Soviet Past to the Post-Cold-War Present | With a foreword by Andrei P. Tsygankov | ISBN 978-3-8382-0851-0

188 *Tomasz Stępniewski, George Soroka (Eds.)* | Ukraine after Maidan. Revisiting Domestic and Regional Security | ISBN 978-3-8382-1075-9

189 *Petar Cholakov* | Ethnic Entrepreneurs Unmasked. Political Institutions and Ethnic Conflicts in Contemporary Bulgaria | ISBN 978-3-8382-1189-3

190 *A. Salem, G. Hazeldine, D. Morgan (Eds.)* | Higher Education in Post-Communist States. Comparative and Sociological Perspectives | ISBN 978-3-8382-1183-5

191 *Igor Torbakov* | After Empire. Nationalist Imagination and Symbolic Politics in Russia and Eurasia in the Twentieth and Twenty-First Century | With a foreword by Serhii Plokhy | ISBN 978-3-8382-1217-3

192 *Aleksandr Burakovskiy* | Jewish-Ukrainian Relations in Late and Post-Soviet Ukraine. Articles, Lectures and Essays from 1986 to 2016 | ISBN 978-3-8382-1210-4

193 *Natalia Shapovalova, Olga Burlyuk (Eds.)* | Civil Society in Post-Euromaidan Ukraine. From Revolution to Consolidation | With a foreword by Richard Youngs | ISBN 978-3-8382-1216-6

194 *Franz Preissler* | Positionsverteidigung, Imperialismus oder Irredentismus? Russland und die „Russischsprachigen", 1991–2015 | ISBN 978-3-8382-1262-3

195 *Marian Madeła* | Der Reformprozess in der Ukraine 2014-2017. Eine Fallstudie zur Reform der öffentlichen Verwaltung | Mit einem Vorwort von Martin Malek | ISBN 978-3-8382-1266-1

196 *Anke Giesen* | „Wie kann denn der Sieger ein Verbrecher sein?" Eine diskursanalytische Untersuchung der russlandweiten Debatte über Konzept und Verstaatlichungsprozess der Lagergedenkstätte „Perm'-36" im Ural | ISBN 978-3-8382-1284-5

197 *Victoria Leukavets* | The Integration Policies of Belarus and Ukraine vis-à-vis the EU and Russia. A Comparative Analysis Through the Prism of a Two-Level Game Approach | ISBN 978-3-8382-1247-0

198 *Oksana Kim* | The Development and Challenges of Russian Corporate Governance I. The Roles and Functions of Boards of Directors | With a foreword by Sheila M. Puffer | ISBN 978-3-8382-1287-6

199 *Thomas D. Grant* | International Law and the Post-Soviet Space I. Essays on Chechnya and the Baltic States | With a foreword by Stephen M. Schwebel | ISBN 978-3-8382-1279-1

200 *Thomas D. Grant* | International Law and the Post-Soviet Space II. Essays on Ukraine, Intervention, and Non-Proliferation | ISBN 978-3-8382-1280-7

201 *Slavomír Michálek, Michal Štefansky* | The Age of Fear. The Cold War and Its Influence on Czechoslovakia 1945–1968 | ISBN 978-3-8382-1285-2

202 *Iulia-Sabina Joja* | Romania's Strategic Culture 1990–2014. Continuity and Change in a Post-Communist Country's Evolution of National Interests and Security Policies | With a foreword by Heiko Biehl | ISBN 978-3-8382-1286-9

203 *Andrei Rogatchevski, Yngvar B. Steinholt, Arve Hansen, David-Emil Wickström* | War of Songs. Popular Music and Recent Russia-Ukraine Relations | With a foreword by Artemy Troitsky | ISBN 978-3-8382-1173-2

204 *Maria Lipman (Ed.)* | Russian Voices on Post-Crimea Russia. An Almanac of Counterpoint Essays from 2015–2018 | ISBN 978-3-8382-1251-7

205 *Ksenia Maksimovtsova* | Language Conflicts in Contemporary Estonia, Latvia, and Ukraine. A Comparative Exploration of Discourses in Post-Soviet Russian-Language Digital Media | With a foreword by Ammon Cheskin | ISBN 978-3-8382-1282-1

206 *Michal Vít* | The EU's Impact on Identity Formation in East-Central Europe between 2004 and 2013. Perceptions of the Nation and Europe in Political Parties of the Czech Republic, Poland, and Slovakia | With a foreword by Andrea Pető | ISBN 978-3-8382-1275-3

207 *Per A. Rudling* | Tarnished Heroes. The Organization of Ukrainian Nationalists in the Memory Politics of Post-Soviet Ukraine | ISBN 978-3-8382-0999-9

208 *Kaja Gadowska, Peter Solomon (Eds.)* | Legal Change in Post-Communist States. Progress, Reversions, Explanations | ISBN 978-3-8382-1312-5

209 *Paweł Kowal, Georges Mink, Iwona Reichardt (Eds.)* | Three Revolutions: Mobilization and Change in Contemporary Ukraine I. Theoretical Aspects and Analyses on Religion, Memory, and Identity | ISBN 978-3-8382-1321-7

210 *Paweł Kowal, Georges Mink, Adam Reichardt, Iwona Reichardt (Eds.)* | Three Revolutions: Mobilization and Change in Contemporary Ukraine II. An Oral History of the Revolution on Granite, Orange Revolution, and Revolution of Dignity | ISBN 978-3-8382-1323-1

211 *Li Bennich-Björkman, Sergiy Kurbatov (Eds.)* | When the Future Came. The Collapse of the USSR and the Emergence of National Memory in Post-Soviet History Textbooks | ISBN 978-3-8382-1335-4

212 *Olga R. Gulina* | Migration as a (Geo-)Political Challenge in the Post-Soviet Space. Border Regimes, Policy Choices, Visa Agendas | With a foreword by Nils Muižnieks | ISBN 978-3-8382-1338-5

213 *Sanna Turoma, Kaarina Aitamurto, Slobodanka Vladiv-Glover (Eds.)* | Religion, Expression, and Patriotism in Russia. Essays on Post-Soviet Society and the State. ISBN 978-3-8382-1346-0

214 *Vasif Huseynov* | Geopolitical Rivalries in the "Common Neighborhood". Russia's Conflict with the West, Soft Power, and Neoclassical Realism | With a foreword by Nicholas Ross Smith | ISBN 978-3-8382-1277-7

215 *Mikhail Suslov* | Geopolitical Imagination. Ideology and Utopia in Post-Soviet Russia | With a foreword by Mark Bassin | ISBN 978-3-8382-1361-3

216　*Alexander Etkind, Mikhail Minakov (Eds.)* | Ideology after Union. Political Doctrines, Discourses, and Debates in Post-Soviet Societies | ISBN 978-3-8382-1388-0

217　*Jakob Mischke, Oleksandr Zabirko (Hgg.)* | Protestbewegungen im langen Schatten des Kreml. Aufbruch und Resignation in Russland und der Ukraine | ISBN 978-3-8382-0926-5

218　*Oksana Huss* | How Corruption and Anti-Corruption Policies Sustain Hybrid Regimes. Strategies of Political Domination under Ukraine's Presidents in 1994-2014 | With a foreword by Tobias Debiel and Andrea Gawrich | ISBN 978-3-8382-1430-6

219　*Dmitry Travin, Vladimir Gel'man, Otar Marganiya* | The Russian Path. Ideas, Interests, Institutions, Illusions | With a foreword by Vladimir Ryzhkov | ISBN 978-3-8382-1421-4

220　*Gergana Dimova* | Political Uncertainty. A Comparative Exploration | With a foreword by Todor Yalamov and Rumena Filipova | ISBN 978-3-8382-1385-9

221　*Torben Waschke* | Russland in Transition. Geopolitik zwischen Raum, Identität und Machtinteressen | Mit einem Vorwort von Andreas Dittmann | ISBN 978-3-8382-1480-1

222　*Steven Jobbitt, Zsolt Bottlik, Marton Berki (Eds.)* | Power and Identity in the Post-Soviet Realm. Geographies of Ethnicity and Nationality after 1991 | ISBN 978-3-8382-1399-6

223　*Daria Buteiko* | Erinnerungsort. Ort des Gedenkens, der Erholung oder der Einkehr? Kommunismus-Erinnerung am Beispiel der Gedenkstätte Berliner Mauer sowie des Soloveckij-Klosters und -Museumsparks | ISBN 978-3-8382-1367-5

224　*Olga Bertelsen (Ed.)* | Russian Active Measures. Yesterday, Today, Tomorrow | With a foreword by Jan Goldman | ISBN 978-3-8382-1529-7

225　*David Mandel* | "Optimizing" Higher Education in Russia. University Teachers and their Union "Universitetskaya solidarnost'" | ISBN 978-3-8382-1519-8

226　*Mikhail Minakov, Gwendolyn Sasse, Daria Isachenko (Eds.)* | Post-Soviet Secessionism. Nation-Building and State-Failure after Communism | ISBN 978-3-8382-1538-9

227　*Jakob Hauter (Ed.)* | Civil War? Interstate War? Hybrid War? Dimensions and Interpretations of the Donbas Conflict in 2014–2020 | With a foreword by Andrew Wilson | ISBN 978-3-8382-1383-5

228　*Tima T. Moldogaziev, Gene A. Brewer, J. Edward Kellough (Eds.)* | Public Policy and Politics in Georgia. Lessons from Post-Soviet Transition | With a foreword by Dan Durning | ISBN 978-3-8382-1535-8

229　*Oxana Schmies (Ed.)* | NATO's Enlargement and Russia. A Strategic Challenge in the Past and Future | With a foreword by Vladimir Kara-Murza | ISBN 978-3-8382-1478-8

230　*Christopher Ford* | Ukapisme – Une Gauche perdue. Le marxisme anti-colonial dans la révolution ukrainienne 1917-1925 | Avec une préface de Vincent Présumey | ISBN 978-3-8382-0899-2

231　*Anna Kutkina* | Between Lenin and Bandera. Decommunization and Multivocality in Post-Euromaidan Ukraine | With a foreword by Juri Mykkänen | ISBN 978-3-8382-1506-8

232　*Lincoln E. Flake* | Defending the Faith. The Russian Orthodox Church and the Demise of Religious Pluralism | With a foreword by Peter Martland | ISBN 978-3-8382-1378-1

233　*Nikoloz Samkharadze* | Russia's Recognition of the Independence of Abkhazia and South Ossetia. Analysis of a Deviant Case in Moscow's Foreign Policy | With a foreword by Neil MacFarlane | ISBN 978-3-8382-1414-6

234　*Arve Hansen* | Urban Protest. A Spatial Perspective on Kyiv, Minsk, and Moscow | With a foreword by Julie Wilhelmsen | ISBN 978-3-8382-1495-5

235　*Eleonora Narvselius, Julie Fedor (Eds.)* | Diversity in the East-Central European Borderlands. Memories, Cityscapes, People | ISBN 978-3-8382-1523-5

236　*Regina Elsner* | The Russian Orthodox Church and Modernity. A Historical and Theological Investigation into Eastern Christianity between Unity and Plurality | With a foreword by Mikhail Suslov | ISBN 978-3-8382-1568-9

237　*Bo Petersson* | The Putin Predicament. Problems of Legitimacy and Succession in Russia | With a foreword by J. Paul Goode | ISBN 978-3-8382-1050-6

238　*Jonathan Otto Pohl* | The Years of Great Silence. The Deportation, Special Settlement, and Mobilization into the Labor Army of Ethnic Germans in the USSR, 1941–1955 | ISBN 978-3-8382-1630-0

239　*Mikhail Minakov (Ed.)* | Inventing Majorities. Ideological Creativity in Post-Soviet Societies | ISBN 978-3-8382-1641-6

240　*Robert M. Cutler* | Soviet and Post-Soviet Foreign Policies I. East-South Relations and the Political Economy of the Communist Bloc, 1971–1991 | With a foreword by Roger E. Kanet | ISBN 978-3-8382-1654-6

241 *Izabella Agardi* | On the Verge of History. Life Stories of Rural Women from Serbia, Romania, and Hungary, 1920–2020 | With a foreword by Andrea Pető | ISBN 978-3-8382-1602-7

242 *Sebastian Schäffer (Ed.)* | Ukraine in Central and Eastern Europe. Kyiv's Foreign Affairs and the International Relations of the Post-Communist Region | With a foreword by Pavlo Klimkin and Andreas Umland| ISBN 978-3-8382-1615-7

243 *Volodymyr Dubrovskyi, Kalman Mizsei, Mychailo Wynnyckyj (Eds.)* | Eight Years after the Revolution of Dignity. What Has Changed in Ukraine during 2013–2021? | With a foreword by Yaroslav Hrytsak | ISBN 978-3-8382-1560-0

244 *Rumena Filipova* | Constructing the Limits of Europe Identity and Foreign Policy in Poland, Bulgaria, and Russia since 1989 | With forewords by Harald Wydra and Gergana Yankova-Dimova | ISBN 978-3-8382-1649-2

245 *Oleksandra Keudel* | How Patronal Networks Shape Opportunities for Local Citizen Participation in a Hybrid Regime A Comparative Analysis of Five Cities in Ukraine | With a foreword by Sabine Kropp | ISBN 978-3-8382-1671-3

246 *Jan Claas Behrends, Thomas Lindenberger, Pavel Kolar (Eds.)* | Violence after Stalin Institutions, Practices, and Everyday Life in the Soviet Bloc 1953–1989 | ISBN 978-3-8382-1637-9

247 *Leonid Luks* | Macht und Ohnmacht der Utopien Essays zur Geschichte Russlands im 20. und 21. Jahrhundert | ISBN 978-3-8382-1677-5

248 *Iuliia Barshadska* | Brüssel zwischen Kyjiw und Moskau Das auswärtige Handeln der Europäischen Union im ukrainisch-russischen Konflikt 2014-2019 | Mit einem Vorwort von Olaf Leiße | ISBN 978-3-8382-1667-6

249 *Valentyna Romanova* | Decentralisation and Multilevel Elections in Ukraine Reform Dynamics and Party Politics in 2010–2021 | With a foreword by Kimitaka Matsuzato | ISBN 978-3-8382-1700-0

250 *Alexander Motyl* | National Questions. Theoretical Reflections on Nations and Nationalism in Eastern Europe | ISBN 978-3-8382-1675-1

251 *Marc Dietrich* | A Cosmopolitan Model for Peacebuilding. The Ukrainian Cases of Crimea and the Donbas | With a foreword by Rémi Baudouï | ISBN 978-3-8382-1687-4

252 *Eduard Baidaus* | An Unsettled Nation. Moldova in the Geopolitics of Russia, Romania, and Ukraine | With forewords by John-Paul Himka and David R. Marples | ISBN 978-3-8382-1582-2

253 *Igor Okunev, Petr Oskolkov (Eds.)* | Transforming the Administrative Matryoshka. The Reform of Autonomous Okrugs in the Russian Federation, 2003–2008 | With a foreword by Vladimir Zorin | ISBN 978-3-8382-1721-5

254 *Winfried Schneider-Deters* | Ukraine's Fateful Years 2013–2019. Vol. I: The Popular Uprising in Winter 2013/2014 | ISBN 978-3-8382-1725-3

255 *Winfried Schneider-Deters* | Ukraine's Fateful Years 2013–2019. Vol. II: The Annexation of Crimea and the War in Donbas | ISBN 978-3-8382-1726-0

256 *Robert M. Cutler* | Soviet and Post-Soviet Russian Foreign Policies II. East-West Relations in Europe and the Political Economy of the Communist Bloc, 1971–1991 | With a foreword by Roger E. Kanet | ISBN 978-3-8382-1727-7

257 *Robert M. Cutler* | Soviet and Post-Soviet Russian Foreign Policies III. East-West Relations in Europe and Eurasia in the Post-Cold War Transition, 1991–2001 | With a foreword by Roger E. Kanet | ISBN 978-3-8382-1728-4

258 *Paweł Kowal, Iwona Reichardt, Kateryna Pryshchepa (Eds.)* | Three Revolutions: Mobilization and Change in Contemporary Ukraine III. Archival Records and Historical Sources on the 1990 Revolution on Granite | ISBN 978-3-8382-1376-7

259 *Mikhail Minakov (Ed.)* | Philosophy Unchained. Developments in Post-Soviet Philosophical Thought. | With a foreword by Christopher Donohue | ISBN 978-3-8382-1768-0

260 *David Dalton* | The Ukrainian Oligarchy After the Euromaidan. How Ukraine's Political Economy Regime Survived the Crisis | With a foreword by Andrew Wilson | ISBN 978-3-8382-1740-6

261 *Andreas Heinemann-Grüder (Ed.)* | Who are the Fighters? Irregular Armed Groups in the Russian-Ukrainian War in 2014–2015 | ISBN 978-3-8382-1777-2

262 *Taras Kuzio (Ed.)* | Russian Disinformation and Western Scholarship. Bias and Prejudice in Journalistic, Expert, and Academic Analyses of East European, Russian and Eurasian Affairs | ISBN 978-3-8382-1685-0

263 *Darius Furmonavicius* | LithuaniaTransforms the West. Lithuania's Liberation from Soviet Occupation and the Enlargement of NATO (1988–2022) | With a foreword by Vytautas Landsbergis | ISBN 978-3-8382-1779-6

264 *Dirk Dalberg* | Politisches Denken im tschechoslowakischen Dissens. Egon Bondy, Miroslav Kusý, Milan Šimečka und Petr Uhl (1968-1989) | ISBN 978-3-8382-1318-7

265 *Леонид Люкс* | К столетию «философского парохода». Мыслители «первой» русской эмиграции о русской революции и о тоталитарных соблазнах XX века | ISBN 978-3-8382-1775-8

266 *Daviti Mtchedlishvili* | The EU and the South Caucasus. European Neighborhood Policies between Eclecticism and Pragmatism, 1991-2021 | With a foreword by Nicholas Ross Smith | ISBN 978-3-8382-1735-2

267 *Bohdan Harasymiw* | Post-Euromaidan Ukraine. Domestic Power Struggles and War of National Survival in 2014–2022 | ISBN 978-3-8382-1798-7

268 *Nadiia Koval, Denys Tereshchenko (Eds.)* | Russian Cultural Diplomacy under Putin. Rossotrudnichestvo, the "Russkiy Mir" Foundation, and the Gorchakov Fund in 2007–2022 | ISBN 978-3-8382-1801-4

269 *Izabela Kazejak* | Jews in Post-War Wrocław and L'viv. Official Policies and Local Responses in Comparative Perspective, 1945-1970s | ISBN 978-3-8382-1802-1

270 *Jakob Hauter* | Russia's Overlooked Invasion. The Causes of the 2014 Outbreak of War in Ukraine's Donbas | With a foreword by Hiroaki Kuromiya | ISBN 978-3-8382-1803-8

271 *Anton Shekhovtsov* | Russian Political Warfare. Essays on Kremlin Propaganda in Europe and the Neighbourhood, 2020-2023 | With a foreword by Nathalie Loiseau | ISBN 978-3-8382-1821-2

272 *Андреа Пето* | Насилие и Молчание. Красная армия в Венгрии во Второй Мировой войне | ISBN 978-3-8382-1636-2